When the Fudge Trees Bloom

When the Fudge Trees Bloom

© Catherine W. Rouhana 2024

Paperback ISBN: 978-1-954779-89-1

emerald-books.com

 Emerald Books

WHEN THE FUDGE TREES BLOOM

MEMORIES OF AN AMERICAN IN THE MIDDLE EAST

CATHERINE W. ROUHANA

To Nagib, with love and gratitude for all the years,

and to Paul, Nick, and Pete, the Original Fudge

LEBANON, JULY 2007

FUDGE: [fuhj] *noun*
A soft candy made from butter, sugar, milk, and chocolate.

"My mother's land has a million fudge trees on it," my husband told me. I giggled and pointed out his mistake, but he brushed it aside. His English was good, but delightfully imperfect. How could he mix up fudge with figs?

"The figs are sweeter than any candy. I will show you."

As the plane made its final approach into Beirut, I remembered his proclamation, spoken in accented English. He looked so like Omar Sharif, despite his broken nose, as he swept the air with one hand. He was good at proclamations. When he gave me the engagement ring, I'd agreed to go to Lebanon, his homeland, with him, but confessed my misgivings. "I'll never ask you to stay in a place where you're not happy," he'd said. I'd believed him. I hastily brushed away the memories, as well as the unbidden tears. It had been twenty-two years since I was last here. I was not the girl I had been when I first arrived in this ancient city, nor the young, scared mother I had been when I last left, fleeing the bombs. I thought fondly of that girl and mother. I shook my head. Could that have been me? Could only eight years define a life?

1

My firstborn, Paul, sat next to me on the plane, much as he had years before. The brave little boy who had shared my adventures had become a stalwart, intrepid man who was fiercely protective of his family. He was handsome with wavy dark hair and kind eyes and a heart of gold. He squeezed my hand, understanding my tears without needing an explanation. My boys were men now, all three with me for this happy reunion. Pete was my youngest, born in Beirut, Nick the second, born in Saudi Arabia, and Paul, my oldest, was born in the U.S. He liked to joke that he was the only one of them who could be president.

I hadn't been on a plane for many years, and I had never had the luxury of flying with adults. But now, with my three sons and Corinne, Pete's fiancée, I walked through the airport empty-handed, one or the other of them having seen to my bags and comfort. And always one of them walked at my side, conversing and joking as he lagged behind the others to accommodate my slower gait.

In years gone by, I had gripped their hands tightly as we made our way through countless crowds in many airports. I had held the little hands securely, protecting them as I shepherded them through the crowds. Now their men's hands, strong and confident, gently took my elbow as I climbed the stairs, carried my bags, or rested on my shoulder to guide me through the throngs.

Paul had announced his engagement after the New Year. He was the bridge between the East and West, giving us the happy momentum to close the gap and banish past hurts.

My emotions had been overflowing for weeks following his announcement. I was preparing for the trip not just for me but for Rosie, Paul's bride-to-be. They would live with me in my home in Baltimore until she was better acclimated, and her limited English improved. I was reminded of my younger self and the advice my sister Betsy gave me as the time drew closer to my departure. "Cath, be like a flow-through tea bag," she said. I laughed, but it was good advice. I would let the experience wash over and through me.

Yes, I had been a flow-through tea bag with all its implications. In the end, I had been drained and emptied, my "essence" released. Who I had been gave way to my becoming, the ignorance of youthful inexperience and idealism chipped away. I had shed my naiveté as I steeped in time and experience to make a stronger brew. I chuckled, thinking that the bag and I had both come out somewhat the worse for wear. The "tea" however, was well worth it. I hoped Rosie would find herself steeped in her new culture, without being drained.

Just looking at a stack of formal invitations she had written highlighted those cultural differences. Nagib sent them to me to be posted in the States, and reading them had started the tears. The composition was very formal but poetic. Very Lebanese, I thought. But I hadn't sent them out. At the last hour, the political situation deteriorated yet again, and my husband pronounced that he could only vouch for the safety of his immediate family. Many of my relatives were very disappointed that they would not be able to attend Paul's wedding.

As I gazed at those cards in my hand, remembering other times long ago, I vacillated between anticipation and trepidation. What would old friends think of me? How would I be received? How would I communicate with Rosie and her family? Would I be good enough? But this time, it wasn't about me. It was a new pair of love birds, coming West this time...

As we prepared to land, I looked down. From a distance, it was paradise. I became lost in memories of a happily anticipated beginning. Memories of a different life.

CHAPTER 1

ZAHLE, LEBANON 1979

It was noon when we arrived in Beirut. The airport was chaotic, and war was evident in the number of soldiers wielding machine guns. They kept careful watch over the comings and goings of the passengers, as well as the bombed-out buildings in the surrounding neighborhoods. I stayed close to Nagib and held tight to three-year-old Paul's hand. This was Nagib's first homecoming since we'd been married four years before.

I looked around, trying to see something I could recognize and relate to—something to anchor me to this new reality. Nothing, however, presented itself. I drew in a deep breath, trying to quiet the nervous butterflies in my stomach. I quietly waited for my husband to collect the luggage and process his American family through the obligatory red tape. What had I gotten myself into?

We must have looked funny standing there, Paul and me, not in anyone's obvious proper possession. At twenty-nine, I looked much younger. I was only four eleven and weighed 105 pounds. I had light-brown hair and a baby face. We looked like two scared children, the older one holding the baby's hand, waiting for some adult to come and claim us. To a casual observer, it was as if we'd been beamed in by mistake from some other existence. It wasn't too far from the truth.

As we waded through customs, I considered the irony of my presence here. My great-grandparents fled Poland in the late 1890s on foot, running from a Russian occupation that was pressing young Polish men into military service. They chose a moonless night, minimizing their chances of being seen. Busia, my great-grandmother, nursed her newborn as they escaped, avoiding the sentries guarding the river border. They knew they would be shot if the baby cried. Now here I was on my first stop in the Middle East, going from stability and peace to a war-torn country and an uncertain future.

Like any airport, this one was full of hustling business-men and yawning travelers, joyful reunions, and tearful goodbyes. But at this airport, corridors were patrolled by armed soldiers who meant business. The walls were covered with bullet holes, and only a small portion of the airport was open.

Outside, the air that September afternoon was heavy. The pungent smell of petroleum fought with the rancid odor of rotting garbage. Beggars and their children ringed the airport, calling for alms while stableboys walked race-horses up and down the middle of the thoroughfare for exercise.

No fool, Paul ran to the safety of his father as soon as the arrival formalities were complete. I found myself alone as I struggled to catch up to them. The immigration officer in Paris had asked Nagib if he was traveling only with his children. He just laughed and said yes. Here, I was quickly singled out as a foreigner by the beggar women outside the airport. They surrounded me now with hands out, cutting me off from my family. Just as quickly, Nagib rescued me, loudly dispersing them as he put his arm around my shoulders and ushered me on.

Nagib's two brothers and a cousin had come to meet us, their joy evident as they hugged and slapped each other on the back. Thank God they had brought two cars, for we had packed almost everything we owned: seven suitcases full. Paul and I drove with Maroun, the younger brother, and George, his cousin, while Nagib and the luggage went with his older brother Gaby. I was comfortable with Maroun. He had lived with us in the States for a while, and Paul was overjoyed to see his favorite uncle again.

Now as the streets of Beirut sped by, I hung from the window to drink in as much of the scene as possible. Oleander was in bloom and anemic-looking banana trees intermingled with date palms along the highway. This was the Levant, exotic and mysterious, its long, rich history full of violence and intrigue, a land where emirs and warlords, saints and soldiers had left their mark.

I had been warned that what I could see of the city from the car window was all that I would see. PLO-controlled Beirut was volatile, and I did not appreciate at the time that this was not a very safe trip for our male relatives to be taking. Civil war had broken out in Lebanon in 1975. We followed the fighting on our honeymoon, and watched as President Sadat of Egypt addressed the Israeli Knesset in 1977. We were hopeful when Egypt and Israel signed a peace treaty in 1979. We indulged in a fantasy of other Arab States, particularly Syria, following suit. We hoped that peace would prevail and that the Palestinians and Israelis would co-exist. But this fight was biblical in its longevity, and, at least for now, that wasn't happening.

It was difficult in 1979 to look at the undeniable effects of the civil war and see the real city underneath. The proud and ancient city that had withstood the invasions of Romans, Crusaders, and Ottoman Turks would survive this clash among Arabs; I was sure of it. And so, I tried to look past the filth and garbage littering the streets, past the makeshift tents on the median strip of the very modern airport road. Past the ten-year-old boys sporting shotguns, and the countless young men guarding the perimeters of camps with Uzi machine guns. I tried to see the jewel that this region was.

The ancient mountain rose before us—tired-looking, oblique and naked. It looked down as if to say, "Ah, I was young and green once." It had been stripped of its famed cedar trees centuries before in order to build, among other things, the Temple of Solomon. This was the land of the Bible and of the Crusades. I shivered with goosebumps when I realized where I was.

Gazing at the mountain, I reflected that the virtue of age is the patience of long, sometimes painful, living. I was never so acutely aware of my country's youth, or indeed, my own inexperience, as I was that first afternoon. Youth revels in muscle flexing. It is strong and aggressive, acting first and often regretting it later. Youth is innocent and idealistic and noble, as I was. This mountain gazing back at me had seen so much. It may have seemed beaten down, but it was dignified, with centuries-old wisdom born of the knowledge of the foibles of men. It could afford to be patient.

As the car climbed into the hills surrounding Beirut, I was stunned by the beauty of the Mediterranean and amazed by the angle of our ascent. We seemed to be going straight up. Used to the gentler slope of the Appalachian foothills, as well as the much subtler inclines, I caught my breath at the dizzying view. Here again the mountain was exposed. I'm not sure what I had expected. But the defense was evidently long gone, leaving the mountain denuded and the city vulnerable.

The road cut straight into the sides of the mountain and spiraled around in a grudging concession to gravity. I was too terrified to enjoy the scenery. Narrow, little more than a donkey path, it widened slightly to accommodate progress. Two small cars passed each other with difficulty, and I held my breath every time we rounded one of the all-too-frequent curves. I was sure that one or the other of the drivers would be on the wrong side of the approach. I was not paranoid. My brother-in-law was driving quite fast and often skirted the outside edge of the mountain to pass a car blocking his way. In 1979, there were no guardrails to give a false sense of protection against falling off the mountain.

After a bit, I resigned myself to the inevitable and tried not to look down. The air was much cooler now and sweeter smelling as we went up into the mountains. The oleander and banana trees had given way to the hardier pines and cedars, and I thought we had left the urban blight and destruction of war behind. Now when I turned around, the view of the Mediterranean and the city was breathtaking.

Paul slept next to me as the two men conversed in Arabic, so I had time to concentrate on my relatives in the front seat. Maroun was a bit shorter than his older brother. His face was round like Nagib's and sported quite a handsome mustache. His Roman nose was, I thought, what my husband's would have looked like if it had not been broken in his youth. He was stocky and carried himself with assurance. He had, I knew, been fighting for one of the militias. Maroun's eyes were friendly and warm, and he laughed easily.

George was also warm and welcoming, in a shy way. He spoke no English, but his humor and good nature shone through. His looks were almost too good to be true, I thought. He was the only child of Nagib's aunt, Nabiha, his mother's sister, and was like another brother. I was taking mental notes to not forget anything so I could detail this trip for my friends back home.

We lost sight of Gaby's car early on, causing a lot of discussion in our own. Evidently, Gaby was the one who knew the road, since his business dealings brought him to Beirut on a regular basis. In my world, this wouldn't have been important. But here, a wrong turn could be dangerous. Luckily, I was blissfully ignorant of the tension in the front seat.

After stopping and reversing direction a couple times, Maroun steered the car onto a one-lane road that took us further up into the mountains. We didn't see any houses along the way as the road narrowed. It finally ended at the entrance to a rough-looking camp. An armed sentry pointed his machine gun at the car, speaking in Arabic. When they answered, he yelled angrily and gestured with his gun for us to leave. Maroun turned the car around quickly and beat a hasty retreat back down the road.

Four years and many Arabic lessons later, I found out, quite by accident, where we had been that day.

When the State of Israel formed in 1948, a flood of refugees flowed into the neighboring countries of Jordan, Syria, Egypt, and Lebanon. The Lebanese government did not allow even refugee status for the displaced Palestinians, since there would be legal implications in international law (U.N. resolution 196, the right of return). They were not allowed to work most jobs or get the necessary papers to become citizens. They congregated together, and camps sprung up in the major cities of Tyre, Sidon, Beirut, the Bekaa, and as far away as Tripoli. Sabra, Shatila, and Tal El Zaatar in Beirut were three of the better-known camps.

By 1975, the Christian Phalange, led by Pierre Gemayel, was a powerful interest group. When Phalangists were shot in a coffee shop by a group of Palestinians, the Phalangists retaliated by ambushing a busload of Palestinians in Ein el Rammaneh. Civil war was born.

From 1976 to 1979, Yasser Arafat was in control of the Palestinian Liberation Organization (PLO). It was during this period that the president of Lebanon, Elias Sarkis, was only allowed into west Beirut with Arafat's permission.

Four years after our misadventure on the road to Zahle, we were living in a suburb of Beirut, and I overheard Nagib telling the story to someone on the phone. He was speaking Arabic but stopped abruptly when he saw my white, shocked face.

"Shit," he said. "I forgot you speak Arabic now."

Maroun, he was saying, had unwittingly driven us into the infamous PLO refugee camp, Shatila. Shatila and its sister camp, Sabra, were the setting for gruesome massacres by the Israelis a few years after our mishap. When Maroun had asked for the road to Zahle, a Christian stronghold, it identified us as the enemy. I shivered, considering how that wrong turn could have ended.

Backtracking, we passed the burned-out hulls of cars and trucks as well as tanks: armed, manned, and ready to fire. These shrines to violence were punctuated from time to time by roadside shrines to the Virgin Mary or one of the saints. Candles burned in petition, and pictures of loved ones papered these alcoves, lest the saints forget what they looked like. Too tired to worry about what I was witnessing, I gave up and put these impressions in the pocket of my memory. Blissfully unaware of how extraordinary our situation was, I settled back to enjoy the scenery. Since no conversational demands were being made of me, I was able to catch my breath before the next onslaught.

Following the peaceful example of Paul next to me, I dozed for the rest of the two-hour trip.

* * *

The slowing of the car awakened me. I had missed the approach to Zahle, Nagib's hometown, as the car safely wound its way back down the mountain. My local friends called Zahle a village, although it boasted a respectable population of around 50,000 people. Maybe they were defining an ambiance or an attitude. Or maybe they meant that the essence of their nationality could be found there. Maybe they were referring to an unsophisticated honesty that was unpretentious. I think, though, they meant that the village was who they used to be.

Zahle is nestled at the foot of the Sanine Mountain in the heart of the Bekaa Valley, an agricultural region. A large percentage of the region's vegetables originate there, from lettuce, tomatoes, and spinach to chard, potatoes, eggplant, and beans. Wheat, their largest crop, is exported around the world. The mountains surrounding it were snow-capped and looked down on the town protectively.

Zahle was known for houses that were the beige of sand, topped by red slate roofs. The townspeople were also known for their colorful language, swearing being an unofficial sport. The town was built on a hill and there was nowhere you could go that wasn't either up or down.

Now off the main road we slowed down and turned onto a narrow street. Men, women, children; donkeys, and chickens milled about. They all seemed to be looking anxiously into the distance. As our car came into view, a shout went up and the crowd gathered around, Nagib's large family came en masse to properly greet his not-so-new bride and three-year-old son. The Americans had arrived. They were exotic to me, and I was exotic to them. After all, Nagib had told me that the Arab stereotype of the devil was blond and blue-eyed.

There was no mistaking my mother-in-law in the melee. She was the big woman at the head of the crowd, swinging incense and chanting in Arabic. Her hair was black and that day she wore it pulled back in a bandana. She wore tinted glasses and, despite a large nose that gave her face character, she was a handsome woman. She was in her element that day. She had been christened Ursula, the she-bear, but after the birth of her first son, she took the proud title of Im Gaby (mother of Gaby), as was the tradition of the region. Salwa, Gaby's wife, called her *Tante*, French for aunt, and I did likewise.

Coming from a large family myself, crowds do not easily intimidate me. This crowd, however, was daunting in its strangeness. The older men were dressed in what I later learned was traditional mountain garb. *Keffiyehs* covered their heads and they wore a sort of pantaloon, tight around the waist, ballooning out from the hips, then tight-fitting from the calves to the ankles. Some carried staffs and I wondered if they were shepherds. Many of the older women were dressed in black, denoting mourning. As I became more familiar with Lebanon, especially Beirut, this dress in young and old alike became a familiar sight.

I was introduced to people over and over as I was pulled this way and that. All I could do was nod graciously, a smile frozen on my lips, and hope there was no test at the end of the day. My mother-in-law forged ahead bearing a screaming Paul, and I only hoped that his father was somewhere inside to rescue the terrified boy.

Someone took possession of my elbow, steering me protectively through the crowd. My savior capably ran interference for me as she warded off hordes of well-wishers wanting to kiss my cheek, stroke my hair, or shake my hand. I didn't see anyone who looked like me at all.

Finally, my escort Salwa, Gaby's wife, led me down a long, dark hallway and into the sanctuary of my mother-in-law's house. The whole journey from car to house had taken less than five minutes, but the newness and strangeness made it seem forever.

The Middle Eastern people are renowned for their hospitality. Knowing this, I was still awed and humbled by the extent of it. Nagib and I, the honored guests, were escorted to the living room and served cold drinks, then left to catch our breath. In the meantime, the women bustled about, warming a large repast that had been prepared earlier and setting the table for the feast.

The room we were ushered into was spacious. We sat in the living/dining area furnished with hand-carved Louis XIV-style furniture, large and ornate, and not particularly comfortable. The far side of the room boasted a heavy, elaborately carved dining set supplemented with folding tables and chairs. The ceilings were high; I estimated twelve feet, and floor-to-ceiling windows covered with heavy drapes let the light flood the room and help warm the cold marble floors.

I watched as the women stacked platter after platter on the already laden table. Until now, I hadn't realized I was hungry. At home, I would have pitched right in to help. But for now, just this once, I was a guest. The men stayed with us, and I became the only woman in a crowded room. They were gracious, though, and attempted to communicate by speaking to me loudly and slowly in Arabic, punctuating their words with exaggerated gestures. They all hoped to make me feel welcome. Eventually, they turned their attention to Nagib. He sat on the sofa, receiving the welcome of well-wishers like an emperor in his glory.

I have never thought of myself as a shy person, but that day stands out as a particularly difficult one. I didn't speak or understand the language, and I felt my isolation tenfold. I was in grave danger of succumbing to self-pity, helped along by fatigue as I sat surrounded by strangers. Sure they were all talking about me, I tried to hide behind three-year-old Paul. The worst loneliness, I was learning, can overcome me in a crowded room.

But help came from the least expected person: my mother-in-law. She had made her objections before the wedding, worried that Nagib would never come home if he married a foreigner. Now, she was magnanimous in her welcome. After all, like it or not, I was family. She came in now, reprimanding Nagib for neglecting me. Leading me into the dining room, she served me herself.

The large table seated twelve comfortably and twenty rather less so, not including children on laps. There was so much food that serving dishes often had to overlap, one on top of the other.

Before us was an awesome array of food. Each dish not only tasted good, but was pleasing to the eye as well. This was the mezze, or first course, the traditional Lebanese appetizers, meant to be the build-up to the main course, but more than capable of standing on its own.

Among the then-unfamiliar food was tabouli, hummus, and my favorite, baba ghanoush, made from grilled eggplant and mixed with tahini, garlic, and lemon juice. There was a dish made by marinating the spinal cord of the lamb in a vinaigrette and various greens, including dandelion leaves and beans. Marinated tongue, sliced thin, an eggplant salad with diced tomatoes, spicy from hot peppers, grilled chicken livers in a marinade, as well as an assortment of cheeses piled onto the table. I drew the line at tasting the raw meats, though. Raw lamb's liver was served, as well as kibbeh nyee, a dish made from grinding very fresh lamb with bulgur wheat and raw onion, a staple of Lebanese cuisine.

"Killi, habibti."
"Killi baad."
"Haram."
"Bint dauphanee kteer."

Perplexed I turned to Nagib for an explanation. Had I offended someone? Laughing, he told me that his aunt was worried about me being too thin and was encouraging me to eat more. Even as we spoke, the ladies were bringing in yet more food. What I had just gorged on had been the appetizers, and Aunt Nabiha was filling my plate again. Unbelievably, they were bringing out platters of shish kabobs and grilled chicken, as well as kofta and kibbeh bil sonieh, (kibbeh in the pan), a ground lamb and cracked wheat dish without which no feast would be complete.

Knowing what I know now, I would never do more than just taste each dish. But that day I was polite, ignorant, and very hungry. I ate my fill, refusing only the raw liver. The ladies were delighted, for they had been cooking for days.

I had just spent weeks getting down to size eight and was, I realized, in grave danger of regaining the full fifteen pounds at one sitting. Taking pity on me, Nagib came to my rescue. He stood, waved his arms around, and proclaimed something in Arabic. I didn't speak the language, but I knew my husband well enough to guess he had said something off-color. Everyone laughed, and the force-feeding ended.

This was truly a family enterprise and labor-intensive. As soon as a dish was dirty, it was whisked away and replaced with a clean one. Young girls stood at the sink washing the plates as they were brought in, recycling them for the guests at the banquet. The sweetness of the teenagers who came to help, both girls and boys, impressed me.

Later that night in the peace and privacy of our bedroom, I mentally reviewed the previous twenty-four hours. So much had happened, and everything was new and different. I had been urged by literary members of my family to keep a diary. It would be a good way to sort out a myriad of new impressions. Tomorrow, first thing, I must find a place to buy a notebook and pen before I forgot the details of the trip and my first day in Lebanon.

"*Haleeb*! *Haleeb*!"

Morning dawned early in Zahle, heralded by the cries of the milkman announcing his arrival as he and his donkey wound their way through the still-slumbering streets. It was 4 am. Milk, like most other things here, was sold by the kilo. Poured out from large cans strapped to the donkey's back, the raw milk was so fresh it was still warm.

The large bedroom window opened right out onto the street. A wrought iron grate covered it to keep out any unwanted visitors. Shutters also hung from the outside, ready if further privacy was wanted. The window itself opened in the middle, like the shutters. Overcome by jet lag, and never one to awaken early, I turned over in the small bed and snuggled close to Paul, trying to go back to sleep. Nagib snored loudly in the bed next to mine, adding to the growing cacophony in the street.

At six, Catholic and Maronite church bells all over the small town began ringing loudly, calling the faithful to worship. Months later, waking for the first time in Saudi Arabia to the early morning Muslim call to prayer, I would be reminded of this morning, musing ruefully that the two religions had more in common than they thought. By seven, businesses all around were announcing the new day. A deafening din ensued as the metal gates, designed to keep out thieves, were raised.

By seven thirty, numerous relatives began making their presence known. One by one they came, tiptoeing into our borrowed bedroom. One needed clothing stored in the large wardrobe, another a towel. Various children needed combs, brushes, and God knows what. There were no built-in closets in this house, and wardrobes neatly hid away clothes and a multitude of other necessities. Finally, Im Gaby crept in to close the window and pull down the shade so that the traveler's sleep wouldn't be "disturbed."

Somehow, Nagib and Paul slept soundly through all of this. To the former, this was a lullaby to his homesick ears after years of struggle and loneliness. The latter, I could only guess, had it in his genes. At eight o'clock, I finally admitted defeat. Climbing quietly out of bed so as not to disturb my more fortunate traveling companions, I put on my robe and slippers, making my way down the narrow marble hall to the kitchen. There I found Im Gaby. She had already been to the six a.m. Mass, then to the butcher and greengrocers to buy supplies for lunch. Now she was preparing the main meal of the day with her niece, Hanani. Both women greeted me effusively, and using sign language and my broken French, they understood that the unfamiliar sounds of the village street had kept me awake.

It was a hilarious breakfast they served me that morning. Unable to communicate well enough to say what I wanted, and unfamiliar in any case with the foods being offered, I left all decisions to my in-laws. Giggling, I ate my toast and eggs with relish, enjoying the antics involved in the elaborate sign language necessary to communicate with "the American".

After finishing my third cup of very sweet tea, I was stymied by my mother-in-law's latest attempt at conversation. Hanani had gone home, and with her the French. No matter how hard Im Gaby tried, this foreigner her son had brought home just couldn't seem to understand. She was obviously frustrated. Salwa, Gaby, and Maroun, the only other English speakers in the extended family, had gone off to work. She gave me a horrified look when I suggested awakening Nagib to translate.

Pausing in her efforts, Im Gaby folded her arms in front of her and shook her head, clearly perplexed by our dilemma. Still, she was not one to easily admit defeat, and gave it one more try. Bending over to hike up her skirts, she began to vigorously rub her two hands high up between her legs, while alternately smelling her armpits. The light dawned. Yes, I nodded enthusiastically. I would love to take a shower.

The shower was an adventure. The bathroom was large and possessed, as any bathroom should, a toilet and sink. Having traveled in France and Italy after college, I could identify the European bidet, but the absence of a bathtub left me confused. My mother-in-law pointed to the shower fixture high up on the far wall. No stall surrounded it, but the floor sloped accommodatingly, allowing the water to rush down the drain at the bather's feet.

Rubber slippers had been supplied to me, and after three attempts, the water, at last, ran hot, telling me that Im Gaby had successfully lit the hot water heater in the kitchen. By this time, Nagib and Paul were up, and the day had really begun.

The days that followed were a whirlwind of new sights, sounds, smells, and impressions.

Im Gaby woke us the following morning at seven. Visitors had arrived and were waiting in the living room. Nagib sat up in bed, exchanging heated words in Arabic with his mother, but I got the tone. He turned to me, saying, "Get

23

up, get dressed, we have to see these people." He was clearly annoyed and tired after our long trip. Bleary-eyed, I rolled over and got out of bed. Was this the custom? I just did as I was told.

Our guests were two old ladies dressed in black with black scarves covering their heads and tied under their chins. They had just come from early morning Mass. The church was at the end of the short street, and they had to walk past our house on the way home. They had come to pay their respects and meet the *arouse* ("bride"). After we were introduced, they kissed me, but clearly agitated, crossed themselves and beat their breasts with their fists. They repeated this process over and over, muttering in Arabic. What had I done?

At first, Nagib spoke calmly while I stood, open-mouthed and perplexed. I'm not too sharp before my first cup of coffee, and I wasn't too sure what I was witnessing. Finally, he'd had enough. Nagib started shouting as his mother diplomatically hurried the ladies out of the house. He continued to fuss at his mother until at last, his sense of humor got the better of him. Laughing, he told me the meaning behind their gestures. Apparently, they were chastising him for marrying a thirteen-year-old! They knew Paul was three and wouldn't believe that I was older than sixteen. The mutterings, he explained, were prayers to the blessed mother, both for my well-being and for the welfare of his soul.

Later that day, Salwa took me to her hair salon. We washed our hair before we left and walked down the street with towels wrapped around our heads. I thought it was strange, but when in Rome... On the way, Salwa taught me a few phrases in Arabic. As one person after another greeted me, I looked them in the eye and said the most useful Arabic word I had learned as yet: "twenty-nine." This way, I could let them know Nagib had *not* robbed the cradle. The ladies at the salon giggled and thought it was very cute.

As the days went by, I had more than enough time to observe and absorb. I already knew that protocol and ritual reigned in the Arab world in an expanding concentric circle of community. The priority is one's immediate family, followed by the extended family, then the neighborhood, and finally the town. The homecoming of a native son with his exotic foreign bride qualified for attention at all levels.

First, the *muktar* (mayor) was expected. After him in close succession came the village priest, the bishop, a family of cousins who had been unable to make it earlier, friends who hadn't wanted to intrude on the family's happiness the day before, and a long line of acquaintances who had come for the gossip, to see the American and to pay their respects.

It was obvious that Nagib was a favorite, and the ambiance on his street was like a holiday. Everyone wanted to come hug him and talk to him. Almost as many well-wishers came to congratulate Im Gaby on her son's proud return. He had left Lebanon to get a college education—the first in his family—and returned with a degree, a wife, and a son.

Ritual demanded that any visitor, after a decent amount of time had elapsed, should be offered a *finjane* (cup) of thick, black, bitter Turkish coffee. Cigarettes were offered as well, it being poor manners to allow a guest to supply their own. If the guest's particular brand wasn't available in the house, a child would be dispatched to fetch them from the corner store. For this happy occasion, sweets and fruit were offered as well, drawing the average visit out to well over an hour.

The days that followed was more of the same, and I feared I'd never be able to leave the house, much less seeing any sights. One after another, they came in an endless stream. Just as one got up to say goodbye, another would appear at the door.

Nagib was sympathetic to my plight. It was, he agreed, senseless to subject me to hours of conversation I couldn't understand. He had been moved to laughter on more than one occasion while watching my frozen smile and stifled yawns. Even though he couldn't be excused himself, Paul and I could duck out whenever we wanted. He would cover for us. When all else fails, I thought, blame the baby.

Freedom was heaven after all the days cooped up inside the house. Often, Salwa took us walking and shopping downtown. Sometimes George and his family would take us riding through the countryside, but frequently just Paul and I would roam the neighborhoods unescorted, enjoying the sights and the mild weather.

The winding lanes we explored were like something out of *One Thousand and One Nights*, the collection of Arabic folk talkes from the Islamic Golden Age. Canopied outdoor bazaars were packed with merchants hocking their wares in the very narrow streets, fruits and vegetables overflowing from their stalls. Flies buzzed around carcasses of sheep and goats, which hung outside the butcher's stall, and women lingered to exchange gossip with the shopkeepers and each other. This was the grocery souk, or market.

The streets were crowded with Bedouin women draped in long caftans, balancing large baskets on their heads. As a child, Gaby came home one day with one of these women and her baby in tow, presented her to Im Gaby, and begged her to buy him a brother. Years later, I jokingly challenged her on the story, but Im Gaby just laughed loudly emphatically denying that the baby was Nagib.

On our walks, we would pass donkeys carrying vegetables, housewares, and tools, and stepped aside to make room for a herd of goats as they made their way in search of grass. We stopped and gawked at craftsmen as they plied their trades in the open, making mattresses, coffins, donkey saddles, tin, and copperware. We walked along narrow streets, which, if I hadn't known better, I would have taken for alleyways. Cars still made it through and, amazing to me, large American sedans seemed to be popular. It was not unusual to see small cars parked smack up against the side of a building, two tires on the curb. There were no sidewalks. All in all, magically unfamiliar.

It was a workout wherever we went. Zahle was built into the mountain, and in the downtown area, steep stone stairways attached lower areas to the higher roads. Amazingly, Paul and I never got lost. But then we didn't venture too far. I spoke no Arabic. and my French, the second language of Lebanon, was pathetic. I was the oddity in the town. My blond hair, blue eyes, and small stature were a dead giveaway. I was gratified, though, to find that no one passed us without saying hello, friend and stranger alike.

There was a garbage strike throughout the country that fall. I hadn't noticed the problem when I first arrived, but now it was painfully obvious in our walks through the neighborhood, as well as in the shopping district. Garbage overflowed everywhere. It hadn't been picked up for weeks, and residents and shopkeepers resorted to dumping trash in the streets and alleys between the shops. To make it worse, toilet paper in Lebanon was disposed of in the trash, not flushed down the toilets.

Huge, reeking mountains of garbage were, unfortunately, a memorable part of that first visit.

I had learned quickly that courtesy in this simple world was paramount. But that courtesy was to be my downfall, leaving me with my most regrettable memory of an already memorable trip. Pleased at my welcome, I was anxious to appear friendly in return. Therefore, when one of the neighbors pushed a bunch of fresh-cut grapes into my hands, I ate them right there on the street. This was a *grave* mistake.

By lunchtime, I was slightly queasy and had the beginnings of a headache. By four, my symptoms intensified, and panic was starting to set in. I had been warned repeatedly by seasoned travelers not to eat anything that was not cooked or soaked in bleach first. I tried to tell myself this was just a cold coming on. After all, with all the changes of the past few weeks, it would be no wonder.

But there was no denying it. I was sick, sick, sick! At bedtime, I wanted nothing more than to curl up and die. I prayed I would be able to vomit quietly, sparing myself the embarrassment of waking the entire household. No such luck.

By morning. I was beyond caring about anything. My fever was 105° F, my head throbbed, and I was in danger of becoming dehydrated through constant purging. Im Gaby took over now. The night before, she had respected my protests that everything would be all right, but now it was different. The search for an English-speaking doctor was on, and the whole neighborhood became involved. In and out of consciousness through layers of fevered sleep, I was alarmed by the number of people in the room. Was I dying? The doctor had arrived, and with him the entire neighborhood. Old women and children craned their necks from the back of the room to see better as the doctor began a perfunctory examination. However, when he put the tongue depressor down my throat, I gagged and then vomited everywhere. I had had enough.

"Get out! All of you! NOW!" I screamed, temporarily forgetting where I was. The doctor, however, spoke perfect English. Turning to the crowd, he calmly suggested they leave.

For several days after that, I drifted in and out of fever dreams. I awakened at one point to find an old lady dressed in black sitting holding my hand and crying. The woman was thin, her face creviced by years of tears. *Now* I must be dying, I thought. But no, this was Aunt Eugenie, the neighbor across the road. Suad, her daughter, was engaged to Maroun. Eugenie was a thin wraith of a woman, with stringy gray hair often pulled back with a scarf over it. Black of course. Aunt Eugenie only wore black. I rolled over and pretended to be asleep.

Days later, after heavy doses of antibiotics, I knew I was getting better when I realized I was starving. I had been living on chicken broth and potatoes baked in the baker's oven for the past week. All I wanted was a Coke and some Lipton chicken noodle soup, the comfort foods of my childhood. Nagib either didn't understand about the Lipton or there was none to be found, so Im Gaby made the soup for me from scratch. Delicious.

At long last I was well enough to get out of bed and eat a real meal. Now the family could finally have the party they had been preparing. Aunt Nabiha, Im Gaby's sister and George's mom, had been planning an event at her house. I had put a serious damper on these plans, and our time in Lebanon was limited, so as soon as I was able to go out, she set about preparing a family feast. We were the toast of the town, and everyone vied for the honor of cooking for us. Aunt Nabiha's house was a one-floor condominium with marble floors, high ceilings, spacious, well-furnished rooms, and a small garden off the back of the house where the children could play. Best of all, they had a modern bathroom, with a bathtub, no less!

There was a festive air at Aunt Nabiha's that day. She and Lodi, George's wife, were pleased with themselves, for they were preparing some specialties not yet served in previous dinners and luncheons. When I walked into the kitchen with Paul to say hello, my eye fell immediately to where the skull of a sheep boiled merrily away in the large kettle, set on a propane-fueled burner that sat on the floor. Its empty eye sockets stared up at me. Still squeamish from my recent illness (at least that was my excuse), I quickly left the room. Aunt Nabiha followed me, though. Approaching Paul, she tried to put something in his mouth as she said, "*Kol zubra.*" Being the mother of a little boy, *zubra* was one word that was in my vocabulary. It meant penis. When Paul refused and ran away, she turned quickly to me and popped the lamb's penis neatly into my gaping mouth. I stood, frozen. Salwa laughed and took it out of my mouth, disposing of it quietly in the kitchen.

When I told this story to my Beiruti friends in Saudi Arabia, they were just as horrified as I had been. That's the village, they told me.

CHAPTER 2

After we had been there for a couple of weeks, Nagib and Gaby planned an all-day excursion to the north to see the famed Cedars of Lebanon. It was to be the only real touristy outing on our schedule. It involved an all-day car trip along some rough terrain, and I was looking forward to it. When the time came to leave, however, I found the family huddled around the radio in the living room. Forty people had been kidnapped on the road to the Cedars, and it wasn't safe for us to take the trip.

I was disappointed, but here you had to roll with the punches. Kindly, Nagib and Gaby put their heads together and announced they were taking me way, way up to see the very source of all the water in Zahle. Water is a precious commodity in the Middle East, especially here in the mountains. They prided themselves on the quality of their water and even bottled it to be shipped out and sold in other parts of the region.

It was not an all-day event as the aborted trip would have been, but I was grateful for an excuse to see more of the countryside. We drove through downtown Zahle and out onto the main boulevard. After a bit, we turned onto a narrow road that took us up and through some small villages overlooking the Berdawni River. I looked around and recognized the tier farming I learned about in third grade. Across the valley, I could see the stone walls that rose up to make a wedding cake effect, spiraling the mountain. We rode past fig trees, grape arbors, and olive groves, and I learned that it takes an olive tree years before it produces fruit. We stopped to let herds of sheep cross the road and bounced up and down as we tried to avoid the many potholes.

The road seemed to be skirting the rim of the mountain looking down deep into the valley, and all the while we kept the river in sight. As we climbed higher, the river snaked smaller in the distance and the scenery became more and more bleak. The day was overcast and chilly, and the colors in my memory are gray and dirty green.

Still, we rode on, the men enthusiastically assuring me that what we were going to see was so special it would be worth a much longer trip than this one. The car kicked up a cloud of dust as we drove, for it hadn't rained in quite a while. Lebanon was famous for its beautiful autumn weather, and the rainy season would come months later. In front of us, in the far distance, loomed the omnipresent snow-capped mountains. The further up we went, the worse the road got, until finally we had to leave the car and walk. It was a relief to get out and stretch our legs after the cramped ride. I have never done well in the back of a car, and the men had ridden up front.

We hiked up a rocky path, framed by mountain laurels and scrub pines. The water was just a trickle as we walked, and the men assured me it wouldn't be much further. As we climbed over one boulder in the middle of the path, Gaby triumphantly proclaimed that we had arrived.

Nagib gave out a *whoop* and yelled for me to come see. Hurrying as best I could, I rounded the bend and joined them at the source: a trickle of water coming out of the rocks. Important indeed, but neither man seemed to see—much less mind—the rotting, stinking corpse of a cow lying smack in the middle of the stream, polluting the water and providing a feast for maggots, flies, and crows.

That image has stayed with me over the years, providing a wordless testimony to the defilement of purity and innocence. It was a fitting metaphor for little Lebanon, weighed down by the stinking corpse of world politics.

Altogether, we stayed in Zahle for eight weeks. We had told his family of our decision to move to Saudi Arabia. Salwa told me that under no circumstances would she ever agree to go. Maybe she knew something she wasn't telling me?

I made good use of the time, however. I sat on a high stool in Im Gaby's kitchen day after day while she cooked. I had a spiral notebook and took copious notes on how to wash the *jej* (chickens), soak the *riz* (rice), and season the *lahme* (meat). Im Gaby was a renowned cook who only ate her own food, even taking it to dinner parties. Her reputation was well deserved. She cooked by ear, and my recipes from that visit are a treasure. Now, if my husband challenges my Lebanese cooking, I can speak with authority: "Your mother made it that way."

As I took notes, she spoke to me in Arabic, and I quickly learned the Arabic terms for the common foods we ate, as well as the fixtures and fittings of her kitchen. It was the beginning of my learning the language. *Mutbuk Arabie*—kitchen Arabic. Life outside her kitchen door was explained to me in Arabic as well, such as the donkey going down the street. "*Hamar*," she said as she pointed for my benefit and Paul's. "*Hamar*." Donkey. Nagib, it turned out, had been affectionately calling me that for years.

He was a jokester, my husband. Before we came, he had painstakingly taught me phrases in Arabic. It was important, he said, for me to greet his mother in her language. I liked this and worked hard to get the pronunciation right. When I finally made my little speech, his mother collapsed in gales of laughter, tears streaming down her face. My pronunciation was perfect. I had greeted her by saying, "Hello, you bitch!"

Luckily for me, she knew her son.

Even though this was a homecoming for Nagib, I was still a tourist. Nagib and Gaby said I had to see the ancient ruins in Baalbek. We would be combining the trip with a visit to the farm of Nagib's cousins in the Bekaa Valley, not far from the ruins. The air was cool during the day, and Salwa and I decided to wear our recently-purchased matching velour pullovers with jeans and leather boots. We both looked very stylish.

Along the way, makeshift huts peppered the side of the road. It looked as if they'd been constructed from discarded corrugated metal and cardboard boxes, or whatever the inhabitants could glean from other people's garbage. They made a poor shelter from the elements. The weather was pleasant—crisp and bright, but winter was coming, along with heavy snow and frigid temperatures. *What then?* I thought. These people were Palestinian refugees, displaced by years of war, belonging to no land, with no government willing to claim them.

We passed farms dotted with ancient Roman monoliths, almost incongruous next to the semi-modern farm equipment. I would have liked to stop and examine them, but my husband was a point-to-point person.

But once there, there was more than enough to examine, and it was humbling to see the Roman ruins up close. The temple columns were unbelievably high, making me dizzy as I looked up trying to see the tops. I don't think I could have felt any smaller. We climbed the rock stairs and poked around, looking at the sculptures and scenes from mythology. It was helpful that I had been such a mythology buff when I was younger. I challenged myself to try to think of the Greek counterpart to the Roman gods depicted here.

When we left the ruins, we stopped at a tourist concession where Paul and I got to ride a camel. It was probably the only camel in Lebanon, since the Lebanese used the donkey for work and transport. I mounted the camel while it lay on the ground with all four legs bent under it, and Nagib handed Paul to me. The challenge was holding onto Paul and keeping my seat while the animal rose to stand. It brought up its back legs first, leaving us at a precarious angle while it then raised up its two front legs. Getting down was even worse. The camel folded its front legs first, leaving us at a more precarious pitch until we were finally down. It was thrilling.

As the air became cooler and the days shorter, Im Gaby announced that it was time to make *labneh bi zite*. Labneh is a soft, tangy cheese made from yogurt. Eaten with toasted pita bread, it was a staple for breakfast. Labneh bi zite, it was explained to me, was labneh rolled into balls and preserved in olive oil. For *labneh bi zite*, Im Gaby liked to use sheep's milk, for the flavor was better when preserved in olive oil. We drove to a nearby farm and after a chat with the farmer, arranged to have the fresh milk delivered the next morning.

The process was simple once you knew the basics. We made the yogurt first. To make it, we heated the milk until it was ready to boil, then left it to cool for a bit. The milk was cool enough when she could hold her pinky finger in the hot milk to the count of ten. At this point it was safe to add a cup of cultured yogurt. She mixed that in and covered the pot with a lid, then wrapped the whole thing in a thick wool blanket and placed it on the counter, away from drafts.

The next morning, to my amazement, the milk had thickened into a beautiful pot of yogurt. Im Gaby then brought out a large cloth bag with a drawstring at the top and, working over the sink, poured the yogurt into the bag. She tied a knot at the top, securing the bag to a faucet over the sink where gravity forced out the moisture. Every morning, she would take the yogurt out of the bag to rinse and salt it. She would wash out the bag, return the thickening yogurt cheese, and take the bag to the faucet. After about three days, it was pronounced ready. She turned the cheese out into a bowl and kneaded it like bread dough. She showed me how to oil my hands so as not to become a sticky mess, and then take small handfuls of the white paste, rolling it into a ball. We placed each ball into a glass jar, added olive oil to cover the cheese, and we were done. I've since seen that cheese in supermarkets offered plain, like we made, or rolled in spices.

The traditional cooking in the mountains had a lot to do with preserving the harvest for the winter. Refrigeration came to the Lebanese mountains some ten years after it became a regular thing in the US. The herbs were dried in the sun and stored in glass jars, to be used in cooking or making medicinal teas. The house across the street from my mother-in-law's had a sod roof. It was not unusual for the neighbor's chickens to be seen up there feeding or nesting, and, in the summer, the sod was brilliant with a small, flowered plant called *babounish*, or chamomile. Grape leaves were picked at a very tender stage and preserved in brine, and small eggplants were stuffed with walnuts and garlic, to be kept in olive oil for the winter.

The preserved foods are collectively called *hawadir*. Nagib told me that he could remember, as a young boy, when his mother put out up to thirteen different preserved and stored delicacies for one winter meal.

The olive oil, a staple of the region, was itself a by-product of the harvest. Years later, living in East Beirut, we had first-pressed olive oil delivered to our house by a farmer. He had processed the oil just that week and brought around twenty gallon jugs to us. The jugs were made of dark-green glass to filter out the sun so they would keep longer. We stored them in the mezzanine over our kitchen, but at that time, other concerns were taking precedence. We left Beirut shortly after that delivery, never to return as a family. I don't know what happened to the oil. I hope my mother-in-law used it.

One day that fall, I was invited to help several of the ladies prepare *kashk*, a Lebanese staple food. Kashk is the final result of combining bulgur wheat with goat's yogurt. I ate kashk on New Year's Eve back at home. Nagib had had a bag of the white floury substance, and we saved it for the holiday. He cut up small beef cubes and browned them with onions, garlic, and diced potatoes. Putting about two cups of the dry powder into a pot, he slowly added water until it became a thick soup. He added the onions and meat and let them cook together. It was delicious and very filling, with a sour tang that I couldn't quite place, until that visit gave me a clue.

The making of the kashk was an involved, labor-intensive part of the traditional village preparation for the lean winter months. The making of this sour flour was usually done in the early autumn to coincide with the wheat harvest. I was told that goat's yogurt is preferred over sheep's or cow's milk because of its tangy taste.

On the day in question, Im Gaby started bustling around early. She looked up at the sky, standing in her doorway, elbows akimbo, and, pointing upward, indicated to me that the weather was good for her plans. She beckoned to me, and I followed her, not knowing where we were going, but happy to have a destination that took me out of the house.

We were joined by Salwa, who explained that we were going to Marie's house to make kashk.

Once at Marie's, we went inside and up a narrow stairway to the sod roof. Already gathered were about eight women, including Lodi, Aunt Nabiha, and Hanani. Marie's daughters, Badr and Lila, were there, as well as Hanani's daughter Claude. A few of the women I hadn't met before but recognized from my walks in the neighborhood. Salwa handed me an apron as she donned one herself and told me to find a spot on the ground.

The women were gathered around a large, coarse rug spread on the dirt. They were either kneeling on it or seated cross-legged at its edge. Im Gaby directed me to join the ladies sitting cross-legged at the edge of the blanket, as she walked over to the other side of the roof to sit on a chair next to her sister Nabiha. Her bad back precluded her from sitting on the ground. They sat with a very large, wood-framed sieve between them, receiving the powdered flour as it was rubbed off of the balls. Using large circular motions, they sieved the powder onto a huge metal tray underneath. Both women wore large aprons over their house dresses, and scarves held back their hair.

I found a spot between Lodi and Salwa, and for the next several hours helped to rub the dried kashk from the outside of what looked like white tennis balls. It was pleasant to sit there with these women, busy at last with a task and glad to be doing something useful. I really didn't know what I was doing, but even so, I felt this was special and unique to the region. I felt privileged to participate, and made a mental note to try to remember the details. I had great faith in Nagib, sure he would be able to explain the process to me and fill in the blanks. Wrong!

The blanket we gathered around was a goat hide, called a *wadiya*. It was large and heavy, and all the work of those two weeks was done on it. Evidently, it kept the integrity of the kashk, preventing other smells from permeating the dough. Back then it was a valued, and valuable, possession within an extended family. Of course, in Nagib's family, the wadiya was owned by Im Gaby. She liked to be in control and in charge. She was the sheikha.

We had been in Zahle for several weeks, and our thoughts were filled with plans for the trip home, as well as painful goodbyes. There was a subtle change in the emotional climate of the house as the remaining days became considerably fewer than the days already spent. "Before you go" was said more frequently now, and it became more important than before not to forget anyone or anything. Now the days were busy, not only getting ready to leave, but the final preparations for the inevitable winter.

The house was downright cold. During the day, I would go outside and stand in the sunshine for a while to warm up, but at night there wasn't much I could do. The men brought out the *barbour*, a cylindrical kerosene stove about two feet high. They placed it in the family room and connected the long exhaust pipe to it at one end and to the hole where the wall met the ceiling at the other. This was the only heated room in the house. We all gathered around the stove in the evenings, watching Arabic TV, visiting, or just chatting. We sat in a line on the sofa, sharing a blanket for warmth, and took turns getting up to go to the cold kitchen for snacks.

Im Gaby put ham and cheese inside large pita rounds and placed them on top of the stove, where the bread crisped and the cheese melted. They were warm and delicious, as well as comforting on cold nights with a cup of hot sweet tea. The smell of the toasting bread combined with the steamy fragrance of the tea lent a safe, warm ambiance to the family gatherings on those cold evenings.

Babies were bathed and readied for sleep in front of the stove, but the adults were not as lucky. The bedrooms were frigid. I was sharing a bed with Paul, but he was too little to add much warmth. I was so cold it was painful, and I couldn't sleep. When my mother-in-law became aware of my discomfort, she took care of the situation straight away. Going into the bedroom, she removed the percale sheets and replaced them with a coarse wool blanket. I slept warm and comfortably after that.

CHAPTER 3

"**C**ome for a walk with me, Nagib," I demanded. He tried to make an excuse. He was an action man and didn't like intimate strolls.

"Come on," I coaxed. "We'll be leaving soon, and I want you to show me the wadi."

Paul joined in to support me, and Nagib finally caved in. He couldn't fight both of us.

The sun was shining on the snow-capped mountain in front of us. Paul and I wore sweaters, but Nagib was comfortable in his long-sleeved shirt. I had been cold in the stone and marble house, but out in the sun, finally moving my legs, I warmed up quickly.

Once outside Im Gaby's house, we turned right, then right again, all the while heading downhill and toward the downtown area. The road was steep, and we were forced to walk in a single file, stretching to hold Paul's hands between us whenever a horse, donkey, motorcycle, or small car came along. There were no sidewalks, just curbs that butted up against the structures along the way. The strike was ongoing, and we passed alleys of garbage. However, I had become accustomed to it and chose to ignore it.

As we walked, I had the chance to observe. What were those metal containers on top of the houses? They were water tanks, Nagib told me. Just like people in the States have fuel oil delivered to their houses, so the Lebanese have drinking water delivered. Water trucks would pull to the side of the building and, using thick hoses, fill these tanks.

By the time we approached the bottom of the hill, Paul was riding on his father's shoulders, his usual throne. I was winded trying to keep up with Nagib's longer gait, and at my request, we slowed down so I could catch my breath. As we walked along the main street, shopkeepers came out to greet us and invite us in for a cup of *ahwhe* (Turkish coffee). We declined each time and continued walking toward the Wadi.

Despite the coolness of the air, I was quite warm by the time we reached our destination, and glad to sit in the outdoor café. The Wadi was a flat area, butting up to a rock cliff. There, a narrow stream of water created a fall, dividing the outdoor café into two natural sections. The water continued its path in what I considered a creek, but Nagib assured me it was a river. Linen-covered tables were situated aesthetically beneath the rock, making this a favorite destination of Zahlewese in good weather.

The dampness of the rock, as well as the shade, soon cooled our skin until I was chilly. We ordered Turkish coffee and sat companionably, soothed by the music of the water, alone for the first time in weeks.

Nagib sat, leaning back in his chair with his long legs stretched out before him. I couldn't help thinking how handsome he was, and how lucky I was to have married such a wonderful man.

I loved to hear him tell stories. There was a reason he was such a favorite. Now, to entice him, I leaned my chin on my hand, looked at him slyly, and said, "So. *Now* tell me. Where did your uncle hide the guns?"

It was a joke between us. When we were first dating, I would flirt with him by whispering in his ear, "Tell me a secret." He would whisper back, "I know where my uncle hid the guns." He never could flirt. Remembering now, I laughed and said, "Imagine. I married you anyway."

"No," he protested. "I didn't make it up. He really did hide the guns, and I was the only one of the cousins he trusted to know the secret."

I've met everyone, I thought. Stories Nagib had told me began to come into context. The more outlandish of them now seemed plausible in this exotic setting.

"Tell me, tell me," I demanded, knowing this was my best chance.

"All right," he answered. Paul slept peacefully on his lap, and he shifted him slightly before he began.

"You met Amu Louis," he said. "He is the sheik of the El-Fahel family, my mother's family. *Sheik* means not only that he is the head of our very large extended family, or tribe, but that he is regarded as a wise man. He earned this title out of respect for his leadership."

"He is married to my Aunt Deebee. Her name means 'she-wolf,' and they called her that because she has blue eyes. By the way," he continued, "they say in this part of the world, blue eyes are a throwback to the Crusades. Amu Louis was also Deebee's first cousin, and of course, my mother's first cousin. They did that a lot back in the old days."

"Anyway," he continued, "the El-Fahel family is and was a very large family, and they all lived in a kind of enclave called St. Anthony's neighborhood. You know my mother's street is St. Anthony's Road, and St. Anthony's church is at the end of the road. That's how they identified the neighborhoods. But just as often, people would call it the El-Fahel neighborhood, because that's who lived there.

"In the ten years prior to Lebanese Independence, Amu Louis was the head of our family's business. The business was very large and very lucrative, and involved all the family, even the women."

"What was the business?" I interrupted, impatient at the deliberate pace of his tale.

He sipped his coffee and, finding it cold, waved for the waiter and ordered more. He made a show of smacking his lips over the fresh brew before he continued, teasing me. Seeing that he had milked my patience for all it was worth, he twinkled his eye at my annoyance and continued.

"The business, sweetheart, was hashish," he answered dramatically, enjoying the look of surprised incredulity on my face. It was the reaction he had been building up to. "Yes," he answered my unuttered exclamation. "My family made their living by trafficking in drugs. They grew, processed, packaged, and shipped hashish throughout the region. This area, the Bekaa Valley, was famous for it. Amu Louis became the best and the most notorious. He earned the respect of many, particularly within the family, because he provided a livelihood for so many. They made good money and were able to care for their families."

He went on to tell me about his uncle's depot. "It was a large house with many rooms," he said, "and an outdoor courtyard where the men would gather to drink coffee and await orders."

"When was this?" I asked.

He paused for a minute, thinking, then answered, "In the late fifties, I think. You have to realize," he continued, "that this involved the women as well.

"Oh, yes," he said, in answer to the expression on my face. "This was a real family business. Everyone contributed.

"The women would sit in a circle on the floor of the depot with the hashish in the middle. Each one knew her specific job; some would sort, others would weigh, while still others cut and packaged. Most of their deliveries went outside the country, with the bulk of it going to Syria.

"The money was brought in bags to Sheik Louis's house. They would bring it in, place it on a table, and leave. My uncle would review it, then sort it, and place it in piles. Meanwhile, the men would pace about outside, excited and anxious, waiting to be called in to receive their cut.

"One by one they came in as they were called. One by one they were paid according to their role in the business and their family need."

"It sounds just like the mafia," I interjected.

"It was a mafia," he answered. "Don't even doubt it."

He cleared his throat and took another sip of coffee. It was starting to get dark in the shadow of the rocks, but Nagib was the quintessential storyteller. He would not be rushed.

"The others trusted him and knew he would be fair in the distribution. In return they gave him their complete loyalty. The society then was almost feudal.

"The feeling on payday was like a holiday. Everyone paid off his debts and enjoyed going shopping. I was young back then, but I still remember shopping for new clothes, and how excited my mother was.

"But nothing stays the same," he continued. "In the early sixties, the government started to enforce the law. You see, the law was always there, but the sheiks were stronger. They had the loyalty of their clans, and the officials were all corrupt.

"Little by little, business became tighter, more difficult. Especially for the El-Fahel clan. That feeling of well-being on the day the money was distributed was gone. Money was tight and everyone worried now about being caught.

"The police started conducting raids on the neighborhood. They knew that Sheik El-Fahel had a shipment in the depot. He was trying to pack it up for delivery, but he knew the police were watching him.

"They were about halfway through packing and loading the shipment when the police attacked. I guess you'd call it a raid in English.

"Somehow, the El-Fahels had some warning. But not by much. My Aunt Deebee, Uncle Louis's wife, ran to call her sisters. Remember, this was a family enterprise. The sisters, including my mother, ran to Deebee's house and started putting up barricades.

"Sofas, tables, chairs, cars. . . you've seen the street. It wouldn't take much to block that little road."

He was right. Amu Louis's house backed up to a steep hill and could only be approached from the front. It was easy to see how the police could be held off for a while.

"When the police got there, they found the barricade, but the women were on the other side with rifles and ammunition, waiting for them. The idea was to buy time for the men to finish packing this shipment and get it out before the police could gain access to the house.

"My mom, with her sisters Badr, Deebee, and Nabiha, held off the police for six hours. When the police finally got into the house, the men, the packing equipment, and the drugs were all gone. They had moved it all out through a tunnel in the back of the house that led to another side of the neighborhood. Cars were waiting there, and they had plenty of time to get everything away."

"But what happened to the women?" I asked.

"Nothing," he replied. "The police never found anything, no one was hurt, and back in those days, they couldn't arrest women. They still talk about this in the town. The women were very brave.

"They were more cautious after that and backed off the business for a bit. The government had extended its authority to the lands where the hashish was grown and tightened up the borders, making life much harder for all the people involved in the hashish trade, especially Sheik El-Fahel.

"Everyone had run out of ideas. That is, until two men, Uncle Louis's nephew Hani and Abu Ali, Aunt Nabiha's husband, put their heads together and came up with a plan.

"They wanted one last hurrah, so to speak. One last big shipment that would set them all up financially, and then each would go his separate way in a legitimate job or business.

"The plan that Hani and Abu Ali proposed took care of the crops while they were growing, as well as the processing and the shipment across borders. It really was clever. They proposed that they sow the field with cabbage seeds. They already had the hashish, but had been unable to distribute it due to the microscope the police had put them under.

"When the cabbages were still young, they placed small packages of hashish into the core of each vegetable. You've seen cabbage growing in the garden. It starts out small, and then the leaves just continue to grow. Within a short period of time, they would effectively surround and protect the main crop—the hashish.

"The elders immediately visualized the rest of the plan without needing to be told. It would be easy to harvest the cabbage crop once it was mature, pack it in crates, and ship it by trucks across the Syrian border, or further if they wanted. So that's what they did. It was a huge crop, and from what I've been told, they all made a lot of money on that one shipment; their last."

"Wow," was all I could muster. "But where was your father in all of this?"

By now dark was setting. Nagib paid the bill and we began the walk home.

"My father," he began, "had nothing to do with it. He was a foreigner, an *ajnabee*."

I was familiar with this word since I was frequently introduced to people, in Arabic, as "the foreigner." I was surprised to hear it, though, in this context. It meant outsider.

"My father wasn't one of them. He wasn't from the El-Fahel family."

"But neither was Aunt Nabiha's husband," I argued.

"That's true. But he was a scoundrel like them. What's more, he knew all the back roads and donkey paths. That, along with his cleverness, made him an asset."

He put his head down in concentration as we walked. I knew this was difficult for him. His father had been dead less than two years, and Nagib hadn't been there to say goodbye. So much had been left unresolved.

"My father," he continued, "was an idealist. He was well educated. That's not a big deal to you. All your family is educated, but remember, Cath, who you've met here. They're simple people. I'm the first to graduate from college; also, the first to go away."

We were closer to his mom's house now, so he stopped and sat on a low wall on the side of the road, patting the spot next to him for me to sit down. "My father spoke four languages," he said. Did I tell you he had fought with the Armenian resistance against the Turks?"

My blank look was answer enough.

"He believed in their cause. For a time, when he was first married, he secretly carried missiles and other munitions on his back across the mountains to the fighters."

"I've never heard you talk about your father before," I said, surprised.

"Yes, well," he answered bitterly, "my father hid behind his newspaper most of the time. My mother ran the show." He rose, carrying Paul, and started walking.

We were back at the house now, and I knew this was the end of the conversation. He had told me a great deal about his family, but I was sorry such a pleasant day had ended on a sour note.

"Hold up a minute," I said, stopping in my tracks just yards from his mother's front door. I grabbed his shirt from the back to stop his momentum. He turned and looked at me in surprise.

"You still haven't answered my question," I said.

His confusion was genuine. "What are you talking about?"

"Where DID your uncle hide the guns?!" I yelled in a stage whisper.

He threw back his head and laughed, and I had achieved my goal. Pulling me close, he leaned down and whispered in my ear, "He hid them in the grandfather clock in his living room."

Straightening up, he leaned his long frame against the wall, and I could see the boy in him, proud and delighted to have been the only one of his generation trusted with this very adult confidence.

"The front panel of the clock was a solid piece of wood," he began. "There was no handle or knob or anything that would make anyone think it could be opened. Amu Louis took me into his living room when I was twelve and showed me that if you pushed on the beveled edge of the panel, it would slide open."

"It was the greatest thing. Imagine a boy just seeing how it magically opened, and then to see all of these guns neatly stashed away.

"Think of the business. Every time his men would make a run, he would gather them into that room and lock the door. As kids, we all thought it was very mysterious and exciting, but we never knew what went on behind those doors. He was passing out the guns."

So now I knew the story behind the guns. But more, the trust my husband's uncle had put in such a young boy spoke volumes about Nagib's character.

I was sorry that we would be leaving so soon. Nagib's story had added dimension to the people I had met. Particularly the older ones. I looked at Amu Louis with new eyes the next time I saw him. Before, he had been another old man to greet, and I tried my best to communicate with my eyes and smile. The language barrier was like a glass wall, or invisible shield, that prevented me from knowing these people better.

Before our *mishwar* (walk or outing), I had only seen an old man, pleasant enough, who walked the town in the morning, stopping at different houses to drink coffee, exchange gossip, or have lunch. Rarely did I see him with his wife, Aunt Deebee. She was too ill then to go walking with her husband, and would die before we were able to go back.

The next day we managed to escape for a rare respite from receiving visitors and family obligations. As we sat on a rock wall, we held hands in the sun and mapped out our plans for the future. Nagib had brought his bride to see his home and it was everything he had said it was. Even the fudge trees up on the *croom* (orchard). He laughed when I reminded him of his previous struggles with the English language, but once I had tasted the figs, I had told him no, fudge wasn't all that wrong. This was the sweetest, richest fruit I had ever tasted. We had plucked it right off the tree, so ripe it broke apart as we handled it.

We decided up there that we would make our fortune in Saudi Arabia. I believed in Nagib's abilities. To me, he was a kind of superhero, able to leap tall problems in a single bound. We wanted to raise our children to be multilingual like their father, and we would build our house right here on the top of the mountain, looking down over the town.

"This is the most beautiful place on earth," I told him as we sat on the hill.

"Can you see yourself living here eventually?" he asked.

I could. He laughed at me when I told him there was something familiar and comfortable about Zahle. Even so, I was nervous. But he calmed my fears, saying, "You know I would never make you stay in a place where you weren't happy." He said this with love and trust, never dreaming that he would, one day, be bound by these words.

As we prepared to leave, I reviewed the past eight weeks in my mind. I had been graciously received by my in-laws. Salwa was even studying English so she could communicate with me. I don't know what I had expected, but what I got was a warm reception from people who went out of their way to make me feel at home. It had been a whirlwind of new foods, sights, smells, and sounds. I had met villagers from the mountains of what they used to call a third-world country. These villagers had spoken three languages, dressed in silk, and had the class to make the American bride feel at home.

When we settled on the plane to return home, I looked at Nagib with new eyes. I saw him for the first time in the context of his culture and family. It gave him dimension. It gave *us* dimension; it enriched our relationship and made our marriage more honest. We made plans together now. No one could say I was going into this adventure with my eyes closed.

CHAPTER 4

BALTIMORE 1979

Nagib was twenty-one when we met, but looked and acted years older. He had a bush of black hair and was fond of bragging that it was so thick he couldn't even get a comb through it. He carried his six-foot-two frame with the confidence of a man who knew he could handle anything thrown his way. His eyes were deep brown, almond-shaped pools, framed by thick lashes. They were always twinkling with laughter. He was the original tall, dark, and handsome archetype, and his gap tooth and crooked nose lent his face character. When I learned he could dance, I was a goner.

I was the perfect foil for Nagib's dark good looks. I was also proud with not fully tested confidence, but any similarities ended there. I was Cathy to family and friends, Kasia to my Polish grandmother and sister Mary. I was petite and blissfully unaware of the amused stares that our "Mutt and Jeff" appearance elicited from passers-by and friends alike. I wore my blond hair as demanded in the early seventies—long and straight, hanging down my back.

We always figured that fate brought Nagib to Baltimore, putting him next door to me. He had originally come to the States to pursue a business degree at the University of Florida in Gainesville, acing his courses in chemistry, math, and French. Although he spoke very little English, he was confident he would work it out. So confident that on one memorable occasion, he went to a McDonald's for lunch. After standing in a long line, he got to the counter and found himself unable to order. All he could say was "Eat." Everyone laughed, and he left humiliated and hungry, but determined. He went straight home, opened a dictionary, and memorized, as he liked to say, "one thousand verbs!"

Although he excelled academically, a broken romance and a timely phone call from a friend in Maryland led him to pack his bags and move to Baltimore. All of his schooling had been in Jesuit-run institutions in his hometown, and he was sure that Loyola College would be a good fit. Despite losing most of his credits in the transfer, he felt comfortably landed.

An innocent invitation to dinner from my elderly neighbor left in my mailbox changed the course of my life. "Come to dinner and bring two friends," she said, "and meet my boy and his two friends."

I liked him from the start, handsome with impeccable manners. He smoked cigarettes and wore Brute cologne, a combination that would stay with me, always smelling like the beginning of love. When he saw me home across the porch, he asked me out and I never looked back.

That first night I asked him how a boy from the mountains of Lebanon had chosen the U.S. to study. He was only nineteen when he came and had never been far from home. His parents objected, saying that it was a lot of money, way too far away, and he didn't speak English! But he was smart, ambitious, and decisive. He had a larger-than-life personality. With only one uncle supporting him, he finally won a reluctant and worried blessing from his parents. His answer told me everything I needed to know about his strength of character.

He was determined and courageous, with a vision for his future that went beyond the village life he was born into. These decisions seemed unimportant at the time, but the ripples would be life changing for both of us. For better or worse, he had taken the first step on the new road he had chosen.

I was twenty-two when we met, a junior at an all-girls Catholic college. Like our apartments, Nagib's school was next to mine. My apartment, in a seedy-chic area of town, catered to students. It was cheap, with easy access to the bus line. It was, conveniently, only four blocks from the bus stop, laundromat, grocery store, and neighborhood eateries. It was also four blocks, in the other direction, to the local bars, adult bookstores, and an X-rated movie theater. The Johns Hopkins University was within walking distance, as was the Baltimore Museum of Art. I didn't own a car, but my roommates and I were not shy to take advantage of Nagib's unselfish aid and strong back. He could frequently be found lugging our laundry and groceries back and forth.

The neighborhood was a mix of elderly residents who had owned their homes for years, young couples just starting their families, and students, as well as a mix of transvestites, drunks, and drug dealers, a neighborhood in flux. It was not unusual to lie in bed at night and hear police sirens wailing, peppered with the percussion of gunshots. I didn't recognize the sound and would just roll over, unconcerned, and go back to sleep.

On any given summer evening, you could find us in groups of two or three sitting on the porch roof, trying to catch a breeze in the typical humid heat of the mid-Atlantic. The house was too old for central air conditioning, and we couldn't afford window units even if the electrical wiring could have stood it. In the Baltimore summer heat and humidity, a second-story apartment could soon become an oven. But it was easy to climb out the bedroom window of the two-story corner rowhouse. It was a perfect spot to catch a breeze or watch the Fourth of July fireworks from the nearby stadium. As dusk began to settle, it was the natural place to sit with a jelly glass of cheap wine and watch the early seventies go by.

A colorful assortment of neighbors paraded through the downstairs apartment over the years of my tenancy: an alcoholic who tried to strangle his young wife with her hair, a family of Romani immigrants, and a prostitute were among the more interesting tenants. We cheered when the drunk's wife fled with his car and the baby, and wondered why in the world the Romani gentleman vacuumed in his pajamas wearing a Fedora, all the while leaving the door open. We felt particularly safe when the prostitute lived downstairs. She entertained quite a few policemen.

Our apartment had only one bedroom, but the kitchen was a large eat-in, with room for at least two cooks at a time, as well as a generous table and six chairs. What richness! A large bay window with a window seat gave a sense of class to the living room. It was a favorite spot to do homework, read a book, watch the neighborhood, or, on occasion, discard the three-month-old Christmas tree. My piano was the centerpiece of the living room, one of the few pieces of furniture not provided by the landlady. It was magical to sit in the window seat, window open, listening to my friend Gus play. One evening, the electricity went off and Gus played, unaware that he was serenading the entire neighborhood. He played by candlelight until the power was restored, shyly gratified by the round of applause that rose from the street below.

When my friend Mary S. moved in, she hung white curtains at the windows and placed framed photographs around the living room. The hardwood floors were mostly fine, but we soon learned not to run down the hall in our bare feet. The tub was the old-fashioned type with claw feet raising it above the floor, and there was no shower. It was a very old house, and we quickly resigned to roaches.

Although I wore jeans and t-shirts, the mandatory uniform of the decade, I did so out of abject poverty. I was the stereotypical struggling student, not out to make a social statement. I worked the necessary two jobs, lived in an apartment with the necessary two roommates, and never seemed to have enough money for food.

Mary S. and I were the first of our group to spread our wings and fly. The apartment was the natural gathering place for our friends. We were poor but happy, and in retrospect, life was uncomplicated.

Mary, like Nagib, had a large, confident personality. She just *knew* things, and if she didn't, she'd find out. Like Nagib, she expanded my horizons in so many ways, like teaching me to drive!

It was Mary who told me about patinas. She said it was the change on a surface, usually metal, caused by age and exposure. I had never heard the word; I had no reason to have known it. Precious metals and their properties were of no concern to me. At the time, I didn't recognize it for the metaphor it would become—that patinas can refer to the soul, the imperfections acquired over time a form of beauty. I just kept Mary's words in my mind for future review.

We had no patina back then. This was our first time away from home, and we enjoyed our newfound independence with starry-eyed enthusiasm. We were smooth: untouched and uncorrupted. We loved everyone equally: the prostitute, the drunk, and the Romani gentleman had every right to be there: live and let live. We believed that everyone loved us. We not only studied the American Dream, we bought into it. We were an industrious bunch and didn't worry about where the money was coming from. We knew we could always work an extra job to cover our expenses. We were proud to be temporarily poor and took it as a challenge. We sensed that the living was in the struggle.

We spent those years studying, working, partying, ruminating, and falling in love. But more important, we were forging the relationships that would support us for the rest of our lives. We had been raised by the children of the Depression, and our values were solid.

Nagib was, in many ways, the antithesis of us. Yes, he was a student. Yes, he worked hard and scraped by. Yes, he was our age. The similarities stopped there. His clothes were expensive and tailored to fit. He was the anti-hippy, always unfashionably groomed and well put together. He wore his dignity like a crown, but took our teasing with good-natured grace.

"This is 1971, for heaven's sake!"

"Do you want to look like a *foreigner?* God forbid!"

Finally, the jokes wore him down. When he did succumb to our ribbing, he presented himself to us for our approval. While he'd been home that summer, he'd had his jeans tailor-made. He was perplexed but amused by our gales of laughter.

He was totally enchanting. He disposed of our cheap Boone's Farm wine and replaced it with Beaujolais, sang to me in French, and kissed my fingertips. He cooked unfamiliar foods for us and told tales of a faraway land.

With a wistful, distant look in his eyes, he described his home and the orchard on the side of the mountain, covered with grapes, cedar trees and ancient artifacts, and filled with the all-important fudge trees. I was swept away.

CHAPTER 5

For us, 1975 was The Year of the Wedding. Our circle of friends bowed to the inevitable, and we went to ten weddings that year. Nagib and I were married in September on a crisp Saturday morning in the chapel at Notre Dame. None of his family were there, only a few friends from back home. He had decided to inform them after the fact and deal with the fallout later. He just told me it was too far for them to come.

The situation in Lebanon was deteriorating rapidly. The Palestinian-Lebanese war had begun, and communication between there and the States was a big problem. This proved to be a constant over the years, even after the cell phone revolution. But in those pre-internet days, it was a major roadblock for Nagib in proving that he was a baptized Catholic, as the church demanded.

Eventually our wedding day dawned clear and crisp, all obstacles overcome. My mom, sisters, and small nieces and nephews gathered at my apartment to dress. We hugged and emoted over an assortment of girly things; hair, make-up . . . *Do you have another pair of pantyhose? Mine just ripped. Do these shoes look ok with this dress?* The photographer met us there to freeze the moment in time.

67

It wasn't a fancy wedding, and we had a few Marx Brothers moments. Although I was at the church on time, my bridesmaids were nowhere to be found. Betsy and Mary had been assigned to bring my car to the church, but it was on empty. No problem, right? Wrong. It was 1975, and there was an oil embargo. Lines at the gas pump were long and restricted to certain days. In the excitement and confusion of the preceding days, I had completely forgotten to get gas. The bridesmaids, also forgetting the gas lines, decided they would stop at the ten-cent store and get the makings for the garter that had gone missing.

Of course they were late. I sat outside the church with my sister Mary, my maid of honor, in the borrowed Cadillac driven by her fiancé Greg. I was a wreck. Seeing my anxiety, Greg, always considerate, reached into the glove compartment and pulled out a bottle of Jack Daniels, offering me a swig from the bottle. I declined.

Even with the delay, though, it was a lovely ceremony. The Peabody Conservatory students I hired to play organ, flute, and violin worked overtime, but we were finally married in the Maronite Catholic tradition; part of the Eastern Rite of the Catholic church, whose members are located chiefly in Lebanon. This ethnic ceremony was countered by a traditional Polish/American reception, complete with the throwing of the bouquet and newly made garter, and the dedication of the bride to the Blessed Mother. As my mother and aunts sang a hymn to the Virgin in Polish, my godmother removed my veil and replaced it with the matron's cap, called a czepek.

We honeymooned in Williamsburg, returning to find our wedding gifts neatly stacked in our new apartment. The cards associated with each gift were neatly stacked as well, separate from the gift they came with. My family didn't want them to be lost, and so kept them all together. Oh, bother!

The first few years of our marriage progressed predictably; we advanced our careers, became pregnant, had our first child, and bought a house. Also predictably, our finances were strained. They were strained even more when I quit my secure job and opened a bookstore with my friend and library co-worker, Janice.

We were young women of the seventies, in a rush to prove our equality, independence, and intelligence. We had a need to prove that we could "bring home the bacon and fry it up in a pan." The feminist gurus of the times told us we could have it all if we only asserted ourselves to go out and grab it. They were wrong.

No sooner had we moved into our two-bedroom rancher than Maroun, Nagib's brother, came to stay. Since the Lebanese war had made telephone communication almost impossible, we had only a week's notice by way of a letter. Nagib's relief was palpable. Maroun had been fighting with the militia, and his brother didn't trust his family to tell him if something happened. They hadn't told him about his father's death until months after.

We gave Maroun the second bedroom and three-month-old Paul bunked with us until we were able to add a bedroom in the basement.

Maroun, like his brother, spoke little English when he came. I was determined to make him welcome, and obsessed over finding a way to communicate. Nagib left early for work every morning, and with him any translation. I solved the problem by sitting myself down across the breakfast table from my brother-in-law and plopping the Larousse Complete French-English Dictionary down in the middle. He laughed and we talked. Maroun, like his brother, was a quick study, and his command of the English language snowballed after that.

He was handsome and charming and soon became a favorite among my unmarried friends and sisters. He was only twenty-four but had an air of confidence about him, not unlike his brother. He was a good listener and gave his complete attention to whomever he was speaking with. His bushy hair, handsome face, and bedroom eyes all came together in a perfect storm. He was sexy and fun and in great demand. He also enjoyed entertaining me with jokes and barbs at Nagib's expense. He adored baby Paul, and he and I quickly became good buddies.

As time went by, Nagib and I became accustomed to the rhythm of life. Our new house kept me busy, and as winter surrendered to spring, then summer, the outside occupied me more and more. The fig tree in the backyard, as well as the grape arbor over the patio, reminded Nagib of his home in Zahle. The pear, peach, and apple trees gave us shade as well as fruit, and I planted gardens around the perimeter of the spacious backyard with tomatoes, zucchini, and eggplant.

The birds helped themselves to a substantial portion of the grapes, but there was still plenty for making jelly at the end of the season. We enjoyed any number of cookouts in the shade of the grape arbor. Our college friends were frequent guests, and after eating, we would watch the sun go down as we drank our coffee and shared the *argilah* (hookah).

We'd been married for close to two years, leading comfortable lives, when I noticed our individual priorities had begun to change. Mine involved "nesting," and his politics. He had started working for the World Bank in Washington, D.C. There, he was befriended by other young and brilliant Lebanese coworkers, and through them, he became involved with the formation of a think tank of the Lebanese intelligentsia in the D.C area. They called it the American Lebanese League, ALL for short. They were determined to do all they could to help the situation in their country. Their activities began to draw him away from home more and more.

In his new role as a member of ALL, it was Nagib's job to find pilots familiar with older-style jets. He quickly found one pilot very close to home—my uncle, a Navy pilot during the Korean War. He had previously asked if anyone in my family had been a military pilot, and I told him about my uncle. The two were already friends, and it took no persuasion to get the older man to our house for a business meeting.

As they sat in my kitchen, each with an untouched beer in front of him, Nagib disclosed the plan for the planes. They needed them flown from Cyprus, where they were parked for safety's sake, to Lebanon. Could he do it?

Tentatively, my uncle agreed.

This discussion gave me chills. Hearing the kitchen table conversation, I realized I had a front-row seat to history in the making. I wanted to know more.

"Really, Nagib," I complained one night over a dinner out, "you don't talk to me. Tell me about what you've been doing in D.C. Tell me about the Lebanese League. I don't really understand. I need to understand!"

Resigned, he leaned forward. "Okay," he began.

The fall of the Tel al-Zaatar camp was one of the all too many horrors that characterized the Lebanese-Palestinian conflict back in the middle seventies. Tel al-Zaatar was a Palestinian militant camp in the hills overlooking East Beirut. The camp had been a thorn in the side of the neighboring villages as well as the Christian forces for some time.

To maintain their armed militias, the PLO enforced taxes from manufacturers in the area, and seized homes and buildings to accommodate the need for military housing and headquarters.

In January 1976, Tel al-Zaatar was placed under siege by the Lebanese forces. It was a bloody and drawn-out conflict that lasted until August of that year.

Six Hooker Hunter fighter planes had been sent to Cyprus for safety, and now the Christian forces were looking around the world for Lebanese nationals, or relatives as volunteer pilots qualified to fly them. The camp was well defended by the PLO, and the strategy was to attack by air.

This is where my uncle came in. He was willing to go to Cyprus for orientation with other recruits and fly a plane back to Lebanon. The Phalangists had prepared a landing strip by commandeering a highway in the town of Halat.

In the end, the joint forces penetrated the Tel-al Zaatar camp, the last stronghold of the Palestinian Liberation Organization, making it unnecessary for the recruited pilots to fly.

This was the chain of events that brought three people at the World Bank together: two Lebanese friends and Nagib. He reiterated that the situation in Lebanon continued to be very bad. They had gotten together to discuss and plan, and ALL was born. It was needed to aid the Lebanese Christian cause. They needed a web, an organized network to gather the thoughts and efforts of the Lebanese Americans across the country—to involve them. The war was ugly, with many elements involved, said Nagib.

"What elements?" I asked.

"Take it easy, babe," he answered impatiently. "For one, as you know, the Palestinians are involved. We are trying to promote a solution to this war that is now gripping our country. We are trying to turn things around so that the Americans side with the Christians in our country."

As he spoke, the light dawned for me. This was bigger than just a few guys getting together over beers after work to commiserate and talk politics. These three strategists had formed a formidable group.

He had been speaking forcefully from the beginning, but as the story progressed, he leaned forward, elbows on the table and fingers tented as he spoke. "There is a group, called the Lebanese Forces, that has just recently come into existence. Its inception has been aided by the Kataeb, or Phalange, with the National Liberal Party, and with Christians from all over Lebanon. The Kataeb is the strongest of the Christian militias. It's led by Bashir Gemayel." His dark eyes flashed as he spoke, and he brought both hands down suddenly, smacking the table with a force that emphasized the power and urgency of his words. "He is our hope, Cath. He is our hope."

Bashir was the youngest of six children born in 1947 to Pierre Gemayel, the founder of the Phalangist Party. The Phalange, while secular, was widely supported by the

Maronites. As the majority sect in Lebanon for centuries, they were constitutionally entitled to hold the office of President of Lebanon. Nagib's description and history of Bashir, as well as the passion behind his words, gave me goosebumps. The emotion of the moment had temporarily overcome him, and he reached for his glass, momentarily hiding behind it as he gulped some water. I reached across the table and squeezed his hand.

I changed the subject after that, and we finished our dinners chatting companionably about Paul, having another baby sometime down the road, our house, and the weather. But the subject had been broached, and I was starting to feel involved. I had a lot to think through!

We picked up the conversation on the way home from dinner and then continued deep into the night. Comfortable in pajamas and cradling a cup of hot tea, I snuggled into the sofa and brought up the subject again.

"Tell me more about Lebanon's government. I'm trying to grasp how it all ties together."

"Okay. It's like this. As you know, Elias Sarkis is president. Remember, he was the governor of the Central Bank prior to being elected. We expected him to be a strong leader, but unfortunately, that hasn't been the case." Nagib paused and sipped his drink. "Sarkis just doesn't have the mass support he needs to deal with this fighting. The country is divided into so many factions! Nearly half of Lebanon is controlled by Yasir Arafat and the Palestinians.

Sarkis just does not have the means or personality to handle the situation.

"With this in mind," he continued, "we decided that the American Lebanese League could be a fast-forward to getting American support based on lobbying. If we do it properly, we could advance the Lebanese cause."

It was two a.m. and my head was spinning, but it was important for me to understand. I needed to know.

ALL was concerned because the Christians were highly vulnerable. Unless or until a UN solution was found, or the Americans intervened, the Christian fighters needed support, both financial and military.

Once the group decided to move forward, he said, they would start by contacting high-profile Lebanese and Lebanese Americans, like the founder of the American-Lebanese League, and a noted philosopher and diplomat.

"Then we will create an office in the press building," Nagib continued, "near the White House, and start rallying the Lebanese together. We'll create a PR campaign, sending information, letters, leaflets, and updates to contacts throughout the country.

"We are trying to find all the influential Lebanese who are in the American government now, like Philip Habib and so many other people who will be willing to help their afflicted country." Habib would become a special envoy to the Middle East in the early eighties, providing an important channel to the Reagan government.

Nagib paused to take a breath and gather his thoughts. He had been so animated and intense, and I thought that he looked a bit pale for such a swarthy man. He took a sip of his tea, now gone cold, and continued.

"One of our goals is to contact people from around the States," he continued, his accent and formal word usage lending a dignified urgency to his story. "We are starting lists and trying to initiate contact. We want to get permission to visit them and ask for a contribution. We want to come out and advocate American support for Lebanon openly.

"This is highly important because it shows support and concern for what is happening on the ground in Lebanon. They don't need money as much as they need the political connection and support. After this, we want to start lobbying through the Foreign Relations Committee, and start getting closer to people in the administration.

"My job," he continued, "is compiling the lists and developing a vehicle of contact. As we generate more and more high-level interest, it is becoming apparent that it is time for us to open an office. We need a central location."

The late hour was taking its toll, and my eyes were heavy. Nagib took notice and finished his tea.

"*Yalla, oomi*," he said, rising himself. He reached over to me and, taking the empty teacup out of my hand, he brought both cups to the kitchen sink where he washed them and put them in the drain to dry.

I looked at him, comfortable with the mundane domestic task just moments after detailing events of international importance, and a sense of well-being flooded over me. The feeling of intimacy was restored by the long explanation, and I was able to sleep soundly, cushioned by the cocoon of my limited experience, American culture, and my general ignorance of all things political.

However, I was deeply moved, that night, at the passion behind my husband's words and the commitment these young men had made. As the tension in their country escalated, these young patriots became more and more determined to find a way to make a difference.

Nagib still didn't talk much about what was going on in his home country unless I asked. Nor did he bring up the plans he and his friends were making to contribute; he never was one for casual talk. He did try to explain the politics to me when I asked, but I didn't feel the fire like he and his cohorts did. I was somewhat removed from the whole situation. After all, I was an outsider-in-law. But still, I felt threatened by the intensity of "it"—that heavy, ever-present cloud hanging over our lives. I chose to not face it, hoping it would go away.

It would be years before I learned that this was when my husband and his partners started playing the big political game in earnest. In 1975, the PLO had support from many of the Lebanese sects, including Sunni Muslims and Druze, a sect of Islam. The pro-Palestinian groups banded together to form the Lebanese National Movement. Inevitably, clashes broke out between this alliance and the Christian groups, which included the Phalange.

In April, two Phalangists accompanying Pierre Gemayel were killed when unidentified gunmen fired on them from a speeding car, and it was assumed that they were Palestinian militants. The Phalangists, assuming the attack was an attempt on their leader's life, retaliated some hours later by ambushing a bus carrying twenty-seven Palestinians, killing them. This was the spark behind the Lebanese-Palestinian War.

In 1976, Bashir became the head of the Phalangist militia after the death of William Hawi. Later that year, he became a leading member of the Lebanese Front, a coalition of several Christian parties, and commander of their main militia, the Lebanese Forces.

The Christians refused to accept any peace offers that included partitioning Lebanese land. Bashir and the Phalange insisted on 10,452 square kilometers, the size of the entire Lebanese territory. He did not want to give up even an inch of Lebanese soil.

"He was the guy," Nagib said, "who people were aware of as coming from the bottom up and then winning the war over the Palestinians. "It was then that we started to introduce Bashir as a solution for all of us, Christian and Muslim. We introduced him," he told me, "not only to the American administration, but to the entire Lebanese community in the United States. We wanted to reverse the perception at that time that this was a Christian-Muslim civil war. We wanted to emphasize that this was a Lebanese-Palestinian war, because the PLO was controlling a good portion of the country. They had a plan to replace our country with theirs."

To many people, Bashir was their hero, their hope, and their inspiration. He was their Moses ready to lead them out from under oppression. Too soon he was to become their Christ, the anointed sacrifice.

Eventually, Nagib and his group began to receive high-level support from the American government, including Robert "Bud" McFarland, National Security Advisor to President Reagan, and Philip Habib, Special Envoy to the Middle East, as well as General Alexander Haig and Secretary of State George Schultz. Although Haig and Schultz were in different Reagan administrations, this was a long process politically, and spanned many years.

Meanwhile, my life was snowballing. I had a new marriage, new baby, new house, and new job. I was trying my hand at entrepreneurism. Janice and I had quit our stable jobs with the public library—jobs that came with a pension and health insurance±—and opened the Bookmark, an independent bookstore. It was located in the neighborhood where we had been serving as librarians. It was a mostly Polish community, and with a nod to my own background, we gave the store a Polish specialty, offering Polish language books, gift items, and artwork. It was far removed from the Lebanese culture I had married into.

Janice and I had the best reasons for going into business for ourselves. By combining our resources and sharing the work/childcare load, we thought we could have the best of both worlds. We arranged our schedules so that one of us was always with the children while the other manned the store. As good as our intentions were, the markup on books was only forty percent, and the Polish specialty books would have been more profitable if we had given them away. Whatever we expected to get out of this venture, we at least added a few nicks to our still fresh patinas.

Nagib was supportive, not only lending his signature to the loan papers saying they could take our house if I defaulted, but also in keeping baby Paul clean, cared for, and happy when I worked on Saturdays. I would always come home to a clean house, folded laundry, dinner, and a happy, tired child. But even with his support, Nagib's attention and loyalty were being pulled elsewhere, and our wallet had taken a big hit.

When corporate headhunter Suhail came to the World Bank looking to recruit someone with hotel and finance experience, he was like an angel sent from heaven. Our financial picture quickly became much prettier. Debt had crept in, but ambition had always been there. We were ripe for the picking.

Suhail represented a Lebanese group called Indevco, owned by George Frem, a wealthy Lebanese capitalist with political aspirations. He had heard about the work Nagib was doing with the American Lebanese League through an associate with the Lebanese Forces. Frem wanted Nagib for his political connections and promising future, and so Suhail set about recruiting him for his businesses in Saudi Arabia.

He painted a tempting picture of life without debt and the chance to save a substantial nest egg in just a few years. All we had to do was move to the desert. *Ha!* For Nagib, it would put him closer to home without limiting his involvement with the ALL group—a win-win situation if ever there was one. For me? Well, I've always loved adventure.

So, the bookstore was closed, the house went on the market, and we packed our bags for this life-changing move. I was leaving behind friends and family, everything familiar, but my loyalty to my husband, and the shine of this grand new chapter decided me.

My sisters cried, my friends tried to dissuade me, but we had determined our path. And so, fully unprepared, we pulled up stakes and shifted to the other side of the world.

CHAPTER 6

DHAHRAN, SAUDI ARABIA, 1980

Saudi Arabia didn't look too bad at first glance. But then, it was nearly midnight when the plane banked over the Persian Gulf to make its final approach to Dhahran Airport. As we circled preparing to land, I could see the lights sparkle off the marble facade, the glitz proclaiming to the world that here was prosperity. Our pilot had warned us that it was forbidden to take pictures from the airplane. For a bit, we were at a height to see just over the building to the modern highway beyond. As in Beirut, date palms landscaped the front, giving a gracious and inviting frame to the grand arabesque-style entrance. But unlike Beirut, these were healthy and cared for.

As soon as we left the air-conditioned comfort of the plane, we were slapped in the face by a thick wall of hot moisture. The air was heavy and oppressive and made us immediately gasp. Welcome to the desert. Nagib carried a sleeping Paul, and we walked into the coolness of the opulent airport. The green and white flag of Saudi Arabia waved above from the rooftop. The Arabic script proclaimed that "there was no god but Allah, and that Muhammad was his prophet." No gunmen were in sight, and I saw this as a positive sign that this was going to be more like Europe or the States. Maybe even a home away from home? Once inside the airport, such a notion was soon dispelled. We joined one of the long check-in queues, and as we waited, I looked around.

Outside, no garbage or debris lined the smoothly paved roads, and everything was pristine. Oil paid for a myriad of services, and people from all walks of life came from around the world for the prospect of a well-paid livelihood: a chance to get ahead. The poor came for a chance at survival for themselves and their extended families back home, and the rich came for the opportunity to become richer. Seduced by dollar signs, the foreign "guests" of the Saudis willingly compromised their ideals and beliefs, put up with physical hardship, and gladly gave up their personal freedoms for a chance at the good life. The Saudis had the money but no human resources or know-how, including labor.

Inside, there were Arab and African men squatting in circles as they waited patiently beside their luggage, and women swathed in black from head to toe, herding their children. Amazingly, the children always seemed to be able to pick out their own mothers from these groups of uniform-looking women.

The men were dressed in long white caftans and wore white or red-and-white-checked scarves on their heads.

A black cord crowned the scarf on some; others wore the scarf turban style around their heads. I was impressed that anyone could keep their balance in that squatting position for an extended period of time. Other groups squatted around their belongings, seeming especially protective of their large copper pots.

Like the Tower of Babel, I heard a cacophony of languages, and above it all, the call to prayers was broadcast over the loudspeaker. Once I had been in the Kingdom for a while, the jumble of nationalities became more commonplace, and I could distinguish the Africans from the Yemenis, the British from the French, and the Lebanese from other Arabs. The Americans were particularly easy to pick out with their casual confidence and comfortable clothes. The one thing we all had in common was that we were the "guests" of the Saudis, and as guests, the men were given a paper detailing the etiquette expected of guests in the Kingdom.

The paper requested that women keep their "beauties" hidden and covered, and that men not expose their "uglies." Although Western women weren't required to cover their faces and heads here in the Eastern Province, they were asked to dress and act modestly, covering their arms and legs out of respect for their hosts. The men, too, were asked not to go around town in shorts, and to cover their arms and legs.

The safari suit was in vogue, and many, including Nagib, wore one. I also saw some Western women waiting next to their luggage. But the Saudi women stood out, swathed from head to toe in black polyester as though in a shroud, revealing only their heavily-kohled eyes. Paul screamed and pointed at a group of young women dressed thus, loudly demanding to know what they were. I shushed him, but not before I heard the giggles of the cocooned teens, signaling their fluency in English,

My blue cotton maternity dress came down to mid-calf. I was pregnant with our second child and would deliver in Saudi Arabia. My wardrobe was limited, so even if I had known that showing bare arms in Saudi Arabia was considered rude, I wouldn't have been able to come up with a suitable substitute. I noticed that the other women were more completely covered. I was the only one whose bare arms were exposed, and I began to feel uncomfortable. It was the first and last time I ever went out in public showing so much skin for the duration of our "visit."

Once we were all processed by customs and had our bags scrutinized and passports stamped, we passed through the building and, like Alice through the looking glass, magically came out the other side into a life that would bear no earthly resemblance to the one we had previously known. Like Alice, we were destined to try to make sense of the absurd, the comical, and the irrational as we navigated the next few years of cultural boot camp.

Nagib had been hired as comptroller for a group of businesses, but the hotel was to be his focus for the time being. He had worked for the Holiday Inn and Baltimore Hilton hotels while in college, ending up as the Hilton's assistant food and beverage manager. After college, he worked in the budget and computing department of the World Bank. The recruiters for this company had come to Washington, D.C., looking for a man who spoke Arabic and had hotel and finance experience. Nagib fit the bill to a T.

Outside, a driver was waiting with a sign saying *Carlton Al-Moaibed Hotel*. He had brought the company station wagon with the hotel insignia written in English and Arabic on its doors. The ride to the hotel was uneventful. It was night, and there wasn't much to be seen in the dark from the car window. The unmistakable scent of petroleum permeated the heavy, humid air. Outside of the air conditioning, I felt immediately dirty.

The road was straight and the terrain flat. The highway smacked of Western engineering, with banked curves allowing higher speeds. As we approached the city, I could see the blinking red and green lights controlling traffic flow. Unlike in Lebanon, here they actually worked, and people obeyed them.

As we drove into the roundabout in front of the hotel, the warm lights from the lobby shone onto the expansive stairs, beckoning us to enter. It was late, we were tired and so alone, but there was life inside, even though by now it was after midnight. A bell boy hurried along the polished marble floor to hold the door for us as willing hands unloaded the luggage, and we carried Paul inside. We had arrived at our new life.

In 1980, the Kingdom of Saudi Arabia was in the midst of a growth explosion. Enormous wealth and prosperity had come to the Kingdom, fueled by the petroleum industry. With this wealth came a push for expanding infrastructure, while maintaining a rigid culture and government based on Wahhabi Islam's tenets. The modern Saudi state came into being with King Abdul-Aziz Al-Saud in 1932. In a short period of time, the Kingdom had gone from a conglomeration of desert tribes to a modern, sophisticated state with a prominent place on the world stage. But even though the newfound wealth was a boon to the Kingdom's citizens, it could not compensate for the way of life that its people had been accustomed to for centuries.

Situated on the Arabian Peninsula, Saudi Arabia is bordered by Jordan on the northwest, Iraq on the north and northeast, and Kuwait, Qatar, Bahrain, and the United Arab Emirates on the east. Oman sits to the southeast, and Yemen to the south. The Persian Gulf lies to the northeast, and the Red Sea to the west. The two holiest sites in Islam, Mecca and Medina, are within its borders, giving Saudi Arabia a unique position in the Islamic world. In ancient times, the Arabian Peninsula occupied a central place in trade between the two great centers of civilization, one in the Nile River Valley and the other in Mesopotamia. Caravan trade routes became the arteries that sustained the sparsely populated area.

For a society previously sheltered from modern progress, it was impossible to make a leap into the twentieth century. Saudi Arabia had built-in social problems, relying on feudal allegiance and rules. I hadn't realized from the start that Saudi was a closed society. Understanding this would take time and painful experience.

The sun came streaming in the large glass window that first morning, screaming that a beautiful day was in order. I couldn't resist its call and gazed out the window while Paul slept. Nagib was long gone, and it was hard to imagine how he had found the energy to be up and about so early after such a late night. I knew he was running on adrenaline.

Outside, the sky was bright blue, ornamented by white fluffy clouds which did nothing to diminish the sun's brilliance. There were no trees in sight, no breeze, and the clouds seemed stalled overhead. Looking down, I noted the bleak landscape, offering almost no relief from the dull brown earth and sand.

Roads cut the desert in cross sections, barely breaking the monotony of the terrain. Long plumes of smoke on the horizon appeared evenly spaced apart—the burn-off from the oil fields. It seemed laughable. The thought that I, an optimistic, adventurous young American woman, could be waking up across the world in the Kingdom of Saudi Arabia was absurd. I could usually find humor in the absurd.

Yet here I was, a pregnant 29-year-old and currently exhausted mother of a toddler. The romance of it all was lost to my fatigue and apprehension, and absolutely nothing was comical.

My surreal, slightly scary situation was sinking in. That first morning, I gathered my courage. I knew I was young and determined. Hadn't my ancestors navigated tougher, albeit less sandy, roads?

Well, here we are, I thought. *Day one of the Great Adventure!* This was *my* adventure. I had goals. I planned to learn Arabic, keep a journal, and practice the piano more. This was an opportunity that most people didn't get, and I was going to make the most of it. Perhaps I'd write my memoirs. I giggled at the thought of an imagined chapter title: "Bedouin Homes and Gardens, or How I Survived the Arabian Nights!" Assuming, that is, that I did survive them!

As if in reminder, the baby suddenly gave a large kick. Right! Just what I needed to get this day started. Down to business. There were people to meet and breakfast to eat! Breakfast first.

A respectful tap on the suite's door drew me from the window. "Good morning, Madame." Nagib had left early, ordering a room service breakfast before he went. The menu was written in English and Arabic, and all the selec-

90

tions were familiar. Lebanese foods like labneh and kinafee were on the menu, but they also offered things that Paul and I were more accustomed to: pancakes and scrambled eggs, European cheeses and pastries, croissants and an assortment of cereal. There was no bacon, though. Pork was taboo here.

Instead, we ordered Cheerios for Paul and a fragrant, steaming pot of American coffee for me. Getting fresh coffee had been an issue in Lebanon, I remembered. We had had to settle for an old jar of stale Nescafe, tucked away on the back shelf of the corner market. This was much better.

I studied our room service waiter as he entered the room. From India originally, he was very deferential. As he spoke, he emphasized his words with a distracting little wobble of the head and a dazzling smile. He carried a large tray laden with our breakfast, and even under this burden, he managed a polite little bow. The workers, I was sure, were probably anxious to look at the new boss and his family.

"Come in, come in," I told him. "Put the tray here on the table."

"Thank you, Madame," he said with his huge, white-toothed grin, giving me another bow.

No sooner had he left than I finally started laughing. Madame! He called me *Madame*! *He* called *ME* Madame!!! What a hoot! I wasn't Madame. To my youthful self, Madame was an elegantly dressed, gray-haired, very tall lady!

I wasn't even thirty! I felt comically insulted. I was a lot of things at this stage in my life. I had traveled, was college educated, married to a sophisticated man. None of that, to my dazed mind, equaled a lady called Madame.

Paul and I toured the hotel. Light poured into the lobby from the recessed, mullioned windows, while low Moroccan couches under the windows made an inviting area for hotel guests to drink their morning coffee over newspapers or while discussing business with a friend.

"Good morning, Madame, good morning, Master Paul," we were greeted by every hotel employee we encountered on the short walk through the lobby. A tall, tuxedoed young man stopped us as we made our way toward the door: "Bonjour, Madame! *Keefeek il yom*? I am Samir, the head waiter for the restaurant," he said in the typical Lebanese mixture of French and Arabic, as he bent over to shake hands with Paul. "Is there anything I can assist you with this morning?" I assured him we were fine, thanked him, and we continued on our way. Paul was a big hit with everyone he met. He wasn't shy about sticking out his hand when he met someone new, and he soon learned that those tours of the kitchen area usually resulted in large chocolate bars or cookies in his pockets. My protests would only result in a smile, a nod of the head, and a "Yes, Madame."

The phone rang right as we got back to the suite. I was startled. I almost didn't answer, thinking it couldn't be for me. But it was Nagib.

"We're invited for lunch at Pierre's today at one," he informed me. "I'll meet you in the lobby at ten 'til, and we'll walk over. It's only a block away."

As in Lebanon, lunch was the main meal of the day. Nagib assured me that several women would be there, and I had been looking forward to meeting them. I wanted to get out and meet people to start my new life. Suddenly a wave of anxiety washed over me. How *could* I meet them? How would I communicate? How would I *dress*?

Apparently, I was now Madame. I had to look the part. "Oh my God," I moaned to myself, "what am I going to do with my hair!? I can't do anything with it!" My hair dryer didn't have a converter for the different electricity in the hotel.

Nagib had his own fires to put out and couldn't be counted on to babysit me. This was it. We had only been here a day. Fear of the unknown fought with my natural optimism. My solution: When worry starts to get the upper hand, take a nap.

At the dot of one o' clock, we arrived at Pierre's, and I faced my first group of strangers. We rang the doorbell twice before a VERY tall woman answered the door. She towered over me. She had a friendly laughing face, twinkling eyes, and *curlers* in her hair! She was Susie, Pierre's wife.

"Come in, come in," she said in accented English. She stood back from the door and waved us in. A bit flustered,

Susie turned to Nagib, exclaiming in Arabic to much laughter. I could guess what had happened.

We, the guests of honor, had arrived first, even before our host. Still, Susie laughed it off and made us welcome. Leaving us alone, she hurried into the bedroom to put on her makeup, take the curlers out of her hair, and call Pierre at the office. *Come home pronto!* Meanwhile, we waited. "There's American time, and there's Lebanese time," Nagib said with a laugh.

After about forty-five minutes, the rest of the party trickled in, Pierre rushing and apologetic. Imagine being late for your own party hosting the new boss! The last guests to arrive were Marita and Rabih. Friendly and kind, Rabih was the youngest brother of the Lebanese owner, George. In his early forties, he was balding on the top of his head and not much taller than his young wife, Marita, who was in her late twenties. She, like Susie, spoke accented but perfect English. She was a beautiful woman, whose curly black hair bounced when she laughed. She glowed and sparkled.

"So sorry to be so late," Marita apologized to Susie. "We had a flat tire." Everyone laughed, but I didn't get the joke until Nagib showed me the house where the Frems lived. It was next door. It was plain to see that they were still "honeymooners."

"Cathy," said Susie, "Marita and I have something in common with you. We're both pregnant!" Apparently, I

94

wasn't the only one with a plan for their stay in Saudi Arabia! The conversation segued into the hospitals in the area, good obstetricians, and babies.

Over lunch, Susie told us about a woman she had met who had been here for several years. "Back then," she said, "when we first came to the Kingdom, they brought people's belongings in containers on barges." The woman told me how excited they were when they got word that their container had finally arrived after several months. Every time they went to the port offices to inquire, they were told *bukra in sha'Allah* ("tomorrow, God willing"). Susie paused for dramatic effect. "They were excited enough," she continued, "that when they were told their shipment had arrived, the whole family went down to the port to watch. The heavy containers were carefully and slowly lowered onto the waiting barge by a crane on the deck."

"But why were the containers being unloaded onto a barge?" I asked innocently.

The water wasn't deep enough for the ship to dock, she told me. The spectators watched and held their breath while the barge rocked back and forth, back and forth, as each additional container was deposited. It looked like the containers shifted somewhat as the barge laboriously poled away from the ship.

"But surely these men knew what they were doing!" Susie gesticulated, emphasizing the drama. "Closer and closer, the barge came to the shore." Soon the family didn't need binoculars to see the workers yelling at each other. As the barge pitched back and forth, they held their breath, praying it would straighten out and dock safely. No such luck.

The men could not correct the listing barge; they capsized, everyone falling overboard. As the owners watched from the dock, helpless and horrified, their container followed the men into the water and then, slipping from sight, sank in the murk.

"What could the family do but shake their heads and go home?" she said, shrugging her shoulders.

Everyone at Pierre's laughed, but I felt a sick feeling at the bottom of my stomach. Our belongings had yet to arrive. Changing the subject, I asked, "What about church?" They looked at each other, then back at me, and told me that the practice of Christianity was taboo in the Kingdom. There was, Susie thought, Catholic Mass every Friday at the American compound, Aramco. It was gated and locked, but if you knew someone, you could get in. She would get the information, she told me. Nagib said not to worry—we could baptize the baby in Lebanon. But I knew it was more than that. Time would tell.

Most of the conversation was in Arabic. I had started learning some words, but I was still in the dark. Susie was careful to include me in the conversation when she could, but she was the hostess, frequently getting up to see to the meal.

Even so, the other ladies were friendly and welcoming, promising to take me shopping and show me the ropes. As a bonus, an Olympic-sized swimming pool was right outside the hotel's bowling alley. A large wall enclosed it, so I hadn't seen it when we arrived. The families congregated there, they told me, on Friday mornings before it got too hot. Thursday and Friday were the weekends since Friday was the Muslim Sabbath. Even so, the men still worked a half day on Thursday. Saturday and Sunday were work/school days. Along with dessert and Turkish coffee, I was getting a crash course on life in the desert.

CHAPTER 7

On my first day in Saudi, I had wanted to go out for a ride and explore the area. As an American, I was used to freedom of choice. I owned my own car and drove everywhere. But in Saudi, driving was forbidden to *all* women, American or not. I couldn't take myself out, even if I had known where I was going. My new friends, however, offered me a place to go, and kept their word.

We began meeting at the coffee shop in the evenings. It was a destination to look forward to, even if it was only a short walk from my room. The coffee shop had hot dogs, hamburgers, pizza, and French fries. It was a good place to feed the little ones and let them run around.

The walk to the shop made me uncomfortably aware that I was still getting used to the climate. What I had seen of Saudi so far was very modern and comfortable. That is, until you poked your head out the door, and the heat and humidity made you run back in. Still, I was better prepared for this environment than Nagib, since I had come from very humid Baltimore. Zahle, surrounded by mountains, had low humidity. It could get rather warm in the summer during the day, but evenings were cool. I've always heard humidity is great for your complexion. Did that apply only if you went out in it?

The following days and weeks came and went. Paul and I had developed our routine: wake up at nine, order breakfast, go for a walk, play games, and wait for Dad to come for lunch. This was fine for a child, but my mind began to hibernate. I found myself sleeping more and filling the rest of the time immersed in books or daydreams. I appreciated that my husband tried to relieve the monotony by sharing interesting gossip and strange news items. However, the job was new and difficult, and Nagib wasn't very available. The days that he had to work late or couldn't come for lunch were hard.

All of this sameness made some casual happenstances seem like major events. A few days after our arrival, Lucky, the doorman, told me I should check out the event in the main ballroom. I walked over and found a crush of women outside the door. All seats in the ballroom had been long gone, and no one could get in. There was a fashion show going on! I was surprised. I had been led to believe that there were no events in the Kingdom—no movies, shows, music, or dancing. This was particularly true when it came to events involving women.

But here we were. A fashion show! It seemed that some things did trickle in, and my excitement spilled over to Paul as I held his hand and tried to see anything. One of the hotel workers saw us, quickly brought a folding chair, and placed it at the end of a row where I had a great view of the stage. Being Madame, I was discovering, had its advantages! With Paul on what was left of my lap, we clapped and cheered with the rest of the crowd.

I had arrived toward the end of the program, and the ladies were really into it. The fashions were from one particular boutique in Al-Khobar. The owner was an Arab woman who designed her own gowns using the traditional ethnic garb of the Arab world as her inspiration. The outfits were beautiful, made with expensive silks in bright colors.

Gold caftans twinkled, while colorful pantaloons, paired with tunic tops, shimmered down the runway. But they had saved the best for last. As in all fashion shows, this one ended with a wedding gown. The level of enthusiasm escalated throughout the show as the producers ratcheted up the glamour by degrees. As the bridal party arrived onstage, the women went wild with excitement. The crescendo of appreciation from this stimulus-starved crowd was deafening. They stood, clapped, whistled, and, new to me, the Arab women ululated, trilling their approval and appreciation.

Disappointed that it was over, I walked away, thinking that this place might not be so bad after all.

Weeks went by, but our little family was still living in the same two rooms while we waited for renovations on the new villa to be completed. It was next door to the hotel in the Al-Ghossaibi compound, whose owners were related to the owners of the Al-Moaibed by marriage. Every foreign company here had a Saudi sponsor. It was mandated. The Al-Moaibeds were the sponsors for the Indevco Companies, one of which was the hotel.

The days passed slowly, and I desperately wanted to move into our place. I was an action-oriented person and wanted to get started on our new life! We needed our own home! Still, as with the fashion show, there were distractions.

The hotel wives dutifully visited every so often. They came, mostly in twos, to pay their regards to the new boss's wife. They came in pairs to offer support to one another, as well as to combine their knowledge of English, little that it may have been.

A typical scenario went as follows:

"Good morning, Madame Cathy. *Keefeek?*" *Kiss, kiss* on both cheeks.

"Come in, come in."

They introduced themselves, telling me their names and which of the employees they were attached to. I would have them sit, then go into the kitchen to see to refreshments. These women would chat with each other while I prepared a tray with Lebanese coffee and coffee cake for them.

While we sipped, my visitors would ask in broken English about Paul, how I was feeling, and when the new baby was expected. In the days before ultrasounds, everyone seemed to be an expert on predicting the sex of the baby, and it was true they had a fifty-fifty chance of getting it right. I knew some words and key phrases in Arabic, and had become quite the actor. As hostess I would raise an imaginary cigarette to my lips, silently asking if they would like to smoke. I puffed away as the ladies giggled, visibly relaxing with the boss's wife. With this rough communication, we found common ground. We were all away from home, and all mothers. And so we muddled through.

I still had our arranged coffee shop date with the hotel managers' wives as well. We fed our small children while the older ones played as the wives waited for their husbands to finish work. The food was a mixture of American and Lebanese cuisine—all in all, pretty satisfactory.

At this time of year, it was too hot for the kids to play outside, and Lucky had warned me not to let Paul walk in the grass out in front of the hotel. The day before, someone found a viper, a particularly deadly snake. Scorpions could also be a problem. They kept the anti-venom for the different poisons in different hospitals. We made sure we kept up-to-date on which ones were where.

Little by little, I eased into a comfortable familiarity with my new acquaintances. Paul, too, had made friends, and we weren't quite as lost as we had been. Even so, little things could get me. One evening while looking for cartoons for Paul, I heard the familiar theme music to *Sesame*

Street and burst into tears. Hormones or homesickness? Pulling Paul onto my lap, we watched together.

We had been in the Kingdom for about three months and my approaching thirtieth birthday found us still living at the hotel. I was spending too much time in our suite and feeling claustrophobic.

"I just want to go out!" I whined to Nagib. He sympathized, but there just weren't too many options. Eventually, we found a place in downtown Al-Khobar and planned a birthday dinner. This was exciting! Desperate to get out, I held out hope that somewhere was life as I had formerly known it.

"Happy birthday," Nagib said as I climbed, ungracefully, into the car.

"Where are we going?" It was a question just to make conversation. I didn't really care where we went, as long as we had to go in the car.

"There's a new German restaurant in Al-Khobar I heard about. I thought we might try it out. You like German food, don't you?" he asked as he slipped the car into gear and pulled away from the curb.

"Fine with me," I answered. German, Swedish, Chinese . . . it didn't matter. I was thrilled to be going out on a date.

It was already quite dark when we left. I hadn't had an opportunity to see any of the sights that Al-Khobar had to offer. I knew it had the best shopping area with downtown streets reminiscent of cities back home. The business area appeared normal, with neon lights advertising their wares in Arabic and English.

"Where is everyone?" I asked. There were people on the streets, but not many.

"I guess the shops are closing early because it's Thursday," he answered. He wasn't much for chatting. He was concentrating on the road, trying to find the landmarks he had been told to look for. Not all of the streets were named.

"There it is," he said, pointing down the street and to the left.

I looked over and saw what he was referring to. Across the street was a nondescript building, dimly lit, with the German name we had been told to look for. It didn't look too inviting, but it was one more adventure inside of another, I told myself. Anyway, we were hungry.

We stopped in front of the restaurant and, leaving our air-conditioned cocoon, stepped out into the now-familiar wall of wet heat. It was comfortable inside, but something was off.

"Are we the only ones here?" I stage-whispered to Nagib.

"Probably they eat late here, like in Europe," he answered hopefully.

The restaurant was dark and cozy, decorated with beer steins and wine barrels, and we were hopeful for a good experience. Our hopes began to dim, however, when it took ten minutes for anyone to greet us. The service went down from there, and the food was worse. Now we knew why we were the only diners here. Still, there were some highlights. Since alcohol was banned, that night I drank "Saudi champagne," a blend of Perrier and apple juice. Really quite refreshing.

We muddled through our meal, laughing and joking, enjoying being alone together for the first time in months. I only hoped it would fortify me until our next excursion. I was certain that this had been beginner's luck, and we would become familiar with the area's nightlife.

A few days later, I found Nagib in the hotel lobby talking to a strange man. He called me over for introductions. "Cathy, tell Samir about the restaurant we went to for your birthday dinner," he said. I was glad to have the subject of conversation supplied to me rather than just resorting to pleasantries. Full steam ahead I went, waxing eloquent in my condemnation of the place, wittily describing the debacle that had been my thirtieth birthday celebration. I finally paused for a breath. Nagib, a twinkle in his eye, looked as if he was about to bestow a prize, announced that Samir was the restaurant's owner! Too late to backtrack, I turned fifteen shades of red and tried to stammer an apology. At the same time, I looked daggers at my husband. He was oblivious to my embarrassment and not at all sorry!

But Samir was a total gentleman. He laughed and told me he had asked Nagib for an honest analysis of the place and was grateful for my candor. Nagib had done this at Samir's request, and he took full responsibility.

A week later, he invited us back as his guests, and the meal was far superior to the first one. I guess Nagib felt sorry for me after the failed evening out. The day after the dinner, he threw an impromptu surprise party for me in our two-room suite.

I celebrated my thirtieth birthday again in the desert with three dozen strangers. Quite a few spoke no English at all. All of them, without exception, brought potted plants as gifts. I was slightly put off by the sheer number of them. In our relatively small living quarters, they looked ridiculous and overwhelming, like we were in the jungle. I later learned that house plants were extremely expensive and valued in Saudi Arabia. Most middle-sized plants cost over $100.

I would be happier to have them when we moved into our larger house, I brooded. If we *ever* moved into our own house. What was Nagib thinking, inviting all these people to this little space? I wanted to go to bed! All of this ran through my mind as I kept a frozen smile on my face and tried to accept these well-wishers graciously. Some I would never see again. Others would be huge players in my life here. But no matter how sincere their birthday wishes, this was a command visitation from the new boss. It was *not* the way I had hoped to begin my next decade.

This was a marker birthday, and I had hoped to have some time alone to collect myself, and then share some togetherness as we compared notes on the beginning of our life here. Evidently, Nagib hadn't gotten the script. I couldn't help being put out with him. It felt a bit like a baptism by. . . fire? No. Chlorophyll.

It took me a little while to forgive Nagib for the disappointment of my thirtieth birthday. Still, over time, my birthday came to be something of a holiday event for the managers at the hotel. With my blessing, it became the blast of spring in a place where there really was very little to look forward to.

Nagib continued to be busy. He had been hired to clean up a mess in the business. Within the employee hierarchy, management and upper-level kitchen jobs, such as chef, were held by Lebanese nationals. Lower paying jobs, like housekeeping, were held by Indians and Sri Lankans. In the absence of the owners, stealing had become rampant. Employees sent whole containers of stolen non-perishable foods, china, silver, table linens, and the like home to Lebanon. My husband gained the nickname The Executioner after he fired eighty employees. Most of the men and women at my birthday party were on a plane home just weeks after the party.

And *finally,* a few short weeks after my birthday, we were moving! Our new place in the Al-Ghossaibi compound was a two-bedroom, one-bath bungalow with a tiny kitchen and combination living-dining room. The floors were carpeted; the plaster was painted white. We would be centered near Nagib's offices in the hotel, and it was an easy walk. This was good for us, as all social and business life emanated from there. I was in heaven after our extremely confining two-room suite. Mentally I prepared to make a home for my soon-to-be larger family.

CHAPTER 8

Busy with moving and all it entailed, I had a daily purpose, and life picked up speed. It was early summer, and too hot for many of us to stay put. Employment for expatriates usually included a yearly ticket home for the employee and his family. Nagib's employee/family tickets were first class, but we wouldn't be going anywhere soon!

Our days developed a pattern. It was pleasant to wind down in the early evening with a walk to the hotel to join the other women and their children in the bowling alley. We chatted and learned more about each other's history, hopes, and dreams, shared child-raising tips, and tracked each other's pregnancies.

My little circle of hotel acquaintances grew as strangers were introduced, quickly being absorbed into our expanding group of friends. The executives' wives all spoke English and were kindly accommodating in translating when necessary, but I knew that if I was going to assimilate, I'd need to become fluent in Arabic. It felt so good to no longer be on hold, and I busied myself making a home for us. Setting up my tiny kitchen was easy. As Nagib was leaving for work the day after we moved in, I asked him if he could take me shopping that afternoon. After all, I needed everything!

109

"Don't worry, sweetheart," he told me. "Today, we'll bring our lunch from the hotel. Give me your list of what you need, and I'll send a driver."

I composed a short list of absolute necessities, handed it to him, and kissed him goodbye. I was surprised when not even an hour later, a hotel car pulled up to the front of the house. Nabile, the driver, began unloading boxes of groceries, pots and pans, dish towels, cleaners, and more. He promised to take me to the supermarket the next day, but he hoped this would do for today. There were advantages to being the boss's wife!

I was happy in our little bungalow. It enclosed us in a protective embrace, sheltering our small family from the elements and the inevitable anxieties of everyday life. It felt like our own little "sea of tranquility" plunked down in the middle of nowhere. It was *ours*. There is a difference between a house and a home, and I was determined that this would be a home.

Compounds, groups of houses in a gated community, seemed to be the preferred mode of regional housing. As compounds went, in Saudi Arabia, this one was rather modest. Most of the housing communities were gated and guarded, but ours was unassuming and humble. There were only fourteen bungalows in this compound, set in an oval. A strip of grass in the middle separated the two sides and allowed room for cars. Most of the villas were occupied, I was glad to find out, and ours was about in the middle.

Best of all, there were lots of children in this community, with plenty of boys around Paul's age. I had already met Milad and Joumana, and they made sure that we met everyone else. Their little boy, Rabih, was as old as Paul, and in the easy way of children, they had taken to each other immediately.

Nagib had told me that Milad's birthday was December 25. Milad meant Christmas, thus the name. Joumana meant pearl. I loved the name, suggesting to Nagib that if our new baby was a girl, we might call her Joumana. He laughed at me. "Joumana Rouhana?"

Enough said. The hunt for girls' names would continue.

We agreed that I would name this baby if it were a boy since Nagib had named Paul. I had chosen Nicholas Alexander. It was a strong name. I hoped it would fit the man he would become, but I hadn't realized that Lebanese custom required that each child, male and female alike, take their father's first name as their second name.

With June came the end of the school year, and the grand exodus of women and children began. The American radio station played Frankie Valli's "See You in September" over and over as we said goodbye to our budding friends, one after the other. After a week or two in what seemed like a ghost town, I began to think that I must be the only Western woman left in the Eastern Province. It was particularly hard on Paul, who didn't understand where all his new friends had gone.

In no time at all, I found myself the *only* woman in the compound, and Paul the only child. I tried my best to amuse us both, but the summer months were long, lonely, and HOT. Interminable stretches of idleness were broken up only by the midday meal, when Nagib would come home for a little while and remind us there was a world outside. In the evening, Paul and I would walk the few blocks to the deserted bowling alley and meet Nagib for dinner to change the scenery a bit. The TV stations didn't start broadcasting until late afternoon, usually around four. We were fortunate that by living in the Eastern Province, we could pick up the Bahraini stations, which were in English.

This was to be the only summer I spent in the Kingdom throughout our sojourn there. I was there on a temporary visa, waiting for the ever-present red tape to be cut. This being the land of slowness and procrastination, it wasn't likely to be soon, and so we waited.

One day followed the next in monotony, each just like the day before. Blue skies, bright sun, 120-degree heat. Wake up, bathe Paul, do laundry, play with Paul, prepare lunch, take a nap, go to the bowling alley, eat dinner with Paul and Nagib, go to bed. Wake up. Lather, rinse, repeat. Still, I tried to be positive in my letters home.

June 1980

Dear Mom,

I have become so lethargic that even writing letters home seems too difficult. But I am REALLY rested! Paul is doing fine. He's a little angry with us right now. He blames us because he had just made several friends here on the compound, and then POOF! They're gone! You should see me, Mom. I look like I swallowed a beach ball! I've picked up some long caftans that are loose and fit over my belly. They're light, cool, and comfortable.

The doctor says the baby is doing just fine, and things are on schedule for the end of October. We toured the hospital, and everything was very clean and modern. It's called the Abdullah Fouad Hospital and is just five miles up the road from us. Nagib has applied for a visa for his mother to come before I deliver so she can stay with Paul and be with me when I come home from the hospital, so don't worry.

I got Betsy's telegram yesterday. The fighting between Iran and Iraq is far from here. Please don't worry. It's unbelievably peaceful and quiet right now, like living on the moon!

We've had some little visitors in the house. I see lizards scampering up the walls from time to time. Someone at the hotel told me not to worry about them; they eat the scorpions!!!

Much, much love,

Cathy

The tension between Iran and Iraq had been developing for decades, but in April of 1980, the pro-Iran al-Da'wa party claimed responsibility for an attempted assassination of Tariq Aziz, the Iraqi deputy Prime Minister. In retaliation, Iraq expelled 40,000 Iranian-born Shiites from within its borders. The war between the two countries began in September of 1980, following a series of retaliations. Iraq invaded Iran after alleging an Iranian artillery bombardment on Khenejin and Mandali on September 4. Both attacked each other's oil fields. We were frequent visitors to Ra's Tenura, north of Dammam and home to one of the largest oil refineries in the world. To my family in the States, Iraq and Iran were just a hop, skip, and a jump away. They were probably right.

The day-after-day sameness was sometimes broken up by visits for lunch from the other managers. Their families gone, they were glad to be invited to a home-cooked meal. More excitingly, our container finally came! What a relief;

it hadn't fallen into the harbor after all. I unpacked my home treasures, excited about potential projects. I drooled over cookbooks, longing to try new recipes. Needlework sat, ready to be made into baby blankets and tapestries. My boxes gave me project after project as I unpacked. Toys, clothes, books—all the familiar home items needed to be examined and put away.

There were some items that never made it through customs. Whether confiscated or stolen, we had no way of knowing. One of these was a beautifully illustrated book on the history of Islam, which my uncle had given me as a going-away present. My classical record albums arrived; the three naked muses on the cover of one album had been colored in with black magic marker, making them more presentable in this restrictive culture. I had already discovered that pork, that taboo word, was blacked out on the back of pepper cans. Imagine the office worker whose job was censoring pepper cans with black marker, sitting in his cubicle, piles of cans to the side. It gave me pause.

At the time, I was too close to the situation to fully appreciate it. In the days before instant messaging, cell phones, Skype, and email, my isolation was complete. Communication with my family and friends was limited to the infrequent and unsatisfactory long-distance phone calls and letters sent by "snail mail."

I had never understood what Nagib meant when he said that Saudi Arabia was a closed society. I thought I would go with the flow and work it out. After all, when in Rome...

Now it was coming to me, up close and personal. Saudi Arabia is a patriarchal society where women are second class, at best. One couldn't just travel about Saudi, touring and seeing the sights. In order to be given a visa to enter the Kingdom, you had to have a purpose, a job. Even so, only men were given work visas, except for a few professions where women were brought in and closely chaperoned. Only the men with university degrees were given family visas.

I knew before we left that women couldn't drive in the Kingdom, but I hadn't realized that I would need a letter of permission from my husband to travel between cities. As outrageous to my American sensibilities as this was, it was mitigated by the discovery that Nagib, as well, would need a letter from his employer to move about the country.

The evidence of the subjugation of women was not subtle. From the black swaths that hid their faces and bodies, to the ban on driver's licenses, women were at the mercy of first their fathers and brothers and later, their husbands. One of the most telling sights during my tenure was a sign outside a new mall restaurant warning NO DOGS OR WOMEN ALLOWED. Shocking as this was, at least I was here temporarily. I was an observer, immune to the restrictions and taboos of the culture. So I thought. The ideals of the culture were everywhere, subtly seeping into the awareness of men and women alike, dulling the Western sensibilities that should have been outraged into a shrugging acceptance.

For me, as for my new acquaintances, these customs and prejudices impacted our daily lives. It didn't matter that I was educated, with a college degree. It didn't matter that I had previously lived on my own and supported myself. It didn't matter that I could drive a car, read a map, play the piano, or change a tire. It didn't even matter that my husband shared my beliefs and distaste for the societal status of my gender. I was a woman, and as such I could not drive, work, or move about freely without permission.

Being the boss's wife had its uses, though. Nagib promised to send a driver whenever I needed to go somewhere. His promise was a comfort, and I knew he would keep it if he could. But even with my husband's permission and a driver, I was constantly reminded that there were so few places to go.

By the end of August, the women and children began trickling back to the Kingdom. Nagib kept me updated each evening until finally, he announced they were coming in a steady stream. Even though this meant the end of vacation and sad goodbyes to their families back home, there was an ambiance of joy and festivity in our communities. Happy reunions were celebrated in every compound, in almost every house. Life was taken off hold, and I was thankfully yanked out of my deep reverie and back into an active reality.

As the return of families in the Eastern Province went from trickle to flood, Paul and I resettled into our daily routine, which expanded to include new experiences. My friend Anna was considered the unofficial mayor of our little compound community. She had taken me under her wing, making it her business to initiate me into the every-day norms of female life here in the Kingdom. She knew the best places to shop for food, craft materials, clothes, and gold. That fall, Anna announced that she would take me shopping in downtown Al-Khobar. I had been cooped up for too long, and this mundane chore took on impor-tance well out of proportion. I was starved for companion-ship.

Anna was Cuban-American, an olive-skinned beauty who spoke English with a heavy accent. She was soft spo-ken and kindhearted. In her early thirties, she wore her dark black hair pulled severely tight in a bun at the nape of her neck, holding her head high as if her hairstyle helped keep it that way.

She was also extremely skittish, startling at sudden noises, panicking if an empty dump truck passed too quickly over a speed bump. The resulting "boom" would send her into a corner, pale-faced, holding her hand to her chest and praying. As I got to know her better, she told me some of her history.

Anna was eight years old when the coup that put Fidel Castro into power in Cuba changed her life irrevocably. Teary-eyed, she told me about her terror the night that soldiers broke down her family's front door in the wee hours, taking her father away with them. Anna herself had been wrapped in a quilt and whisked away by car, though she didn't know by whom. Ultimately, she was smuggled safely to an aunt in Florida, who raised her. She was never to see her family or home country again, nor to learn what became of her father. As she told me her story, I cried with her, barely able to comprehend an existence so alien to my own upbringing.

But that was later in our friendship. This day, we rode and chatted as Anna pointed out the sights. To our right we saw development; buildings, housing businesses, compounds, and the like. To our left, we could see the Persian, or Arab Gulf as the Saudis called it, in the distance. Barges carrying containers bobbed up and down on the gentle Gulf swells, queuing to be unloaded. The omnipresent sand stretched parallel to the road, dirty and unattractive. Unlike the beaches at home, one was not inspired to walk down to the shore. Closer to the road, we noticed that tar had been poured over the gray sand—an attempt to keep it from blowing and reclaiming the highway.

I was surprised to see the road littered with stopped automobiles, pulled over onto the side. Men knelt on carpets beside their cars, bowing and praying, facing the desert with their backs to the vehicles. The call to prayer droned loudly from the minarets that dotted the landscape. *Allah u akbar*, "God is great," was a familiar phrase, coming at arbitrary hours. Anna explained about prayer times. When the call sounded from the minarets, it let the faithful know it was time to stop everything, turn to Mecca in the east, and pray as one. The cars pulled to the side of the road were a common sight, their former occupants kneeling and praying on their mats.

"You'll get used to it," she told me. The tilt of her head and the expression on her face left no doubt as to what she thought of the practice—a total annoyance. Still, Anna knew a way around it. Since prayer times changed every day, they were published in the daily papers.

"I checked in the newspaper this morning," she said. "The prayers will be over soon, and we'll have plenty of time to shop." Anna had also checked the price of gold in the newspapers. She could get some gold jewelry at a bargain, she told me, in the market. Timing was crucial.

The usual practice was to close the stores at the call to prayers. If you were unlucky enough to get caught halfway through your grocery shopping when the call began, then you had the choice to leave your cart and wait outside until business resumed, or just come back another day.

This practice was not taken lightly. Saudi Arabia's government and laws were, and are, based on religious law. Several years later a Canadian friend, a Muslim, had kept working during the call to prayer. He was in the middle of a project and didn't want to stop since he had a deadline he was trying to meet. The Mutawa (religious police) caught him, and he was sentenced to be whipped. It was serious.

Stepping out of the car in downtown Al Khobar, we gathered our thin, black *abayas* around us, the dark polyester absorbing the humid heat, not letting it go. This was the traditional outdoor garb of the women of the Eastern Province, assuring modesty when out and about. The thick air smelled heavy, belying the bright blue sky. The air-conditioned car had let us pretend the heat was tolerable.

I hurried through the market after Anna, not wanting to lose her. She was a woman on a mission, but turning back to see where I was, she burst out laughing.

"You look like your eyes are going to pop out of your head!"

Whose wouldn't? I thought. We were in the middle of the downtown section called the gold souk (market). Everywhere I turned, I saw gold in the shop windows. Not just a tastefully arranged display of jewelry, but gold chains, watches, and bracelets hung closely together, seeming to cover every inch of the display area, as thick as syrup. They stood, shop after shop, one next to the other, with no shoe store or restaurant to break up the mesmerizing, shimmering opulence. So much gold was on display that it seemed unreal.

Halfway down the block, Anna let me know that we had reached our destination. All business, she marched into the shop and up to the counter. We were greeted by an Indian clerk, who bowed slightly in deference to the American ladies and asked how he could help us this morning.

Anna went straight to work, producing the morning's newspaper clipping that gave the price of gold per ounce. He confirmed the price, and Anna went to work selecting a bracelet. She tried one after the other, asking for my opinion. I did my best, commenting on the design or delicacy of each piece, but to my eye, one was as good as the other. She finalized her purchase, very pleased with herself, and we left.

Outside again, she explained that many of the Kingdom's "guests" followed the gold market, as she did, and considered jewelry purchases a wise investment.

It reminded me of a story Nagib had told me. He had a friend who worked with him in Washington, D.C. The friend and his wife had high-powered jobs that took them to live in London and travel a lot. They had a jewelry collection that was worth thousands, and they were rather paranoid about protecting it.

Anna grinned as she saw where my story was heading. Nabile, in the front seat, cocked his head, listening.

"It happened that while his wife was away on business, he was unexpectedly asked to take a trip for work.

He didn't have time to take the jewelry to the bank, so he wrapped it well in paper and hid it in the freezer.

"When she returned," I continued, "she went on a cleaning spree. What better time than when her husband was away and she had some time on her hands?" Anna gasped and put her hand over her mouth. Nabile was grinning from ear to ear.

I paused for dramatic effect. "You guessed it," I said. "She cleaned the freezer and threw out all of their investment that he had hidden there."

Anna couldn't stand it. "Didn't he leave her a note? Didn't he talk to her on the phone?"

"Evidently not," I shrugged. "When he came back and discovered what had happened, all hell broke loose! They spent almost a week digging through the landfill where the garbage was dumped, trying to find it, but they never did. In the end, they divorced."

Anna paused for a moment, aghast. "That's what happens when a husband and wife don't talk to each other," she pronounced. "Unbelievable," she said, shaking her head pensively. "Unbelievable. The moral is to always talk to your spouse!"

By now, we had reached our next destination, a not-so-glittery part of downtown where more practical everyday items could be bought. Anna finished up with her purchases, then pressured me into buying a pair of round, black onyx earrings. They weren't terribly expensive, but simpler, understated, and elegant. I liked them a lot. I kept those earrings for twenty-five years before I, unfortunately, lost them. I would think of Anna with a smile every time I put them on.

CHAPTER 9

As my pregnancy advanced, I took comfort in our research into the Abdullah Fouad Hospital in Dammam. We had found it clean and furnished with the most modern equipment, and the staff mostly spoke English. It wasn't hard to find women who had given birth there, and I had been quickly reassured.

This was the decade of natural childbirth and Lamaze. The doctor who delivered Paul in Baltimore was the same one who had delivered most of my brothers and sisters. He didn't hesitate to give an unequivocal "no" when we requested that Nagib be allowed in the delivery room. He had allowed him in the labor room with me, but asked Nagib to leave when the birth was imminent. He told us that he didn't think most fathers really wanted to be at a birth, but were coerced by their wives.

This time, I made it perfectly clear to Nagib that I would only deliver in Saudi Arabia if he was present with me at the birth. I envisioned all kinds of mix-ups resulting from language problems and I at least wanted a translator, if not an advocate.

My friend told me that my fears were warranted. She had delivered her baby three years before in Beirut, and had

had quite a few complications during her pregnancy. Her doctor was one of the best, though, and she had complete confidence in him. She went into labor in Beirut in 1976. The phone system at that time was antique—propped up, literally, by two-by-fours. Unable to contact her husband, she took a taxi to the American University Hospital of Beirut. She left word for both her doctor and her husband to meet her there.

The political tensions were high at this time. Going to the American University Hospital of Beirut necessitated crossing the "green line," an imaginary line separating mostly Christian East Beirut from mostly Muslim West Beirut. That day, the hostilities escalated and the military later closed the road. This was her first baby, and she was scared. Everything was complicated by the shells raining down around the hospital, and her worry for her husband's safety. But at least she was in her own country, and she spoke the language.

As her labor progressed, it became more obvious that this would not be an easy delivery. She was alone, but lucky. She arrived at the hospital before the roads closed. No member of her family, nor her doctor, could cross the green line separating the two warring sides of the city. The resident on duty that night was American. After examining her, he turned to the nurse and, thinking his patient didn't understand English, said he guessed he'd have to do a C-section. The nurse gasped and answered, "But do you know how?" She sat up in the bed as best she could. Grabbing the lapels of his lab coat, fiercely, through gritted teeth, she demanded that they get her doctor. NOW!

She never knew if it was luck, fear, or an act of God, but her doctor materialized shortly after that to save the day and deliver a healthy baby boy.

We had checked out the hospital and found the doctor, but try as he might, Nagib could not get a visa for his mother. Who would stay with Paul when it was time to deliver? The officials kept telling him, *bukra, in sha'Allah*—tomorrow, God willing. Blame it on God and look up at the sky with a shrug.

Now that the women had returned, so did the compound coffee mornings. Joumana's friend Nadine lived at the entrance to the compound, and I was invited to her house for just such a morning. Nadine was Lebanese, a bit older than I, but it was hard to tell. She was tall, thin, and very stylish, but her skin was old-looking; pitted and sallow, probably from smoking. Her English wasn't quite as good as the other Lebanese women I'd met. She spoke with a heavy accent, and was sometimes hard to understand.

Wearing a new light-brown caftan Nagib had picked up for me at the bazaar, I waddled up to Nadine's house. It was comfortable and soft, but I still couldn't help thinking that I looked somewhat like a walking circus tent! Joumana stopped by my house on her way so I wouldn't have to walk in alone.

I was amazed at how many women were pregnant. Nadine was, and Joumana and another woman, Cristae. This party was like a little United Nations meeting; six or seven countries were represented. Joumana and Nadine were from Lebanon, Cristae was Australian, Wendy from England, Dawn from Cornwall, Tahseen from Pakistan, and Josephine from Syria. Carmen and Anna were from Cuba, but called the U.S. home. We all gathered in Nadine's living room and drank coffee and ate croissants and homemade pound cake.

Nadine's home was the same floor plan as mine, as were all the compound houses. Yet it was amazing how different cultures and tastes could transform the same space. Her house had a lot of Lebanese-type décor: carpets, copper trays, tapestries, numerous cushions, and argilehs. Nadine liked to smoke the argileh.

This particular coffee morning had a purpose. I had already seen incredible displays of gold jewelry at the bazaar with Anna, but this was a new one on me—expensive jewelry being sold at someone's home! It was like a Tupperware party. I found it fantastic and unbelievable, but also quite appropriate to the country. Plus, it was fun. I met quite a few new women who didn't live in the compound. We drank coffee and ate cake while the saleswoman brought out diamond rings, sapphire bracelets, and the like. We tried them on, oohing and ahhing. I tried a sapphire ring, and it looked pretty on my finger. Joumana encouraged me to buy it, but I told her I had no money.

"What?" Joumana yelled at me. "Your husband is the boss! Call him NOW!"

I did, and the next thing I knew, a bellboy from the hotel rang Nadine's doorbell with an envelope full of Saudi riyals for me. I bought the ring and the bracelet that went with it, an unfamiliar, luxurious experience. If the folks back home could only see me now, I thought.

Even so, I still couldn't believe all the diamonds, sapphires, and rubies I saw at that party. My mouth hung open. Once again, I was Dorothy in Oz.

About a week after Nadine's "Tupperware party," a box arrived for me at the hotel. It was from America, and I could see by the return address that it was from my friend, Mary S. How like her, I thought, assuming it to be baby gifts. I sat right down on the floor in all my hugeness to open it.

Yes, there were baby gifts inside, but, to my amazement, the gifts were from all my friends. Mary had thrown a baby shower for me, in absentia. Enclosed were not only the wrapped gifts, but all of the cards, paper plates, and party napkins. Down on the bottom of the carton I found a letter they had sent, as well as a tape. They had recorded the *entire* party! I crawled over to the stereo, popped in the tape, and, without getting off the floor, sat listening as I read the letter. At the end of the tape, they all sang Roy

Rogers' theme song, "Happy Trails," whose lyrics included "Until We Meet Again."

Happy Trails. That's what it's all about anyway, isn't it? When Nagib came home for lunch shortly after that, he found me sitting on the floor, crying, looking at the gifts and listening to my tape. How I missed my friends.

My due date was fast approaching and there was still no visa for Im Gaby. As before, we heard, "Tomorrow, God willing." For now, at least, it seemed God was not willing.

Even though everything wasn't in place for the birth, labor started. Anna kept Paul for us. He was happy to spend the night with her son Chris, and he loved Anna, who was very kind to him. My neighbor Tahseen had come over earlier in the day, and when she found out I had started contractions, she polished my toenails for me. I had done my fingers but was having trouble reaching my feet. Knowing what to expect, I was more apprehensive this second go-round. My labor this time was longer, but less intense. Nagib timed the contractions and told me to breathe, which helped. Nick's birth was proving much easier than Paul's had been.

The staff was busy that night; six women were in labor. All the women started out in the same ward, separated by curtains, but one by one they were wheeled to the delivery room, leaving the rest behind. Nagib was the only father who stayed. The Jamaican nurse assigned to us seemed to take his presence in stride. At one point, she snuck in a cup of tea for me to sip on. This was forbidden, and whenever a doctor appeared, she quickly whisked it under either my bed or on someone else's.

Dr. Sayed came and went, telling Nagib that it would be hours yet. By now, all the other women on the ward had delivered, and we were alone. Unable to stay awake, Nagib had just put his head down on the bed when my abdomen rose and fell in an aggressive manner. Nagib woke up and, panicking, begged me not to push. But this had nothing to do with me; the baby was coming.

Nagib ran down the hall, flagging down the only nurse left on duty. It was after midnight, the lights had been dimmed, and he could see no one else around. The nurse came on the run. After examining me, she pushed the heavy bed into the delivery room, abandoning us to find the doctor, running at top speed. Nagib's face turned the same shade of sickly green as right before our wedding.

Our son Nick has always been a take-charge, proactive kind of guy. His entrance into the world was no different. His father was all set to deliver this second son when the doctor sprinted in, pushed him aside, and made a catch worthy of a tight end. No slouch in the lungs department, little Nicky announced himself to his parents with gusto, a trait he displayed often over the years.

Happily, my stay in the hospital was only two days, and I was anxious to get home. The food was inedible, even the breakfasts. I had chosen cold cereal with milk for my first hospital meal, but as I poured in the milk, up came little bugs, floating to the top like cream in coffee. After that, the hotel catered anything I ate in the hospital. But food aside, I missed Paul and wanted to present his much-awaited brother to him.

A steady stream of well-wishers seemed to line up at our door to congratulate us on Nick's birth. Even though I knew that much of this was dictated by strong cultural protocol, it was still very nice.

All the ladies in the compound came to coo over baby Nicky, as did the company managers and their wives. I wasn't prepared for the visits. I had only met these men and their wives once, and very quickly. Many didn't speak English, but I was getting good at the key phrases for such an occasion. Nagib's business acquaintances came as well, and for many of these, it was my first introduction to people I would count as friends for the rest of my "visit" to the Kingdom.

One of these men, Nabile, was older than us by at least twenty years, maybe more. He took Nicky in his arms, looked closely at him, and decreed that this would be a very handsome and forceful man. A few years later, the sister of one of the manager's wives took one of three-year-old Nick's hands. Looking at his palm, she gasped and told me that he would be a force to be reckoned with, and a great help to his brother.

The Lebanese are great proclaimers, and I was touched and impressed. I would always say thank you, then put these things away in my heart. Strangely, only Nick has been the recipient of these fortune tellings over the years. Something about the boy's demeanor made people stop and take notice. It had gotten so extreme at one point that, while in Lebanon, his father would shout at people that they were bringing the "evil eye" down on the boy.

I was new to Lebanese baby traditions. Paul had been born in the States, with his father's family many miles away. Maroun had been with us, but he was a twenty-four-year-old man. What did he know? No, in every culture, I think it's the women, particularly the older ones, who keep the traditions alive. Everyone brought a gift for little Nick, most of them some sort of gold jewelry.

Nagib's new bosses sent ten solid gold coins, and Abdul Aziz, the Saudi owner, sent a large, antique gold coin. Per Lebanese tradition, we served each one of our guests a spicy rice pudding called migly. Migly was made from rice flour, sugar, cinnamon, and ground caraway. The spices made it a light brown color, but the top of each serving was covered with shredded coconut, ground pistachios, pine nuts, and walnuts. I hadn't ever seen it before, and it was really quite pretty. The chef at the hotel made it for us. Im Gaby, of course, would have made it for us if she had been able to come. But still, I soon became very fond of migly.

Nagib hadn't given me a baby gift when Nick was born. I really didn't care; Nick was his baby too. I didn't think anything more until the other women started asking me what kind of jewelry I'd gotten. I never said anything about this to Nagib, so I was doubly surprised when the piano arrived one afternoon. After all, I *had* told my mother that I would spend my time here having a family, learning Arabic and improving my piano playing. It was a totally thoughtful and sensitive gift, and I was thrilled.

Nick proved to be a popular guy in the compound. The ladies all came to coo over him, and for the most part, he was agreeable. His brother liked him too. Toward the end of my pregnancy, he had exploded in frustration to the doctor, "Oh, just cut him out of there NOW!" Paul was a forceful child who was used to being able to manipulate situations to his advantage. When he was three, he saw the ocean for the first time. As the waves rolled in, he held up both hands, palms toward the water, and loudly shouted: "STOP!" We held our collective breath for a heartbeat, he was so commanding. My uncle George still says the ocean had to think twice about it.

Paul was just a month shy of four when Nick was born. He had been asking for a little brother for a while, and now that Nick was finally here, he just didn't understand why this tiny being wouldn't get up and play with him. But the anguish of school kept Paul occupied most days.

He had started the previous month. He looked so small, holding his lunch box and waiting for the driver on his first day. It was a bonus that his best friend Rabih would be riding with him. Paul's friend Chris was starting school that day, too, and after the children left, I took baby Nick and walked over to Anna's house in tears, looking for tea and conversation. Paul's first school day was a landmark, and I needed comfort. If we had been in the States, it would have been delayed for another two years, but we had chosen the French school, and the French system started children at age three.

Paul started school already at a disadvantage; he didn't speak French. Nagib and I were hopeful of raising our children to be multilingual. Our plans to settle in Lebanon would require a knowledge of French for their school system. Arabic would be needed then, too, and this school offered an after-school program in Arabic for the Lebanese children. La Petite Ecole Française, or the French School, was the choice for the company children, including Rabih.

Paul *did* have some advantages. He was blessed with a wonderful teacher who loved him. Madame Ava was a young Lebanese woman who, thankfully, also spoke English. She gathered Paul gently under her wing and took it upon herself to report to his father on a weekly basis.

Some of her reports were as poignant as they were funny.

"Today, class, I want you to draw a picture of a rabbit," she told the small students, in French, of course. She went around the classroom, standing by each student as they proudly showed her the picture they had drawn of the *lapin*. When she got to Paul, he was assiduously working on his art project and was just ready to put the final changes to his drawing of a house.

"That's a very nice house, Paul," she told him.

"Thank you, Madame," he answered in French. We had been coaching him on that one.

"But Paul," the teacher continued, this time in English, "you were supposed to draw a rabbit. Where is the *lapin*?"

"But Madame, I did make the rabbit," Paul answered.

"But where, Paul? Where is the rabbit?" she asked.

"Madame," our son answered, "he is behind the house."

Ava couldn't stop laughing as she related this story to Nagib. And when he told me, neither could I.

It was still very hot when Nick was born that October. The temperature stayed around 105 to 115 degrees, and the humidity stayed consistently in the ninety percent range. Anyone who wore glasses had to remove them immediately on going from the cool air-conditioned inside to the sauna of the Saudi outside. Their glasses would fog over completely and immediately when the humidity hit. I heard some people had dropped eggs on the sidewalk, trying to prove that it was, indeed, hot enough to fry an egg. The swimming pool had a cooling system installed to keep the water from getting too hot, and the waters of the nearby Persian Gulf felt like bath water.

There was really nothing to be done but endure. I hadn't been in the country a full year yet, so I was unprepared for the sudden change. I still remember the November morning, a few weeks after Nick was born, when it happened. I was changing Nick's diaper, and Nagib was getting ready for work.

Paul had gone to the front porch to see if the car was outside to take him to school. We were surprised when he came running back to us, very excited, shouting that something wonderful had happened, and we should come immediately! We didn't know what to expect, but ran outside with the little boy. Lo and behold, a cool wind was blowing! The air was dry and comfortable, and felt nothing short of miraculous. It was like waking up to an unexpected snow back home. We were all excited for the change of season, and other welcome changes that blew in with the wind.

With school started, we settled into a routine of breakfast at 7. Then it was time to wrestle with Paul to get him fed and ready for school. It was a shame that it took two adults to get one four-year-old dressed and into a car to go to school, but he made it clear every day that he much preferred to stay home.

Work was going well for Nagib. And me? Well, I was happy to have my body back. I took care of the children, prepared the meals, and kept the house. In between those chores, socializing with friends was a pleasure. My surroundings began to seem ordinary, but I could still be surprised. Car wrecks on the side of the road were left on pedestals like monuments. Each car had a large sign attached to it, which warned against careless driving. The owners of the cars couldn't get them back for repairs, either. They were confiscated. I missed driving, but Nagib put off getting his license as long as possible. I believed he was worn out from all the driving he had done back and forth to D.C. every day. Turned out, he just enjoyed being driven everywhere.

Our driver Nabile once told me that if you hit a camel on the side of the road, you'd better hope that your car could still run. If the camel's owner was still around, he'd take your car, your wallet, and anything else you had of value. Camels were a special commodity and very expensive. You could sometimes see them from the road, walking their funny gait in a line on the horizon.

Every day, I passed huts on the side of the road as we approached the hotel. Hut was a generous description for those makeshift abodes. They looked rickety and crude, but all had large tv antennas coming out of the top, and people would sit outside, in their large Cadillacs, watching TV. I'd guessed they weren't too worried about rain. In my letters home, I tried to relate this new world.

Dammam, Saudi Arabia

November 1980

Dear Mom,

Sorry I haven't written for so long. In a way that's a
good thing. It means I've finally found my groove over
here! The other women on the compound are great.
We have eleven different nationalities represented in
this enclave! We get together at least three or four
mornings a week to have coffee, sew, and talk. Sometimes as the whole group, other times just one on one.
We all have children and a lot of them are around
Paul's age.

My friend Dawn is from Cornwall, and married to an
Austrian. They have two teenage daughters who have
been begging me to go shopping and leave Nick with
them for an hour or so. It's getting close to Thanksgiving, so I think I might take advantage of their offer!

Funny thing happened here the other day. As you
know, I can't drive here. I had to take Paul and Nick
to the pediatrician for a regular checkup. Nabile drove
me there. It's a fairly undeveloped part of the region,
and there aren't any street signs. I don't know how
anyone finds their way around. Anyway, when we got

there, I was about to get out of the car with the boys, when I looked behind me and saw a herd of cattle coming down the street. Long-horned cattle. They were HUGE! You better believe that we stayed in the car until they had gone by.

We put in all new kitchen cabinets this week. They're dark blue. It really makes a difference. I'm having about fifteen people to dinner for Thanksgiving, so I'll give it a good workout!

Much love to all. I really miss you!

Cathy

CHAPTER 10

Since Im Gaby had been unable to come after Nick was born, Nagib sent a young Sri Lankan man named Mahinda to help me clean. The housekeeping manager at the hotel had trained him, and we arranged for him to come three times a week. It was a luxury, and I couldn't help feeling guilty. Yes, I had two small children, but I wasn't working. However, all the other women had some help during the week. Mahinda came for a couple of hours three times a week only, and vacuumed and cleaned the bathroom. The house was small, and we weren't terribly messy. I tried to put my mental anguish away.

The arrival of Mahinda gave me a measure of freedom. I was able to step out across the compound to visit with one friend or another for coffee while Nicky slept and Paul was in school. Even if I didn't go far, at least I was going somewhere. These few stolen hours were a blessing, particularly so soon after Nicky's birth. My new friends linked me to another world as well—that of fashion.

As I had seen from the show several months before, fashion was very important to the female world in Saudi, and they were experts. Take silk. I learned about silk in grade school, how it was produced by silkworms and made into thread and then fabric. I had never given the word or the substance much thought beyond that. What else did I need to know? A lot, apparently. The Lebanese ladies of the Eastern Province took it to another level.

Raw silk, Parisian, Chinese, and Italian; some mixed with other fabrics and some of far inferior quality to others, at widely varying prices. You could find them all in Al-Khobar. Vibrant, shimmering hues, earth tones and jewel tones, subtle and beautiful. Silk was never the wrong thing to wear.

As the boss's wife, I had had to learn quickly about the luxurious requirements of the position. I now knew about wearing expensive jewelry—sapphire rings and gold bracelets, diamond necklaces, and more. I already knew that the gold sold here was eighteen to twenty-two carats; more valuable than the fourteen I knew as the standard in the States. But there was still the dress code to master.

"I like your dress, Cathy. Where did you get it?" one Lebanese hostess asked me at an evening soirée.

"Oh, I just got it the other day at the dress shop in Al-Khobar," I replied. It hadn't been expensive, but I thought it had some style and looked good on me.

"Really? Which shop?" she asked. And then the inevitable, "Which designer?" The dress was not designer, but it wasn't any of her business. I tried to change the subject. Not to be thwarted, she reached behind me and pulled out the tag to read.

"Hmm," she said, "it's very nice anyway." My education in designer clothes, and the snobbery associated with them, had begun in earnest.

I learned all about French and Italian lines of dresses, shoes, sweaters, and everything else. I was a quick study and reveled in my newfound affluence and position. It was fun to buy clothes, particularly these oh-so-stylish, beautiful garments. I never worried about overdressing. The ladies always called around and set the tone of an evening ahead of time. It was a fast-paced, intensive sort of crash course, but it was a lot of fun!

Fudge: A delectable marriage of bitter and sweet, when cooked just right, yields a tender and delicious confection.

Life was sweet. New baby, new job, new friends, new country. A prosperous and comfortable future shimmered in front of us. I settled in, prepared to do my part to make this adventure a success.

Happiness is being part of the gang in Saudi Arabia! announced the T-shirt I found in one of the bazaars. The shirt was yellow with brown trim around the sleeves and sported a picture of the Peanuts gang doing a happy dance to Schroeder's piano music. I bought it immediately and wore it often. It was true! Happiness was, for the time being, being part of the gang in Saudi.

All the women of the compound had much in common and bonded quickly. We were all of an age, mostly early thirties, and had young families or children on the way. We all had families who were far away and missing us. Many of our husbands were from different countries than we were. And of course, we were all foreigners to the Kingdom. Time didn't hang so heavily as we enjoyed these new friendships.

Some mornings we would call around and agree to meet at the pool, or a couple of us would go shopping if someone could get a car and a driver. That someone was usually me, and it was a rare day when Nagib had to tell me no.

But we always fell back on the coffee mornings. They were the staple of female social life, and luckily for me, English was the common language. Eventually, we developed the coffee morning into a sewing circle. It was Wendy who sat down with a catalog from The Stitchery, in Massachusetts, and took people's orders. She paid for it on her credit card and had it shipped to her house. I ordered a large, pre-stamped kit for Crewel embroidery. It was to be a colorful and vibrant floral arrangement. It looked beautiful in the catalog, and even though I had never done anything like this before, I felt confident that I could learn. There were plenty of people available to advise me.

It was a happy day when the box arrived. Wendy called us all the night before to invite us to her house in the morning when she would distribute the goodies. Whenever we gathered after that, we would embroider, crochet, or knit. We worked as we watched our children, gossiped, and reminisced about home. The toddlers would play together while the mothers took turns rocking and comforting each other's babies.

At times, I would be invited to coffee mornings by the women in the hotel community. This way, I was introduced to all the company wives affiliated with the hotel. Some of them spoke no English, or very little. Under Joumana's tutelage, I could now get by in Arabic, at least the pleasantries.

Whenever I hosted a morning, I would prepare large thermoses of American coffee and set out my china cups on a pretty tablecloth. I would either make something from scratch or order cake from the hotel. It was all very civilized. We liked to exchange recipes at these gatherings. Josephine's specialty was cheesecake, but she was an across-the-board wonderful cook. Tahseen, who was from Pakistan, made some unusual (for me), dishes, such as cardamom-flavored carrot pudding. I diligently recorded these recipes as they came up and added them to my collection of Im Gaby's treasured recipes.

As I tackled my job of nesting, homemaking, and learning about new foods, Nagib was tackling his: trying to elevate the hotel's cuisine, specifically the hotel's bowling alley. He was full of ideas, confident that he could make them work. He commanded respect and wasn't afraid to shake things up if he had to.

There was a formal restaurant in the hotel as well as the coffee shop. As the wives were fond of feeding the children their evening meal in the bowling area, I was much more familiar with the quality of the food there. I knew what Nagib was trying to accomplish, so one day when Paul's hamburger came to the table with soggy, undercooked French fries, I brought it to Nagib's attention. He tasted the offending food, made a face, and, taking the plate, told me he'd be back in a couple minutes. He took the plate to the kitchen, where he patiently told the chef what was wrong and how he should cook it in the future.

The chef was an older Lebanese man who wore his stringy long gray hair pulled back in a ponytail. This, along with his stained apron, gave him a somewhat greasy appearance. But it was his pointy-toed snakeskin cowboy boots that caught my attention. He must have had them for a while—the snakeskin was peeling off.

A week later, when the French fries again arrived at the table soggy and inedible, Nagib again took the plate back to the kitchen. This time there was nothing polite, only yelling and screaming. I was hesitant to order the hamburger and French fries after that, and I was right. They came to the table as before, unappetizing and unappealing. This time, Nagib asked Paul if he was finished with his food. Calmly carrying the plate back to the kitchen, he threw the china dish at the chef's feet as hard as he could and fired him on the spot. They hadn't nicknamed him the Executioner for nothing.

Christmas 1980 was coming and my friends in the compound took turns babysitting Nick, while Nagib and I shopped. Parties were planned and menus discussed. It was important to try to include every nationality's holiday tradition, from plum pudding to eggnog. The air was filled with excited anticipation.

When I finally persuaded Nagib to take an hour off to shop, I was careful to check the paper for the prayer times. The week before I hadn't checked. I had a cart full of groceries when the lights started blinking and they began shooing people out of the store. I didn't want another incident like that to ruin our Christmas outing.

Nagib didn't like to shop, and he didn't like to take rides to explore the countryside. But Christmas was different. I had gone with Anna, her husband, and their son for a ride through Al Khobar to look at the lights. The lights had been strung just like the Christmas lights at home, across the streets and on the buildings in celebration. It helped to get us in the Christmas spirit. Ironic, isn't it? The lights had been strung to celebrate the "coming of the King," while we were preparing to celebrate the coming of another king. It was strange to be in a country where Christianity was taboo.

This was a particularly hard time of year to be away from home. I was a Christmas girl, and I had never been away for the holiday before. Hard as it was to get used to shopping around the call to prayers, it was harder still to celebrate the season without church bells or pine trees. We bought a very expensive artificial tree and decorated it. I played Christmas music, trying to make a festive family atmosphere. Bustling about helped stave off pangs of homesickness, at least for the time being.

Nagib went to Beirut ten days before Christmas. It was the first time I had been alone since we arrived; I would get used to it over the years, but this first trip was difficult. He was going to meet with the owners to present the budget of the four companies for the next year. He had good news to report and anticipated a generous bonus.

He assured me that the trip would be four days long, five if he traveled up to Zahle to see his mom and brothers.

I didn't feel too alone. I was busy with the boys, and all of my women friends were nearby. They tried to look after me while Nagib was away, and I was invited out to lunch frequently. Nighttime was the hardest, but I was usually so tired by the end of the day that I would collapse into bed and sleep until Nicky woke for his feeding.

The camaraderie in the compound was never more evident than at this first Christmas. We came from such varied and diverse backgrounds, but Christmas was a real unifier. In the absence of parents, siblings, or familiar home comforts, we adopted each other and came together to make a unique holiday. Although we focused on the children, it was the adults who were homesick. And so we made plans.

Wendy was having a party the Friday before Christmas, and I was confident that Nagib would be there in plenty of time. Santa was to make his rounds around the compound, too. To the British, he was Father Christmas, to the Lebanese, Baba Noel, and to the children who went to the French school, he was Papa Noel. Over the next few years, I would learn the words to "Petit Papa Noel," "Angels We Have Heard on High" in French, and "Jingle Bells" in Arabic. But everything was for the first time, and very sweet.

Yet the reality of living in the Middle East was hanging over my head. At the time Nagib left to present his fiscal budget to the home office in Beirut, I was more isolated from the rest of the world than I had ever been. I didn't watch the news, and the hotel said they had not received their most recent shipment of the only English-language newspaper. Happy in my little orbit, I was largely unaware of anything outside of my boys and making a life for us in this strange world.

Consequently, I didn't know that anything was amiss in Lebanon until I tried to telephone Nagib at his mother's house. The phone lines to Lebanon had never been good, and I was used to trying for days before getting through. This time, I got lucky. When Nagib came on the line, however, the story he had to tell shocked me. They had hunkered down in his mother's hallway while missiles rained overhead. The Syrian army, in what would become known as the Battle of Zahle, surrounded the town, the occupants now under siege. He was all right, but he didn't know when it would let up, or if he'd even be able to leave anytime soon.

I had called on the off-chance that I might be able to get a line, even though I knew the chances were slim to none. It was silly. I wanted to hear his voice, using the excuse that we needed some medicine for the children that you couldn't get in Saudi Arabia. It was a totally fatuous, spur-of-the-moment, "I miss you" phone call.

Nagib, of course, assumed that I had heard what was going on. He had no way of knowing that his staff had been keeping the English-language newspapers from me, saying the shipment hadn't arrived. This made the first minute of our conversation odd and at cross-purposes; him reassuring me, and me making small talk. It took a minute before we both caught on.

Even though I heard what he was saying, it took my brain until after I had hung up to catch up. I sat on the floor for a while, shaking, not able to cry. After a bit I became angry, realizing that I was the only one who hadn't known. Everyone in the hotel and in the compound must have known. They had access to the outside world through the Voice of Lebanon Radio. I did not have that same access.

I went through the next few days in a cloud of fear. Once the other executives knew that I knew, they gathered around to support and console. Now, the newspapers arrived on my doorstep in the early morning. I received daily updates from various people, letting me know the latest news as it came over.

The women of the compound and the hotel were wonderful. I had numerous invitations to lunches and dinners, and I went to all the festivities as planned. I was able to suppress the anxiety when I was with other people. But the nights were difficult, when I was alone with my thoughts of "what if."

Christmas Eve had always been *the* special day back home. My family had been raised following the Polish traditions. On Christmas Eve all nine of my siblings, as well as their families, would gather at my mother's house for the *Wigilia* (vigil) dinner. My mom would prepare the traditionally meatless meal, just as her mother and grandmother had. Hay would be placed under the tablecloth to remind us of the manger, and the youngest child would watch out the window to announce the appearance of the first star, signaling the time to begin the meal.

Before sitting down to eat, we would break the *oplatki* (pronounced op-wat-ke). These were thin, white rectangular wafers, about six inches long and four inches wide. In Polish custom, they are distributed on Christmas Eve. We would stand in Mom's living room, wafers in hand, breaking off pieces and offering them. These wafers are meant to signify family unity, and we shared ours, kissing and saying Merry Christmas and *Wesołych Świat*, in Polish.

After dinner, we gathered in front of the Christmas tree, turning off all lights except those decorating it, and my father would read a prayer blessing. Afterwards, we sang carols in both Polish and English. But always, the highlight of the evening was the nativity pageant the youngest children would perform for their gleeful audience. In my family, I was famous for playing the donkey to my brother Tom's Virgin Mary.

We took delight in planning the perfect gift for each other, and surprising our parents with special things we had all pitched in on. Yet our celebration was more about gathering family and putting aside stress and problems, in ritual remembrance of the holiest of families. Christmas Eve had always been a night of love and merriment, and I promised myself that my husband and children would have that blessing wherever our travels took us. Home would be wherever we were.

It was very hard that first year away from home in a Muslim country. As of then, I had never experienced war, and it was hard for me to imagine my beloved husband taking refuge in a hallway, his life in danger.

At five p.m. that Christmas Eve, Paul was in our family room resisting dinner. It was a nightly tug-of-war. I had prepared fish sticks and macaroni and cheese for him, two of his favorites, but he didn't want to eat. He was upset by his father's absence, and in turmoil over the anticipated visit of Santa/Papa Noel/Baba Noel/Father Christmas. He was tired and excited.

When the knock came at the door, I left Paul in order to answer it. Standing on my doorstep, as planned, was a man dressed in a long, burgundy velvet robe. He wore black boots, a crown on his head, and carried a tall staff in his hand. He was accompanied by my neighbor, Wendy, who introduced him as Father Christmas.

The man worked with Wendy's husband. He was a bachelor, glad to have this bit of magical family activity. I turned to look at Paul and found him staring, mouth agape, eyes wide with amazement. He had heard other children in this international community speak of Father Christmas. He knew who Father Christmas was, but being only four, he didn't have a locked-in mental picture of what he should look like.

Father Christmas stooped down and spoke to Paul. He gave him a small gift and told him that if the boy ate all his dinner, he would come back in the night, after Paul was asleep, with many more.

There was no discussion after that. Paul did an about-face, marched into the house, finished his dinner, took his bath, and went to bed. Father Christmas left me a gift as well. I got a phone call from Pierre at the hotel shortly after Paul and Nick were in bed, saying that Nagib had called. He had been able to leave Zahle in a diplomat's limousine

and would be home before midnight. My relief was inde-
scribable. I never questioned that this was our own, personal Christmas miracle.

As momentous as the build-up to that Christmas night
had been, what followed has been ingrained in family lore.
Nagib arrived home around eleven p.m. We were invited to
a birthday celebration at Milad and Joumana's house, but,
of course, had declined. All the hotel executives were going, as well as the neighbors in the compound. We hadn't
made any babysitting arrangements and Nagib was too
tired to go out, so we sent our regrets.

Nagib had news from Lebanon, and our little community was very disappointed at our refusal to come. They
urged us to walk down to the party for just an hour. "Leave
the kids alone. They'll be okay. You're just a few houses
away." I knew that quite a few of our new friends were inclined to do this, but we wouldn't risk our children. And,
selfishly, I wanted my husband to myself for a while after
our scare.

But the Lebanese close to us were hungry for news,
both from the political arena and the business side. The
phone rang off the hook even at this late hour, threatening
to wake the children, and disturbing our reunion. Nagib
spoke patiently with his executives, giving the news in a
nutshell while promising more details the next day, a workday even though it was Christmas.

It was almost midnight when the excitement finally settled down and the phone stopped ringing. Nagib and I took our tea into the living room and, at last, settled down to talk about what had just happened to both of us. The plastic Christmas tree lights were glowing, and the sweet smell of fresh baked cookies and Polish babka, baked that morning, hung in the air. The night was finally quiet, accented only by the carols playing softly on the stereo. Tired as we were, we weren't ready to end this holy night.

Christmas Eve was just turning to Christmas morning when the doorbell rang. I opened the door and, for the second time that memorable night, I let in Santa Claus. This time, it was the Santa I recognized. It was John, the new food and beverage manager who, with his wife Lorraine, had visited me after Nick's birth. He had recently arrived for work from Kuwait, but his family hadn't yet received their visas and were Christmasing in England. John was dressed as Santa for the party at Milad's, and since he had to walk by our house to get there, he stopped and rang our doorbell.

But Paul didn't know all of that. He woke up when the doorbell rang and peeked out from his bedroom doorway. From his vantage point at the end of the hall, he had a perfect view of Santa's back as he chatted with his father. I saw Paul and hurried to put the wide-eyed boy back to bed, but years later, as an adult, I overheard him tell his little cousins about the time he *really* saw Santa Claus. Even though he knows in his head who it was, the child in his heart still leaps when he thinks of that magical night.

We had a party at our house on New Year's Eve. Our house was small, but it only made the ambiance that much cozier. All the executives and their wives came. We ordered prime rib and lobster as well as the Lebanese staples of hummus, kibbe balls, and tabouli. Everything, of course, was catered by the hotel. Nagib managed to obtain some scotch—Johnny Walker Red, the only non-bootleg alcohol to be found in the area. It was $200 per bottle. We wouldn't serve or drink the *sadiqi*, the homemade alcohol more easily available. Literally translated, it means "my friend," but it had an unfriendly side. We'd heard too many stories of people becoming sick. I made eggnog, using the very strong recipe in the *Joy of Cooking*. I just substituted Scotch whenever it called for any kind of alcohol. Most of our guests had never had eggnog before, and it was a huge hit.

It was a feast that we spread out for our guests, but more importantly, the mood was jubilant. Nagib made it back safely from Lebanon with hopeful news. He had met with the owners and brought back tidings of great bonuses. We were looking forward to a new era, and trusted that the group gathered on that last night in 1980 would be able to turn these businesses around. We all wanted to make enough money to realize our individual goals, dreaming of a time when we would be building our own homes in a more hospitable country.

Nagib hadn't been able to shop for Christmas presents for me as planned, but he had bought a bottle of Opium perfume and a gold necklace and bracelet on the plane. We danced closely that night, our dreams still intact. The music was French and slow. It was a special night, and if I close my eyes and think about it, I can still smell the perfume and feel the love.

CHAPTER 11

I had become used to the absence of entertainment sources in the Kingdom, at least not what Westerners were used to. Besides the coffee mornings and the occasional party, there were no plays, live concerts, or movie theaters; no clubs where you could dance or gather. Of course, drinking alcohol was against the law, but I was surprised to find out that any form of recreation that mingled males and females or "excited the senses" was taboo. Anything that gave sensual pleasure was considered sinful and therefore banned. Even the prayers from the minarets to call the faithful in this country were sung in a monotone so as not to appeal to the ear. The only legitimate pastime for couples in this country was eating. Surprisingly, there was a dearth of good restaurants in the region.

So when Nagib instituted the Thursday night barbecues, the response was overwhelming. Tables with crisp, white linens were set up around the pool. The lights shimmered off the water while tuxedoed waiters hustled about carrying trays of bottled water, soda, and Saudi champagne. Buffet lines formed on the side and featured shish kabobs, Gulf shrimp the size of lobsters, prime rib, and kibbe balls, among the many dishes offered. Spicy falafel burgers were fried as you waited and served piping hot. Hummus, tabou-li, and baba ghanoush were staples at the mezza table for those who still had room, and the dessert table overflowed with *aish el soraya*, a flat creamy cake topped with syrup and crushed pistachios. There was Black Forest cake, tarts, rice pudding, and Pierre's favorite, New Orleans–style beignets, fried fresh and covered with powdered sugar. The rich aroma of savory spices mingled with the decadence of sugar and fried dough; it was dizzying. The spicy fragrance of the frying foods, combined with the salty breeze, almost made me forget where I was.

People came to say hello and compliment both the dinner and the Carlton for a job well done. For Pierre, Su-sie, Nagib, and me, it was as if we were entertaining five hundred of our nearest and dearest friends. The barbecues had begun in early March and immediately headed for great popularity. It was just the thing to bring the commu-nity of expatriates to the Carlton, to showcase the cuisine of the revamped kitchen and display the artistry of the new chefs. The dress style of the day for women was designer jeans with high heels and silk blouses, accessorized with expensive jewelry, super-coiffed hair, and exquisite make-up. Those of us who had just recently delivered were happy to be back to our normal bodies, clad in our now-slinky clothes.

The men were comfortable in safari suits—perfect for this climate. March was one of the best times of the year in the Eastern Province. The humidity was gone, and a cool breeze blew over the diners. There were times when we took along blankets to snuggle under as we listened to soft, jazzy music. We shared our hopes for our futures and spoke of our oh-so-different pasts those nights, sure that we would be friends for many years to come. I can remember laughing until I cried with Joumana and Milad and Susie and Pierre. As we sat back in our chairs, reveling in the music from Spanish guitars, we could have been anywhere.

The food alone would have been treat enough, but Nagib had gone so far as to find amateur bands to play every week. They were made up of workers from different nationalities and different walks of life. Filipino, Lebanese, and European bands rotated in and out, entertaining us from one week to the next. The most popular of all, Abdo Mounzer, was the recreation center manager at the hotel. He went on, post-Saudi, to become one of the most famous composers in the Arab world. We counted the days from Friday until next Thursday.

The expatriates in the area had been starved for this sort of fun, and the barbecues were a huge hit every week. They became the talk of the town, and in the end, that proved our undoing.

I didn't go to the barbecue that final night. We were six weeks in, and I figured I could skip a week. Nagib was in Lebanon on business, and I just couldn't see going without him. I went to bed after I'd settled the boys for the night when the ringing of the phone surprised me out of a deep sleep. It was Hosni, Aida's husband. He kept saying, "Where's Nagib?" I told him that Nagib wasn't there; he had gone to Beirut. "Thank God," he said, relieved. I had been struggling to wake up, but with this exclamation, I sat straight up. In answer to my worried questions, he told me that the Mutawa, the religious police, had raided the barbecue that night and arrested dozens of people. He didn't have details, but I knew it wasn't good. Would Nagib be arrested at the airport on his return? What had happened to my friends? Were they arrested? Deported? Physically punished? There was no more sleep that night.

After Nagib returned safely, he spent hours sequestered with his executives. An air of apprehension hung over our community. When hot weather forced the barbecues indoors, it had caught the attention of the Mutawa. That night they had come into the lobby and asked to be let into the dinner. The hotel employees could have denied them entrance and asked them to leave. It was a costly lapse in judgment. The Mutawa proceeded to create havoc indoors, brandishing their signature wooden staffs and clubbing any man within reach. Women screamed and fled as these white-garbed, bearded fanatics rampaged.

Some of the men had their visas confiscated, and some were taken "downtown." The women were not in physical danger, but faced deportation. The formal complaint accused the hotel of allowing "lewd behavior, with bare-chested women, drinking, and carousing." The complaint was issued against Nagib, John, the food and beverage manager, and the Saudi owner. Nagib wasn't worried. He believed it would come out in court that the Mutawa had lied, and that the hotel employees were innocent. But he hadn't been in the Kingdom long enough.

The drama dragged on for several weeks while both sides postured, and Nagib and his advisors conferred at countless meetings. I realized later that he had played down the matter to me so I wouldn't panic. At the time, he was seriously concerned, but that concern was for the business he had been hired to promote. Neither he nor his lawyers were prepared for the outcome of the initial hearing.

When they went to court for the first hearing, the judge listened to the complaint made by the government, but did not allow the hotel attorneys to get through their opening statement before he cut them off. Time and again, the lawyers tried to make their case, and time and again the judge shot them down. Each side became more and more heated and loud until the judge ordered Nagib's lawyer to shut his mouth and not say another word. In essence, they were left defenseless. From there on out, it just got worse. In the end, Nagib was sentenced to two months in a Saudi jail and John to two weeks.

The court imposed heavy fines on the hotel and also ordered the restaurant to be closed for two weeks. This included painting the doors to the restaurant red and chaining them shut. A hotel without food service cannot function, and this would literally close the hotel for those two weeks. But at the time, none of us were too worried about the hotel. It would survive. It was the men we were concerned about.

Of course, this didn't evolve in a day. First was the initial hearing, then an appeal, then another and another. Abdul-Aziz was recruited to plead our case. As a Saudi citizen, he was entitled to directly appeal to the king. We were afraid it might come to that, as our pleas fell on deaf ears.

I was in the States with the boys for the summer when Nagib called to say that I'd better cut my trip short and come back. It looked like he was going to jail. My heart dropped into my stomach. I had never truly believed that the worst would happen; my faith in Nagib's ability to come out on top was complete. I had told my mom what was going on to try to prepare her; nevertheless, the shock and concern showed on her face. She was more worried than I had been. I armed myself with a two-volume Kissinger biography for Nagib to read in jail, and returned to the Kingdom.

In the end, Abdul Aziz went to petition the king in Riyadh, as was his right. He was our last hope. We held our collective breath until he called from his hotel room. The king had pardoned everyone and wiped the slate clean. We found out much later that the argument used with the king was based on intentions. Abdul Aziz had emphasized to the king that Nagib, all along, had acted with good intentions. He told the king that Nagib had kept the barbecue night a family event, giving people a pleasant place to gather. In praising Nagib's good intentions and many talents, trying to show that Nagib was an asset to the development of the Eastern Province, he threw in that Nagib had been the one to develop the dental clinic, providing much-needed services to the citizens of the Eastern Province.

That night, we celebrated with our friends and employers. It had been a close call, but in the end, it turned out ok. What a story we'd have to tell our grandchildren, we said, relieved.

Nagib and I survived that crisis, but it took its toll. An angry Mutawa continued to harass the hotel. Politics played a big part in Saudi life, and the Eastern Province was known for its discontent. Finally, Abdul Aziz and the Lebanese owners of the hotel bowed to the inevitable and accepted the original penalty of closing the restaurant for two weeks.

The other casualty of this crisis was the loss of John as the food and beverage manager. He had come too close for comfort and told Nagib no job was worth it. They packed up and left a month later. John's wife, Lorraine, was the first friend I had to say goodbye to over there—the first of many.

CHAPTER 12

Nagib threw a party to celebrate my thirty-first birthday, my second in the Kingdom. Parties continued to be most of our entertainment, and my birthday had become a big deal. Our guests could be assured of some alcohol, at least scotch. This party was lightyears from the previous year's when I was scared, pregnant, and didn't know anyone. This year, I was ready to boogie!

I had my hair highlighted for the occasion. I'd lost a lot of weight since Nick was born, and I felt good, like myself again. Everyone who came was a friend, and all had a great time.

It was hard to think that we had been here a year. So much had happened! Now we had *children*. Imagine. I will forever remember the first time I said to Nagib, "The children are asleep." Wow! Having that second child felt like another significant step toward reaching our goals. Nick underscored our happiness and determination to create the life we wanted, and Paul was ecstatic to finally have his baby brother.

Very few of the people who came to the party last year were there this year. For that matter, a great many of those who came last year weren't even in the country anymore. What a difference a year made!

George, Nagib's longtime friend and best man at our wedding, now worked for the hotel. Nagib would turn thirty a week after my birthday, and George was bound and determined to throw a surprise party for him.

I said that Nagib might not want one since we just had a big bash for me, but George insisted. He gathered the other managers, his group of co-conspirators, and went to work. The hotel owned a large house in the corner of the parking lot. It was popular with businessmen and Saudis who wanted privacy. This, they thought, would be the perfect venue for a surprise party.

Nagib had broken his foot two days before playing basketball. He broke every bone on the top of his foot and was in terrific pain. He didn't say much, but it showed on his face in the gray, putty-like pallor. He still went to work every day, but the injury made the situation with the party even more absurd.

I worried about him, and I worried about the party. I called George after the accident, thinking they'd cancel, but the executive brain trust at the hotel were determined to go through with it. I hoped they knew what they were doing. I couldn't imagine how they planned to get him there, but they assured me that everything was under control.

Rosario, the front desk manager, called our house around seven the evening of the party. We were relaxing as a family, and I answered the phone in the living room when it rang. Nagib's foot was in a cast, and it was painful for him to get around, so when I told him Rosario wanted to speak with him, he said no. Let Pierre deal with it. Guiltily, I said it was an emergency; he really would have to speak to Rosario.

Nagib hobbled to the phone, fuming. After much cursing and yelling in English and Arabic, he slammed down the receiver, saying there was an emergency at the hotel and he'd tell me about it later.

"Oh my God," I thought, "he's going to kill them!" At the very least, I was sure they'd be unemployed by morning. The car was already out front waiting for him. As soon as he was out the front door, face purple with anger, Mahinda came in the back door, ready to babysit the boys. A second car waited for me, but we weren't fast enough and I missed the surprise.

When I got there, I took Pierre aside. "What in the world did you tell him to get him over here?" I whispered.

Pierre started chuckling. "It wasn't me, Cath," he said. "I wash my hands of the whole thing!" He grinned, emphasizing his words with his hand pushed forward, palms up and facing out.

Now that it was safe, he was enjoying the escapade immensely.

"It was George's idea," he went on. "You know that this villa was rented to three Saudi men for the week?

Well, George and some of the other men had the idea to tell Nagib that those Saudi men had become drunk and rowdy and that the police somehow had become involved." He grinned from ear to ear at the look of horror on my face. Chortling, he continued. "When Rosario called your house, he told him about this 'problem.' When Nagib wouldn't cooperate, they had to tell him that the men were being arrested. They said that the Saudis had started a fight. The police wanted to know where the alcohol came from and WHAT kind of an establishment was being run here. They wanted to speak to the manager right away." I knew George had planned the party; I hadn't known about the ruse. After his experience with the Mutawa, this was guaranteed to bring Nagib to the party at a run. It was demonic, brilliant, and perfect.

Nagib's blood pressure did finally settle down. He enjoyed the party and forgave them for their trick. After all, he was a huge prankster himself. In one short year, he was already renowned for stealing women's shoes at parties. Beware if aching feet made a poor lady kick off her stylish heels. Nagib would steal just one of them as he said his goodbyes, leaving her and her hostess to search for the missing one. In the end they always called Nagib.

The villa had a large living area, and with the furniture pushed back against the wall, it made a great party room. We danced the night away while Nagib presided over us in an overstuffed armchair. With his leg elevated, he looked like Kookaburra, receiving gifts and birthday wishes. I remember that party, with all of its hilarity, every time I look at the German barometer his staff gave him as a gift.

We had been in the little house on the Al-Ghossaibi compound for over a year when Nagib told me that the penthouse had become available, and we would be moving into it. It was just on the other side of the hotel, about six blocks on, and an easy walk. The penthouse was on the top floor of a semi-high rise owned by the group. In addition to the apartments, it housed the dental facility and a travel agency, both run by the group and managed by Nagib and Pierre.

When Nagib took me to see it, I was impressed by the room size. There were three large bedrooms, each with its own bath, a large family room connecting to an immense double living area, and dining room. The living/dining area was open and bright, with windows wrapping around the outside walls. There was a huge eat-in kitchen with a laundry nook and yet another bathroom next to it.

It struck me as absurd that a family of four would have a bathroom for each family member. I had grown up in a three-bedroom row house with one full bath and a rudimentary half bath in the basement. I shared it with nine siblings and two parents. We were definitely living in the land of excess here in the Kingdom. What richness! Four bathrooms were nice, but they would also have to be cleaned. Thank God for Mahinda.

The entire apartment was carpeted with expensive wall-to-wall gray Berber, and the walls were covered with textured fabric-like wallpaper. This had been Abdul Aziz's apartment for entertaining. The doors on the ground floor locked at night, and a concierge kept watch for unwanted visitors. It had been a good place for drinking and other illegal activities. Now it would be our home.

However, we couldn't move in until the outside walls had been reinforced. Nagib had found that if you leaned on the outside wall of the dining room, the walls shook and swayed. This understandably made him nervous. Evidently, the building codes were a bit more lenient than we were accustomed to. While he was having the walls reinforced, he had the workmen put up an iron fence to top off the four-foot-high balcony wall. Nagib reasoned that with the way it was, any energetic child could easily scramble to the top.

The penthouse was nicely furnished and supplied by the company. We decided to keep what was there and supplement where needed. This time, everything was high-end Italian. Two complete sets of living room furniture were tastefully arranged in the double living area. Until now, Mahinda had worked part-time, not needing to come more often to the little house. The rest of the time, he worked in the hotel. Now, he was happy to be working in the 'big' boss's house full-time. This gave him a certain prestige with the other workers. Nagib was known to treat the men from India and Sri Lanka generously and fairly.

It was all very exciting, the idea of this plush apartment all for us. My head was swelling at the same time it was spinning. At last, I began to see myself as others did, fitting myself into my role as Madame. But in retrospect, it would have been nice to choose our own furnishings and put our own mark on a home, temporary though it was.

At the time, I didn't realize that even that short distance would remove me from the everyday intimacy of my female community of friends. They would no longer be next door or across the way. Looking back, I should have hesitated to remove myself from the close network that had been established behind the protective walls of the Al-Ghossaibi compound. But it wasn't that far, I reasoned, just a short walk.

I didn't like housework and had never been particularly good at it. With someone to clean the house, do the laundry, and iron the clothes, it was easy to become Madame. Mahinda even ironed Nagib's underwear. The king-sized sheets were sent to the hotel laundry to be washed and ironed. Our family was growing, and Nagib's position demanded a suitable abode in which to receive and entertain. At the time, it seemed like a good idea to move. I was much too easily seduced by the glamor of it all.

The change was subtle at first. But now I had to make an effort to see my companions, and Mahinda had effectively taken over the housekeeping. The days slowed considerably. From my penthouse balcony, I had a close-up of flat, empty vistas of colorless terrain, without even a blue or red bird to liven it up. It was relieved only by puffs of black smoke from the oil burn-off. From one window, I could look down on the Carlton's pool and tennis courts. Dhahran Airport was in the distance, with not much to obstruct the view. I found myself longing for a storm cloud to relieve the monotony of the constant blue sky and brilliant, relentless sun. A lot had changed since we arrived, but not the lifeless landscape.

All of this washed over me, not like an ocean wave or even the gentle lapping of a lake, but rather the soothing waters of a hot bath. Like the lobster in the lobster pot, it lulled me into a semi-stupor, anesthetizing and creating a cloud of steam around reality. Time no longer had meaning.

Life had become outside of time, and outside of reality. There was no hustle or bustle here. Everything continued at one speed: slow. *Bukra in sha'Allah.* Tomorrow, God willing. But God, too, was half asleep, lulled by the oppressive heat, fatigued by the humidity, and so... *bukra in sha'Allah.*

One Friday afternoon, the Sunday of Saudi life, we went out for a drive along the coastal highway. A large sign, prominently placed, caught my eye. *CELIBATES ONLY.* I laughed. How could they know? Later, at the much-awaited opening of the new mall in Al-Khobar, another sign proclaimed *NO DOGS OR WOMEN ALLOWED*.

Sometimes the absurdities of Saudi life, such as the signs, were funny and harmless.

However, the message that prompted these mandates was not funny and warned of a larger social issue in this patriarchal society. Women were the property of their husbands and fathers and must abide by their rules or suffer consequences, sometimes dire. Even Nagib, as a working alien, was under the protection of his company and couldn't move around without their permission.

Intellectually, I understood that I was here under the auspices of my husband, without rights. But I still felt like an American woman: a person with choices, rights, and autonomy. For me, this was temporary.

It wasn't only the Saudis who kept an iron thumb on women. The female community had been buzzing for weeks, anticipating the next International Women's Group meeting. The only damper on our excitement was that Tahseen's husband wouldn't allow her to go. We had all tried to convince Wasi to relent. So, I was surprised on a rare cold, rainy day when Tahseen came over, glowing. Her husband had agreed to allow her to join the International Women's Group. It only met once a month, and the next week it would be the talk of the compound. She said he only agreed if she would go with me. He knew, of course, that I would have reliable transportation, but he also felt comfortable with who I was. I was thrilled, and we celebrated with a cup of tea and homemade cookies.

The International Women's Group was fun. There were several hundred members, originating from almost everywhere in the world. Women went in groups to the meetings to listen to speakers, look at exhibits, eat lunch out, and take a rare respite from the doldrums of daily living. The woman who wrote *At the Drop of the Veil*, a book about an American woman who married a Saudi in the fifties, spoke at the meeting a few years before. I had read that book before I ever met Nagib.

The atmosphere in my first gathering was charged and invigorating. The meetings were held at a local hotel and focused on projects. We were all challenged to find and send in recipes from our native countries: family, traditional, fancy, or easy... all categories. There had to be committee leaders, and it was time for elections. Nominations were made, platforms shared, and our group left for a rare women's lunch out.

While we ate, we shared our thoughts on the meeting's main points, advising each other which one of our many dishes we should share with the cookbook. We also agreed on our candidate for the next month's election: Antoinette, an Australian known to some of us through bridge games. We didn't linger since children would be arriving from school, and I had promised to get Tahseen back early. But all in all, it was a highly satisfying event.

A few weeks later, I found myself called upon to mediate another situation that required a woman. When Abdul Aziz wanted to host a small dinner party for the American consul, Nagib was told to make it happen, and he arranged a gathering at the hotel restaurant. I elected not to go since I had a bad headache. Nagib supported my decision, saying I would probably be the only woman there anyway, since Marita had just delivered, and Abdul Aziz's wife didn't usually attend these types of events.

Fifteen minutes after Nagib left, he called with an urgent demand. "Come NOW!" The representative of the American consulate had brought his wife, and I was needed. I threw on clothes and was semi-ready by the time the Carlton car arrived. Mahinda, "requested" by Nagib to watch the already sleeping boys, got out, and I got in.

I'll never forget the look of utter relief on her face when she saw me walk in. It was nice to talk to someone from back home, and it turned out to be a pleasant evening. The only downside was that Abdul Aziz left before dinner. Nagib was furious! Not only was it insulting to the guests—after all, they were there by his invitation—but he'd left Nagib to smooth things over.

But even in this otherworldly adventure, we needed to attend to the regular and the mundane. All expatriates must have passports, no less Nick. The first order of business was to take proof of Nick's birth and nationality in order to obtain an American birth certificate. Rosario, horrified when he heard I hadn't yet been to the American consulate, announced that he would take me personally. It was going to be a nice morning outing to start the weekend. The skies were bright blue and the sun shone brightly as Paul, Nick, and I set out with Rosario.

The consulate was located in the Aramco compound. Aramco stands for the Arabian American Oil Company. Now called Saudi Aramco, this state-owned oil company is the largest oil corporation in the world, with the largest crude oil reserves. In 1938, after a four-year search, oil was discovered in Dammam, just north of Dhahran. The company changed its name from California Arabian Standard Oil Company to Arabian American Oil Company (Aramco). In 1948, Standard Oil of New Jersey purchased 30% of the company and Socony Vacuum purchased 10%, leaving Standard Oil of California and the Texas Oil Company with equal 30% shares.

In 1950, King Abdul-Aziz Ibn Saud threatened to nationalize the country's oil facilities, forcing Aramco to agree to share profits fifty-fifty. In 1973, the Saudi Arabian government acquired a 25% share of Aramco, increased it to 60% by 1974, and finally acquired full control of Aramco by 1980. The name was changed from Arabian American Oil Company to Saudi Arabian Oil Company (Saudi Aramco) in 1988.

The compound was a gated community—much, much larger than any of the other ones I had seen. It was more like a small city. According to Rosario, you had to know someone in order to get in. The guard at the gate would call that person to verify that you were expected and then buzz you in. Driving into the Aramco compound, I was shocked to see American suburbia-type lawns, with sprinklers going full force to keep the grass green. The neighborhoods were designed like in the States, with streets making grids and parking on the side of the road.

I saw a woman driving a car down the road. *Holy cow!* I couldn't believe my eyes. Just another block away, women in shorts were working in their gardens. Rosario laughed at my wide-eyed wonder and kindly drove me around to see the little American community. He told me that they even had a church in Aramco and if I wanted to go on Friday, he'd get the name of the person of the week who could buzz me in. The icing on the cake was when he pulled over to the side of the road and insisted that I drive. I was surprised at what a thrill it was. Maybe I'd been in Saudi longer than I thought.

Before we got inside the consulate, I was stopped by a Marine guard who thought he had discovered a threat. He ordered me to take everything out of Nick's diaper bag, where, unbeknownst to me, Paul had packed his plastic machine gun. Oops! The young Marine tried hard not to laugh and let us in.

As diverting as the trip to Aramco was, that time we were unsuccessful in getting a birth certificate for Nicky. Paperwork got in our way, and it would take several tries before we were successful.

CHAPTER 13

We were Advent people, the expatriates in this country. We were a disenfranchised community, waiting and hoping for something else, something better. None of us would put down roots here. It was a lucrative holding tank.

We fought to hold onto our faith, to not be sucked into a sea of ennui. Our circumstances sometimes presented solutions we would never have dreamed of. Through word of mouth, Marita had discovered Father Andre, the only Roman Catholic priest assigned to the Eastern Province. Father Andre was in the Kingdom on a teaching visa and worked during the week at Aramco. On the weekends, he traveled around the province, ministering to one community after another. This was highly illegal and done under the greatest secrecy. Because of this, he told us, he could only be with us once a month.

We began to meet in secret every Thursday night. Solemnly, the executives of the hotel and its sister paper company, with their wives, began to gather at our penthouse apartment once a week for a Catholic liturgy.

We gathered that first night to meet the American priest and to celebrate Mass. It was one of the most solemn and emotional liturgies I've ever had the privilege to attend. We were like the early Christians, meeting in secret in the dark of night, behind locked doors. We were breaking the law.

Babysitters had been hired, and we made sure that our boys were asleep before people arrived. If the children talked about this in school, it could mean a harsh punishment and deportation for everyone involved, particularly the priest. He could have been whipped and then imprisoned.

The women involved, if caught, risked deportation. The men risked varying degrees of corporal punishment and imprisonment, as well as heavy penalties for the companies that sponsored them. Nagib was also taking a big risk. As the CEO of the companies employing the worshipers, as well as the fact that the service was being held in our house, the consequences for him would have been severe.

After that first Mass, at Father Andre's suggestion, we held a meeting. Father Andre told us a little about himself. He was a missionary from a small town in Wisconsin assigned to our area. He explained that he could only be with us once every month, since he was on his own, and the territory he was responsible for took him miles away every week. At first, we were disappointed, but he soon made us understand that we could still meet and worship every week without him.

He advised us to hold a weekly Communion service. He would consecrate enough hosts to last for the three weeks of his absence, and then return to say Mass the fourth Monday of every month. I was in the kitchen making Turkish and American coffee for the group. Mahinda could not be there for this secret service, even though I trusted him completely. In my absence, the group voted that I should be the one to keep the Eucharist in my house, and to distribute the Communion at our service every week.

It made sense on many levels that I should be the Eucharistic minister. Since the services would be held in our home, nothing would be transported back and forth every week. Also, I was the boss's wife. I was proud and honored to be chosen, for whatever reason.

Father Andre gave us a copy of the liturgy to Xerox and use at the services. They were in English, but the few women who didn't speak English said they didn't mind. They knew the prayers by heart in Arabic or French.

Monday nights became sacred to us all. We kept the Communion services short and prayerful, everyone going home directly after. But once a month, when Father Andre came, it was special. Every household would come carrying a covered dish for a potluck dinner after the Mass. Nagib insisted on playing cards afterward. I lost that argument. I always felt that it was slightly disrespectful, and Father Andre never stayed long after he ate. I felt that conversation would have been more appropriate, but I was outnumbered, and cards it was.

We had been meeting this way for a few months when Father Andre brought the Pope's representative with him to one service. We were forewarned and ready to receive him. He was also American, on his way to meet with Pope John Paul II about the state of affairs in this bishopric. Top on his agenda was Muslim-Christian relations.

The men in our group were not shy in their efforts to make him understand that Lebanese Christians were an endangered species. After all, who was better equipped to speak? When was the Pope going to speak out? Why hadn't he been to Lebanon to see and support them? The emissary had come looking for a large monetary contribution. It was well known that if Saudi Arabia had nothing else, it had money. Wasn't that what this expatriate life was all about? He did get his money that night from Rabih and Marita, although probably not as much as he had hoped. But he also left with the words of the people in his ear and more information than he had had before. We could only hope that he would pass it on.

Pope John Paul II did finally visit Lebanon before he died. He made his historic visit on May 10, 1997, the first pontiff to be in Lebanon since 1964. According to Lebanese news, it was the first *official* visit since the first Pope, the apostle Peter. The excitement and awe for the papal visit cut across political and religious lines. Muslims, Shiites, Sunnis, and Christians of every denomination poured into the streets of Beirut to greet the future saint. He was met with a twenty-one-gun salute, and the air rang with hundreds of church bells at the same time, marking the momentous occasion. It united the factions in Lebanon in a way nothing else had in decades. I like to think that the seed for this visit might have been planted in our penthouse in Saudi Arabia that night.

Father Andre's visits added sense and normalcy to our routines. It was shocking when he announced that his Archbishop was moving him to Israel's West Bank. He was a quiet, simple man, and I think our group reaction gratified him, while at the same time it embarrassed him. The last Mass he celebrated with us was quiet and sad. Never a stable community, the year had seen an exodus of familiar faces and friends. We had all said too many goodbyes, and now, our priest was leaving us too.

After the Gospel reading, Father Andre talked about the light of a single candle relieving even the blackest dark. In the face of our grief, he was happy to be going into a new situation—a more dangerous one. He would miss us, but he was sure we would be all right. There were others who needed him more.

A candle in the dark—a simple, poignant image—cliché but it spoke to me in my isolation. It was one of the many gifts that I put into the pocket of memory to take out and look at again in the future. I had been brought up and educated Roman Catholic. I had a strong faith, but my relationship with God was personal, not dependent on ritual or rules. I carried it with me wherever I went, like a talisman. Sometimes it took a back seat, but other times, like now, I needed it front and center.

Still, our priest's departure felt like an abandonment. We saw Father Andre going into a dangerous situation, risking his comfort and safety for a community forgotten and discarded by the world. He had a cause, and we applauded his mission, never stopping to admit that one of the abandoned, forgotten communities was ours. Father Andre was our spiritual glue. We had been lulled by an empty environment of sameness until his arrival. When he left, we suffered a spiritual void, feeling in danger of losing our souls.

His abandonment would be the first of many. People were preparing to jump off the wagon and "get out of Dodge." The gold rush was peaking, and executives were beginning to see their bonuses and perks start to decline. The Saudi economic development plan that had recruited top performers began in the middle-to-late sixties. Working in the desert back then had been a true hardship, with many areas without electricity or phones, and it had been necessary to offer outrageous incentives to recruit the best. The plan had been in five-year increments, with the last period aiming for self-sufficiency. We were approaching the peak now, and many who had made their careers in the desert were looking toward the future.

Our only purpose, it seemed, was to endure for a while in order to accumulate wealth. We were all here to worship the Golden Calf, but at what cost? Were we hypnotized? Brainwashed? Terminally stupid?

One by one, I saw my friends leave, never to see them again, leaving an unfillable void where their companionship had been. In our make-believe lives, Andre had been real.

And so Andre left, and with him, it seemed, went God. We made a feeble attempt to continue the prayer service after he left, but something always got in the way. But it went deeper than that. Maybe the commitment to prayer once a week had helped keep our humanity in perspective. Now that commitment was gone, once again leaving a void soon to be filled with anxiety and depression.

CHAPTER 14

After Father Andre left, I tried to keep my internal candle lit, not just for myself, but for Nagib and the boys. I tried to find pleasure in small things as I watched life come and go from my kitchen window. Not much life, of course: this was the desert, but I saw the comings and goings of the hotel staff, tennis players on the courts right below me, and an occasional car passing by.

Sometimes I was rewarded with something worth watching, like the rare and powerful thunderstorm rushing towards us. One rainstorm actually closed the schools and made a huge mess. The drainage and sewer systems weren't set up for a sudden, large volume of water, not to mention the unusual hail and flooded streets. The hotel staff set out planks from our building's front steps to the street, making a bridge over the highest water so Paul could get to the car.

Once, we watched as several villas in the compound below us burned to the ground before the rarely utilized, inexperienced Saudi fire department arrived. Once they did arrive, it took quite a while before they figured out how to hook up their hoses. Some of the Lebanese hotel staff had gone to lend a hand, later reporting that the firefighters were so inexperienced, they declined any help when the hoses were finally turned on. One employee just shrugged and waited, watching, while the initial power surge of the water rushing through the hose knocked the fireman backward off the wall he'd been standing on.

I watched spectacular sunsets over the desert daily. It was a sight worthy of awe and almost made the slow days and weeks bearable. Almost. At least they heralded the end of another tedious day, their beauty giving hope for tomorrow.

But mostly, I watched for Nagib as he made his way home for the afternoon meal or at the end of the day. My connection with the compound friends had ebbed, through distance and my own growing alienation. Our penthouse move had put us in proximity of the company employees and their wives. Their conversation tended to be more political and business-oriented, and of course, conducted mostly in Arabic. I was slowly being nudged to the outside, and a seed of self-doubt and insecurity began to grow.

I was more dependent than ever on Nagib as my conduit to life outside the apartment, outside Dammam and outside the Kingdom. The real world. I looked forward to his stories, anecdotes, and confidences. This wasn't new for us. He had begun when we were first married by looking for and clipping strange or funny blurbs from the Washington newspapers when he worked for the World Bank. Most memorable was the tiny article about a severely constipated elephant at the zoo. When a case of laxatives didn't work, a firehose was brought in to administer an enema. Ouch!

On this day in 1981, I was rewarded. Nagib came home from work looking like the cat that had swallowed the proverbial mouse. He told me he had news, but, teasing, made me wait until we sat down to eat. He told me that a Saudi man had come into the hotel that morning at ten a.m., asking for the general manager. The man was tall, slim, and comported himself well. When ushered into Nagib's office, he introduced himself as a government agent, a general.

"What I'm about to tell you must be treated with the utmost secrecy," he told me seriously.

I mentally rolled my eyes high up into my head in anticipation of having to pull this story out of him piece by piece. He was nothing if not dramatic, the quintessential storyteller. But this time, I found out he was on the up-and-up.

"It seems," he began, "that the queen mother of Saudi Arabia, the king's mother, is coming to the Eastern Province. She wants to stay at the Carlton with her *ENTIRE* entourage." He rolled his *R*s, adding dramatic emphasis.

It didn't take a genius to jump to the conclusion that this would be awesome for business. I had been here long enough to know that someone of the queen's stature would be traveling with a boatload of people: servants, bodyguards, friends, and family.

They were coming in four days, and the government agent requested that Nagib move all of his current guests into other area hotels. Security was a sensitive issue. The royal family and members of the Saudi government were Sunni Muslims, the majority in Saudi Arabia. The minority Shiites were found predominantly in the Eastern Province.

The history of the Shiites there wasn't a happy one. A recent protest had resulted in a bloody street massacre in the Hassa area. What better way to retaliate than against the king's own mother? It was imperative to protect her and discretion was part of that.

The requirements of the advance security team were a logistical nightmare for Nagib and his staff. They managed to move their guests and cancel the next week's reservations as well. They told the guests that the water system was being revamped and there would be no water for a period of time. It was necessary to invent a lie, since the truth was closely guarded.

Despite manic preparations, the owners and managers of the hotel were honored to be chosen by the queen. Evidently, the Carlton was known throughout the Kingdom for its Lebanese cuisine. This, we were told, was the reason she had chosen us. The chef was proud and vowed to outdo himself. Abdul Aziz was beside himself with joy and excitement at the honor.

The day after the announcement, the government advance team arrived to coordinate the event. They went over the hotel, evaluating the accommodations, and then assigning the rooms. They worked from a list, starting with the queen mother and her daughters and worked down to the servants who would be attending to her. Everyone needed his or her own place, and everything had to go smoothly.

The man in charge sat across from Nagib's desk, sipping tea as he chatted affably.

"If you need anything," he told Nagib, "just call me. I have the list."

He never mentioned money, but it was understood between the two men that money was not a problem. Nagib knew that the hotel would probably do better if there was no negotiated price.

The day the queen arrived, Paul, Nick, Mahinda, and I were glued to the dining room windows. A long procession of expensive cars—Cadillacs and limousines—lined the road in front of the Carlton. They waited, flags flying, for their turn to disembark in the front turn-around. It was the most exciting thing that had happened here, but despite our bird's-eye view, we were unable to see anything but black-swathed figures in the procession.

Back at the hotel, everything was chaotic. Only Nagib, in his status as manager, was allowed to greet the queen mother, and that from a distance. As people started to disappear into the elevators, two armed guards took up their stations on either side of them, and two in front of the stairs. Snipers were posted on the roof of the hotel, and guards stood at every entrance.

The executive staff had known for the prior two days what to expect and had each briefed the people under them that morning. The chefs had been baking and cooking for hours, anticipating the needs of the distinguished guests and their army of attendants. Everything humanly possible was done to ensure the comfort and privacy of this particular guest. The special gold-plated flatware and Spode china with the Saudi national emblem engraved in gold were taken out of storage, along with the sterling silver salt and pepper shakers and Baccarat stemware.

During the queen's visit, the wives and children of the executive staff were asked to stay away from their usual haunts at the pool and bowling alley. We had no interaction with the guests and could only watch as the servants went in and out of the hotel.

My family, however, did have a chance to contribute toward the success of the Queen's visit. In the 1980s, in Saudi Arabia, videotapes were rare and mostly frowned upon. Most of the tapes in circulation were pornography. So, when the general came to Nagib's office on the second day, it was with a strange request.

The queen mother, he told Nagib, always traveled with several of her favorite video tapes. She therefore required a VCR and wanted a TV with a much larger screen than the one in her suite.

The staff searched high and low for acceptable machinery. None were available in the storerooms or on the premises of the hotel or its sister companies. Finally, Nagib came to our house with two hotel workmen. We *did* have the larger TV and VCR. They exchanged ours for a smaller one from the hotel, and after asking Paul and Nick if they minded lending their VCR to the queen for a couple days, they left with the much sought-after equipment, and peace reigned in the hotel.

Since it was taboo for any male to see the uncovered face of an unrelated female, there was a lot of necessary scrambling for that week. Whenever the queen mother wanted to move around the hotel, one of her servants would give advance notice. Anyone along her planned path was required to duck into an office and close the door until after the all-clear sign was given. The same was done on her return.

On the fifth day of the queen's stay, our phone rang at two in the morning. At that hour, it could only mean a problem, so Nagib quickly answered the bedside phone with much trepidation. He held his breath as the number of things that could have gone disastrously wrong raced through his mind.

The night desk manager was on the other end. He apologized for the disturbance and assured Nagib that everything was all right, but told him that the princess, the queen's granddaughter, wanted to speak with him personally.

I didn't realize that I'd also been holding my breath through the conversation. I had reason not to trust the system here, and I knew that our welcome could sour at any minute. I also understood enough Arabic to know that this time, at least, the world wasn't coming to an end. Nagib ended the conversation, replacing the receiver with a bang. He sighed as he threw back the covers, reassuring me that everything was all right. He dressed quickly, explaining that our guests needed him, but he didn't know what for, and he recommended that I try to go back to sleep. Fat chance!

Nagib was dressed and downstairs in less than five minutes, but even so, a hotel car was waiting on the street to drive him the short distance. When he arrived at the hotel lobby, several young women were waiting. They were all draped in black from their heads to their feet, so as not to pose a threat either to themselves or to Nagib at such a late hour. Their spokesperson explained that they were waiting for someone, and even as she spoke, a limousine pulled up to the curb in front of the main lobby. Another black-draped female emerged, and, after a great deal of teenage squealing and hugging, it was clear that this was another princess.

Nagib had been asked to open the recreation area so that these sleepless teenagers could bowl or play billiards, or just sit and gossip. He and the general accompanied the girls. Nagib thanked his lucky stars that he knew where all the light switches were, and that the bowling alley was fully automated.

As soon as the lights went on, the girls asked for the ladies' room and went off in a giggling mass of flapping black. When they emerged, there was no resemblance to what had gone in. They had each changed into cut-offs and t-shirts. They were also braless. They had emerged freed from some kind of bondage, running around and screaming in youthful exuberance.

One of the princesses, the one who came late in the limousine, started flirting with both the general and Nagib, speaking fluent English. She was the daughter of the prince of the region, the head of the Eastern Province and the cousin of the king. Nagib was in a dangerous position. Even he didn't know what would happen if he were found out, and he prayed that he and the general would make it through the night without any mishaps.

The girls remained in the recreation center until 5:30 in the morning. They then changed clothes, donning their black coverings again, and headed up to their rooms to sleep. Nagib was not as lucky as they. His adrenalin was still pumping from the danger he'd been in and could still be in. Seeing the faces of the princesses was bad enough, but being alone with them at night . . . It was better not to dwell on the possible consequences. He went to his office to begin his day's work, fervently hoping no one had seen them. The princesses had asked him to keep their secret, and he did.

On the final day of the royal visit, the hotel was again abuzz with the bustle of packing and moving many people. Suitcases, crates, dress racks, and people filled the lobby and lined the halls, waiting to be loaded and transported. Men shouted orders as cars pulled up to receive their cargo and passengers in front of the hotel. Standing at the entrance supervising, Nagib hoped that his TV hadn't been inadvertently packed. He would be in trouble with Paul and Nick if it had.

At one o'clock in the afternoon, the queen mother decided it was time to go. Her bodyguards led her to the front entrance and then lined the path to her limousine. Her majesty stepped out of the elevator and headed toward the main door. Nagib was standing between the door and her limousine, waiting to bid her goodbye and wish her a safe trip.

She walked up to him and, stopping suddenly, lifted her veil and looked at him with a beautiful smile. She stepped toward her main bodyguard, the general, and reached out toward his sword. She took him by surprise, and before he could react, she unsheathed his curved scimitar and handed it to Nagib, thanking him for his care and hospitality. The general was not pleased, but Nagib treasures this memento to this day. I always thought that she knew what the girls had done, and this was her way of thanking Nagib for keeping them safe.

Three days after their departure, the hotel received a generous check to cover expenses incurred during that week. Added to that amount was a tip of 82% of the total bill, to be distributed by Nagib to his staff for their care of the queen mother and the princesses during their stay in the Eastern Province.

CHAPTER 15

W hen new hires arrived at Aramco, they were issued the materials and instructions to build and use a still. Rumor had it that some of the Americans over there produced some right good liquor, even something fancy like peach brandy.

Nagib and I really weren't drinkers, but it would have been nice to have a glass of wine now and then, so we asked around and found out what we needed. We put jugs of fermenting liquid in our laundry room and let it do its thing.

The hotel management had brought in a consultant, specializing in hotel décor, to advise on how to enhance the appearance of the rooms and lobby without spending a fortune. He was German, but based in Cairo. He was away from his American wife and children and appreciated being invited to our home.

But more than anything, he appreciated our "green wine." *Green* because it hadn't yet matured and had a rough, strong taste. He said it was his favorite. Of course, hospitable beings that we were, that wine never did mature.

While Werner was with us, we had occasion to entertain several other Germans who worked for the airlines. One man told me, politely enough, that Americans didn't have a cuisine. Well! It just happened to be the second week in November, and I invited him for Thanksgiving dinner on the spot. Nothing like a challenge.

I had come to the Kingdom well-armed. I had a collection of cookbooks—some bought at second-hand stores, some from my bookstore, and still others were basic books that had been gifts at my wedding showers.

I wasn't a novice at cooking Thanksgiving dinner, but the norm had always been to enjoy it at my mother's house. This time, I was cooking for twenty. Undaunted and energized as I always am by the holidays, I began searching the cookbooks for menu ideas. Of course, turkey with my mother's bread stuffing would be the main event. My guest of honor was German, so sauerkraut was a must. Hadn't corn been a major player in the first Thanksgiving? Corn pudding and cornbread, then. How American can you get?

After consulting with Nagib, I put oyster stew at the head of the menu. He assured me that oysters would be available. The dessert was the easy part. Pecan, apple, and pumpkin pies would round out the banquet, but I still needed greens. I stuck in Brussels sprouts and a broccoli casserole for good measure. They would have cranberry sauce at the local Safeway, I hoped.

I wasn't worried about cooking for a large number of people. I cooked for twelve when I was a teenager on a regular basis. I also didn't have to worry about preparing the house. Mahinda would do that, and Nagib would send over some young men with tables, chairs, and table linens. They would even set the table and add decorative touches. Sometimes I really enjoyed being the boss's wife!

We set up the tables outside on our humongous balcony. It was November and the temperature was a clement seventy degrees. It would go down in the evening, and the ladies would want wraps, but the timing was perfect for an outdoor event.

Nagib told me that the chefs and hotel staff were at my disposal, but I really wanted to do the cooking myself. In the end, I had to concede that my oven was too small to cook everything and have it ready and hot when we wanted to eat. So I had the chef roast the turkey.

Since it was a Thursday and the beginning of the weekend, the men would arrive home at around noon. I invited my guests for two. A hodgepodge of nationalities was expected; Tahseen and Wasi from Pakistan, the German men, Franco, who was Lebanese/Italian and his wife Cristae from Australia, Wendy and Peter, who were British, a Canadian couple, and several of the Lebanese from our group, as well as David and Lynn, a British dentist and his wife.

We gathered for drinks and appetizers in the living room while waiting for latecomers. In the meantime, Mahinda and the tuxedoed waiters kept the food warm. The turkeys had arrived, golden brown and perfect. The chef had carefully pulled back the skin and expertly carved the birds. He then replaced the skin so you couldn't even tell it had been disturbed. I was very impressed. I had never heard of such a thing, much less seen it.

While we waited, I noticed that the usually bubbly and vivacious Lynn was not in a good mood. It was apparent that something had upset her. She was my friend, so I sidled up to her and asked if anything was wrong.

"Well," she began with a pout, "how can you ask me that when you've asked us here to celebrate defeating us?"

It took me a minute before what she had said could sink in, but when it did, I threw back my head and laughed. She was confusing Thanksgiving Day with Independence Day, I explained. I set her straight and her smile returned after that. We had a good laugh over it, and the incident gave me a perfect segue to explain the origin of the tradition of the holiday. Lynn wasn't the only one in the group of guests who was confused.

The sun was low in the sky when we served dinner, and we were rewarded for our patience with a brilliant sunset. We laughed and talked our way through the different foods, eating too much, as is required on Thanksgiving Day. The Germans thanked me and conceded most graciously that the Americans did indeed have a cuisine. I in turn thanked them for helping me celebrate the holiday so far away from home.

Werner came back to town in December. We laughed at his disappointment that we didn't have any more wine and told him that it was his fault since he drank all the green wine the month before. His American wife accompanied him this time. I couldn't imagine how he had gotten a visa for her, but I was delighted to have her company. She had smuggled in two pounds of bacon and some pork chops as a gift for us. I almost cried, I was so excited. I decided to save the bacon for Christmas breakfast as a treat.

Werner's wife Peggy was just as excited to find a Safeway supermarket that sold all the American foods her kids missed. She was especially happy to find the makings for tacos.

Over a cup of coffee, Peggy described everyday sights in Cairo. She told me that she drove in Cairo, but it was hardly worth it. The streets were so packed with people that it was extremely difficult and slow.

Beggars were a common sighting, she said. The eyes of the infants they held were covered with flies. Infection was rampant and blindness often the direct result. Even though the villas in Cairo were nice and comfortable, it was not uncommon to see someone squatting to defecate right outside the house. She was impressed with how clean and organized it was here.

Later that month we were surprised by a visit from Nagib's friend Phillipe. People didn't just drop in on you in Saudi Arabia; it was not a destination country. But he was on a mission from the World Bank to Lesotho in Africa and had been commissioned to try to talk Nagib into coming back to the World Bank. He told us that Lars, Nagib's former boss there, had asked him to. And so, he stopped here on his way. In his easy style, he told us that he had tried to place a call to Lesotho, using the long-distance operator. The Saudi operator told him there was no such place! He finally got through by placing a call to the London operator, who in turn placed the call to Lesotho. Evidently there *is* such a place!

Another World Banker stopped by on his way home from a mission to Yemen. This man could also drop in almost anywhere in the world, because he carried the United Nations passport of the World Bank. He gave us a bag of green coffee beans. He said the ambassador always gave him coffee beans, and in the past, he gave it to his mother in Lebanon. But his mother finally told him that she didn't want them because they were too much trouble to roast. She'd just as soon buy her coffee pre-roasted.

It took years before I realized how naïve I had been. *Stopped by* the Kingdom of Saudi Arabia? It was on the way? Really. No, this man had another mission as well. The business that had been started in D.C. with the development of the American Lebanese League was going as planned. I just didn't know the plan.

Nagib's current boss, George Frem, yearned for political involvement. He had handpicked Nagib in order to get close to Bashir Gemayel, the rising star of the Christian

Front. Thus, Nagib's job in Saudi. This visit was to shore up the plans.

The decision had been made with another World Banker to include George Frem in Bashir's cabinet once he was elected.

After the assassination of Bashir Gemayel, George Frem had no choice but to call on Nagib. Nagib was one of the trio recommended by the State Department to keep Bashir's plan in effect with Bashir's brother, Amin, now being sworn in as president.

Bashir's death had left my husband heartbroken and numb. The young soldier had been their hope, their leader. Nagib had personally worked with Bashir and hosted him a few years back in the States. He had been a friend, full of youth and vigor. Now he was gone, like so many others in this war. Their dreams once again shattered, they had to somehow muscle on without him. My husband hid his grief as he bravely resolved to keep Bashir's vision for Lebanon alive. But at what personal cost?

CHAPTER 16

Our family routine had become established. Paul left for school in the morning. By the time Mahinda arrived at nine, I had Nick fed and bathed. Mahinda would bring me my coffee in the living room and watch Nick while I drank it.

Sometimes there would be a coffee morning or a bridge game. Often Susie or Elonca, my Dutch friend, would come over, or I would go to them so Nick could play with Sami or Tatiana. I knew I was lucky to have regular access to a car and driver. We had found out through word of mouth that there was a Lebanese woman here who had worked as an archeologist. She was giving classes on the history and archeology of the area. This was an unprecedented opportunity; there was nothing here for women to stimulate learning. My friends and I were quick to sign up before the teacher's quota had been met. It seemed to us to be extremely relevant, an opportunity to stretch our rusting minds a little bit.

The class was held only once a week for about an hour, but it quickly became very important to me. The four or five ladies in the compound who were attending with me depended on me for a ride, and every week the Carlton station wagon would faithfully make its rounds.

We were about four weeks into the course when the car just didn't show up. I called Nagib every fifteen minutes, and every time he told me that he'd send the car as soon as it came back from the morning marketing. It was the first time that this had happened, and I was shattered out of proportion to the situation. I can remember standing at the dining room window, waiting, watching, and crying. I knew I was being ridiculous, but the overwhelming sense of dependency, combined with intense cabin fever and boredom, flooded over me, leaving me totally despondent.

Just a few days later I found out I was pregnant again. The baby would be due in January, and I had a feeling that this one, too, would be a boy. That was okay with me. I loved little boys, and we were certainly set up for them. Still, a little girl would be nice. Nagib really wanted a girl.

We had moved Paul from the French school to the American school, the Dhahran Academy. It was a bit of a longer ride for him than the French school, but we thought he would be happier there studying in English. The previous year at the French school had been very difficult for him.

A driver from the hotel took Paul to school in the morning and then picked him up at two. He was the only child from our group of companies going to the Dhahran Academy, so this was a special trip for the chauffeur. Paul was usually home by 2:30 to have his meal and see his father before Nagib went back to work.

So, of course, when there was no Paul or driver by three, we were nervous. We called the school and were told that Paul had been picked up on time. We called his friends and were told by their parents that they hadn't seen any accidents on the road.

After pacing for another twenty minutes, Nagib called for a car to go looking for them. His face was black with tension and worry. When I demanded to go along, he was emphatic that I wait at home. I teared up, but he made it clear that if I cried, he would completely fall apart. "Stay calm for Nicky and the one you're carrying," he ordered.

I pulled myself together and watched from the window as Nagib's car screeched at breakneck speed around the corner and onto the highway. Now I had to worry about him, too.

I paced and prayed, waiting for some news. Forty-five minutes later, Nagib called me from the police station to say he had Paul, everyone was all right, and I wouldn't believe his story, because he hardly believed it himself. He would be home within the hour and would give me the full update then.

I hung up the phone, only then allowing myself to cry.

After a tearful reunion with Paul, who was tired, hungry, and cranky from his escapade, Nagib told me what had happened.

There had been a car accident the day before, involving a hotel vehicle. It was minor, but the car was incapacitated. Nagib saw it on the road as he retraced the driver's route, and rightly guessed that the two things were connected.

It turned out that there was some paperwork in the car that the hotel needed. Since it was on the way, the driver was asked to stop and pick it up on his way back from getting Paul. He had done just that, but as he got back into the front seat, a policeman pulled up behind him. The policeman arrested the driver, accusing him of breaking into an abandoned car. The driver showed his hotel ID and tried to explain his mission, but the Yemeni policeman wouldn't hear any of it. At least, the driver begged, let me take this little boy home. No such luck.

And so began the great adventure that Paul always referred to as "the time I got arrested." The policeman took his time at the scene of the former accident, and then took the two "prisoners" twenty minutes north to Dammam to the scene of another accident, before he took them thirty minutes south to the police station in Al-Khobar.

By the time Nagib found Paul safe and sound, he was beside himself. The police chief was known to Nagib and was able to calm him down, but not before the distraught father raged on the policeman who had caused us so much worry. He lifted the man by the front of his uniform shirt and pushed him against the wall a foot off the ground, all the while lashing him with expert Zahlawee verbiage. Anywhere else in the world, Nagib would have been arrested. However, the police chief merely intervened, saying matter-of-factly that they gave their policemen radios just for such circumstances, but they refused to use them.

"Now you see," he told Nagib, "why we don't issue them bullets."

Nagib was right. The story was unbelievable, and neither of us could picture it being played out in either of our native countries.

Not to be outdone by his son, Nagib came home for lunch one day and made a shattering announcement, once again changing the direction of our lives. We were moving to Beirut. George Frem had been appointed to a ministerial post in the new government and he needed Nagib. We would only have two weeks to pack and get ready. That meant I was on my own as far as packing and closing the house was concerned. Nagib would be crazy busy in his office. He had to finalize everything at the hotel and have all in order and ready for Pierre to take over, for the time being at least. I would have Mahinda and anyone I wanted from the hotel staff, but the brunt of the work was still on me. He wouldn't be leaving his job here. He would go back and forth between Saudi and Lebanon, working both jobs. That meant I would be alone with the children while he traveled.

I was relieved when Mahinda agreed to come with us. I would need him when the new baby came. I was stunned, and not a little scared. I talked to Susie, reassured when she told me that throughout the troubles in Lebanon, there had never been any fighting in Jounieh, where we'd be living. Two positives—it would be nice to be with family again, and I would be able to drive.

The suddenness of this change took all of us by surprise and set the business, temporarily, on its ear. Firming up contracts and briefing Pierre, packing his office and trying to get a handle on what would be expected of him in Beirut had Nagib's head spinning. He knew I could handle it from my end. I'd done it before.

By now I was in my seventh month of pregnancy, and there was some trepidation on our part as to whether I'd be allowed to fly. But it was a relatively short flight.

In the end, it all happened so fast I didn't even have a chance to say goodbye.

CHAPTER 17

BEIRUT, LEBANON 1982

As the plane banked left and made its final approach, I looked down on the once-grand city with trepidation. The presence of armed soldiers throughout the airport made me anxious. Once again, we gathered our bags and our sons, greater in number this time around, soon to be greater still. We were here now to start a new life . . . again. We had discussed our future at great length many times. Nagib wanted to be part of his country's renaissance, always hopeful for the end to hostilities. It was exciting to be in a country that housed not only family, but some liberties that I had been denied in Saudi. I planned to work once our children were older, maybe as a teacher. We wanted to settle here.

Nagib pushed the baggage cart forward with one hand while he held onto Nick's leg with the other. It was Nick's turn to be enthroned on his father's shoulders, the place of honor that had been Paul's alone for so long. Paul didn't seem to mind. He took a proprietary protective interest in his brother's every move. Now he walked next to me, holding my hand with one of his, his knapsack in the other. I knew better now than to look right or left, but stared straight ahead, ignoring the outstretched hands of the inevitable beggars. I had become a seasoned traveler.

The trip from the airport was short but tense. This was an area filled with displaced refugees, plagued by poverty. South Beirut could be volatile and dangerous. This time we were traveling to Jounieh in East Beirut. It was overcast and drizzling that bleak November day—not an auspicious welcome home for us, but after countless days of relentless sunshine, welcome nonetheless.

The car did not climb this time, but we could see the mountain as it loomed before us, powerful and imposing under the weeping gray sky. In other times it had inspired poets and dreamers to write of lofty things. It had made men and women look upward and think of God, as I now did. It had given them hope. It now gave me, heavy with child, the courage to plan another life.

But with awe came a sneaking dread. Despair was in that mountain. Bashir Gemayel had been assassinated within the past few months, his killers slithering back to hide in the shadows. They left behind a flood of tears from the bereft, and we counted ourselves among them now. It was worse still for those who had no tears, whose days and nights were haunted by dreams of unspeakable violence. Hate and longing for vengeance lived there as well, pushing out compassion and tolerance. It did its best to quench hope; eating at the soul of the nation like a cancer, paralyzing and wearing it down.

I feared that we, too, could become another casualty of this civil war.

I shivered, shaking myself out of my morbid reverie. Surely there was strength here as well. These people loved their country and families with fierce loyalty. Theirs was a strength born of hard, unremitting work—not expecting wealth, only to celebrate now and then. In spite of the blight that had come, these were the heirs of a long, proud history, and an inspiring one. They might flee the mountain, but they would not forget. Many would spend the rest of their lives remembering and fighting to come back.

We had returned to Beirut, this time to live. In November 1982, people were hopeful for peaceful change. Nagib had been offered a post within the new government, while still keeping tabs on his Saudi job. I was eight months pregnant and apprehensive about the political situation. Everyone assured me that there had never been any problem in "our" part of Lebanon; Jounieh had been pretty much untouched.

After a half hour drive, Eli helped Nagib carry the bags up the stairs to the third floor apartment that would be home. Though the building had an elevator, the electricity was off when we arrived. This was something we would have to become accustomed to. Paul bounded up the stairs, following his dad with energy. I brought up the rear more slowly, holding Nicky's hand. This was not amusing.

The apartment the company provided was in a building overlooking the autostrada, the main coastal thoroughfare. The building was on a hill, elevating the condo and affording us a good view of the Mediterranean. It was convenient to the main part of town, and shopping was within walking distance. If we had been situated in Paris or London, or almost any other capital city in Europe, we would have been living in an enviable location. However, in war-torn Lebanon, this was not the case. We had been assured that a very suitable house would be made available to us by the company. The apartment was to be furnished comfortably with everything we needed. One of the owner's sisters had lived there, so we were unconcerned, sure that it would be more than acceptable.

But when we finally arrived, there was no way around it; our new housing was a disappointment. The place was just plain shabby. The floors were everyday marble, faded and worn; the plaster walls were dingy and needed paint badly. The ceilings were quite high, and the smallish front room had French doors leading out onto a small balcony. But the paint on the doors was chipped and peeling and I knew, with my sons, that the balcony would soon become an issue of concern. At least the lock worked. Inside, a narrow hallway led to three medium-sized bedrooms, furnished with large armoires. At the end of the hall was the only full bathroom. The half bath was located in the hall just outside the kitchen.

I was tired, apprehensive, and very pregnant, but I didn't cry until I saw the kitchen. Something about the oven not having a temperature setting was one thing too many for me. I couldn't help it. Tears began to stream down my cheeks, unbidden. The pent-up emotions of the past few weeks could not be stopped. Nagib couldn't have been nicer. He stifled his own dismay, seeing the writing on the wall. Gathering me up in his arms and kissing the top of my head, he said, with all seriousness, "It's all right, baby. Do you want me to bring your mother?"

"My mother!" I wailed. "*My* mother? No way!" I sobbed. "My mother wouldn't know what to do either! Bring *your* mother!" And so he did.

Im Gaby came a week later, dispelling the mystery of the oven, but not before an apple pie destined for Thanksgiving dinner burned to a charred, unrecognizable glob. She showed me how to control the temperature by turning the knob on the gas can, connected to the oven by a short hose, to give more or less gas. This still left me with a lot of guesswork, but at least we could function.

I was determined to keep life as normal as possible and make yet another new place a home for my husband and our boys. I was reminded of the Little House books. Throughout the series, Ma Ingalls carried a china figurine from log cabin to sod house, from the wilds of Wisconsin to the plains of the Dakota Territory. Laura Ingalls wrote in her books that this figurine came to represent home to the children. With Ma as my example, I placed our familiar knickknacks around the apartment, making a home.

Thanksgiving was around the corner, and the American holiday seemed a good time to begin my normalcy campaign. Frozen turkey could be had. Some items had to be done without, but we were able to find sauerkraut, a Baltimore must. Mashed potatoes would be no problem, and vegetables were abundant in Lebanon. All I needed were the ingredients to make my mother's traditional bread stuffing. It was a simple recipe, calling for few ingredients, all of which were to be found on a daily basis in any American kitchen. I was able to purchase the spices I needed, and bread and onions were to be had, but the celery eluded me.

The stuffing was somehow important to me. It felt like the cornerstone of what I remembered as our family feast. It was out of proportion to all reason. But then, who cared about reason? I had the right to be unreasonable.

After much searching, I finally found a sorry bunch of celery in another town. I paid the equivalent of $30 for it, but at the time, it seemed worth the investment. One of the American women I later met in Beirut advised me to grow it from seed on my balcony, as she did. As always, the most important ingredient of a happy Thanksgiving was the gathering of family and friends to eat and celebrate.

Nagib's brothers and their families were appreciative of the feast.

Meanwhile, we made plans. I joined the American Women's Group of Beirut and bought a car. I was able to see the friends from Saudi Arabia who had moved back to Lebanon and became engrossed in plans to build a house on land that we bought in the mountains just above East Beirut, since Nagib would be working in the area. After the forced dependency in Saudi, I felt free.

I wasn't worried about having to depend on anyone in this foreign country. I had made great strides in learning Arabic, and could communicate well with Im Gaby and the Arabic-speaking ladies in Saudi. My French, on the other hand, was rather poor. I had never had to use it and hadn't studied for years. Funnily enough, whenever I spoke Arabic with shopkeepers in East Beirut, they answered me in French. I went so far as to ask one young lady if she didn't speak Arabic. She huffily answered that *of course* she spoke it, she was Lebanese! After that, the transaction went forward in Arabic.

The Lebanese of East Beirut were known to be French educated. Indeed, I was amazed to find how dependent they were on the French language. Shortly after we arrived, Nagib's cousins came to visit. They were younger than he, the youngest still teenagers. Once, Im Gaby asked the girls what time it was. They answered her in French, she didn't understand, and they were unable to tell her in Arabic.

Ironically, it was I, the *ajnabeia* (foreigner), who was able to translate.

West Beirut, on the other hand, is the home to the American University of Beirut. English is the foreign language most frequently spoken there. Unfortunately, as the war progressed, we had fewer and fewer reasons to go into West Beirut, and many reasons not to.

As we acclimated that first month, a quick and intense journey through Thanksgiving and Christmas kept me occupied. I was building a protective cocoon of bustle and purpose around the shock of yet another major life change. After that, pregnancy and delivery took over.

As difficult as the transition had been for the adults, it was hardest for Paul. Nagib used all the influence he could muster, and Paul had been accepted into the St. Joseph's School in Cornet Shahwan. It was an excellent private school, said to be the best in the area. It used a Canadian curriculum and was run by nuns. They taught equally in French, Arabic, and English, which we found very attractive. Paul was only six. He had had some French schooling, and he spoke English. However, he hadn't had any reading instruction in English, and Arabic was going to be a challenge. We quickly hired a tutor to work with him.

At this amazing school, music and literature were taught in French, math and science in English, and religion and history in Arabic. My mother, a retired reading teacher, was amazed when she saw Paul's school books.

Since Paul had gone to the French school in Saudi Arabia, his skills in reading English were nonexistent. French was still difficult for him, and he was lost in Arabic. For Paul, the days were long and hard, and when he returned home, he still had homework in three languages to deal with. His tutor, a college student, arrived on the first day bearing the gift of a toy car as a present, ensuring a quick bond. After that they were fast friends.

Paul's ordeal was complicated by the fact that the electricity went off every evening at six p.m. I once found myself on the elevator with Paul and Nick when it went off for the night. Luckily, the concierge heard us. We were about three feet above the floor, and I was able to hand the boys down to him without much trouble. I, on the other hand, was very big and clumsy. I managed, but not easily. And after that, we took the stairs.

Paul did his nightly homework by candlelight until we purchased a small camper's gas lamp. Compounding his difficulties, the school was extremely strict. Besides his tutor, his other saving grace was an American teacher who took him under her wing and tried to help him fit in. She was a young widow with two boys of her own, supporting herself by teaching. Her husband had been an airline pilot who flew for the Middle East Airlines between Beirut and Kuwait. He was killed in an automobile accident in Kuwait. She stayed for a year after that, for his parents' sake.

Nagib's brothers came down for Christmas with their families. Maroun and Suad had just had their first child, a little girl, in early December. They went back to Zahle after the holiday, but Gaby and Salwa stayed for a while with their children. Nick and Paul slept in the double bed with Nagib to give their room to their relatives. I was too huge to share a bed.

Peter was born in January of 1983 at Notre Dame Maternity Hospital. The phone in our apartment worked one day but not the next, and I had been worried that I might not be able to get in touch with Nagib at his work. I could see the hospital from our apartment, but how would I get there if I couldn't contact anyone? I wasn't anxious to walk there in labor. However, accommodating from the first, Peter arrived on a Thursday night when his dad was home.

After an easy three-hour labor, Peter was delivered and the doctor put him into his father's arms. Nagib then brought him to me, and together we marveled at the perfect little body of our third son. We hadn't yet agreed on a name. Nagib wanted Michael, but I had a nephew with that name. I wanted Joseph, but *he* had a nephew by that name. But when his father looked into his face for the first time, he declared, loudly, that *this* was Peter. Meaning "rock," it was an inspired choice. Our third son has lived up to his name. He is the rock that anchors our family, a strong and gracious man, and a blessing to all who know him.

My three sons were delivered in three different hospitals in three different countries. My delivery in Beirut was the easiest. This was a maternity hospital, and everything was done to accommodate the mother and newborn. Afterward, Paul and Nick were allowed to see their new brother. It was amazing how big they seemed.

Life settled into a new ebb and flow after Peter's birth. We got used to the daily loss of electrical power and adjusted accordingly. We had bought a car for me, a used Volvo. I had wanted a Mini, thinking it would be easier to navigate the narrow alley-like roads here. However, Nagib wisely bought the armored Volvo, knowing how people drove in this congested town. We found a fast-food restaurant, new to the area, called Winner's. It was a McDonald's-type place where hamburgers and French fries topped the menu. Its customers boasted women in mink coats, who waited patiently in line to enjoy this novelty to their region. For us, it was a little piece of home, and something Paul considered a treat.

Peter was just a few weeks old when an earthquake struck the Beirut region. I had gotten up to feed him in the middle of the night. As I dropped awkwardly back into the bed, holding him, it seemed that the headboard was hitting the bed, not the other way around. It took a couple of seconds before my sleep-deprived brain registered exactly what was happening. I lay in bed, too exhausted to get up and do anything. Anyway, what *could* I do? I tried to go back to sleep, hoping I was imagining things. I wasn't.

I called out to Nagib in a soft whisper, then louder when he didn't respond. By this time, Im Gaby joined us in our room, confirming my fear; it was an earthquake. The shaking didn't last long and, exhausted, we went back to bed. All of my childhood I had had a "bugaboo" about floods, tidal waves, and earthquakes. It seemed all my fears were being realized.

Before we slept, I jokingly told Nagib that if there was a tidal wave, that would be the last straw and I would leave. The next morning, we heard that the epicenter had been a mile or so out to sea. Had the quake been any stronger, there would indeed have been a tidal wave, killing hundreds of people who had run to the beach for safety.

Suad, in Zahle, had felt the rumbles and awakened in a panic, thinking they were under attack. When told it was "just an earthquake," she relaxed and went back to sleep.

As we settled in, seeking a rhythm of ordinary family existence, I was insulated from the woes of the outside war by my newness. I had few friends, fewer language skills, and a total absorption in my new infant and his young brothers. But, as in Saudi, the outside world soon found a way to impose itself on me.

CHAPTER 18

The man who stood on the other side of our door was small. Back bent as he spoke quickly with Im Gaby, his gravelly tones made his words unintelligible to my novice ear. His shoes were split in the front from long wear, his clothes gray and dusty, and his jacket looked several sizes too big for him. It was bought, it seemed, in a more affluent time. It was obvious from the tone of the doorway conversation that a negotiation was going on. Hand signs and language that seesawed back and forth made me wonder what this old man could have that she might want. We had never seen him before.

When she finally shut the door, she turned to me and simply said, "*Haleeb.*" Pointing to the back of the house, she made me understand that this man lived somewhere behind us. More importantly, he could bring us fresh milk. Nagib later confirmed that this was so. The milkman lived directly behind us, and we could see his farm off the back balcony. I had never noticed this before, but Im Gaby and Mahinda, the smokers, spent a good deal of time on the balcony. They had noticed. And so we arranged to have fresh milk delivered to the house twice a week. Previously we had used powdered milk, and I was looking forward to enjoying the taste I was used to.

In my mind I pictured neat, capped bottles left in front of our door before anyone got up. The milkman who made his pre-dawn rounds was a thing of the past in the U.S., but I remembered. I could still call up the memory of milk delivered every other day, bringing the bottles into the house on bitter cold winter mornings, and the look of the caps as the frozen white liquid pushed its way out of the bottle. Sometimes the bottle would break, and my mother would put it back into the crate on the back porch, ready for the milkman to replace.

Mom would have five or six gallons of milk delivered at a time, a necessity for our large family. I still remember struggling to make room in the refrigerator, and finally making them fit, a difficult task.

I was happy about this new arrangement. With three young boys, milk was an absolute necessity. Even so, I was surprised when I opened the door a week later to find the man standing there, bearing two tin buckets. The buckets were attached to a yoke he wore across his shoulders. They were heavy, but he managed the weight, bowing forward under it, seeming resigned to it.

He looked at me and said, "*Haleeb.*" I looked around for the bottles. Again, he said "*Haleeb,*" this time raising the buckets slightly to bring my attention to them. Im Gaby materialized behind me and took matters into her own hands. She directed the farmer into the kitchen, where he carefully set the buckets down on the floor. She brought out a large kettle, and without further fanfare, the man poured the milk into the kettle. She paid him and he left.

The milk would now be my responsibility, but raw milk was not something I was prepared for. I still depended on *The Joy of Cooking* as my bible. It told how to do everything from making sour cream and cheese to curing meat. And, thank God, pasteurizing milk.

We followed the advice of the cookbook, boiling the requisite time to make it safe for the children. My grandparents had had a farm, and now I remembered drinking the milk there. My sister and I relished watching my grandfather milk Betty the cow, and even tried milking her ourselves. But when that same milk was offered at lunch, we turned up our noses. We didn't like it; we were city girls, not used to the rich taste. In the end, my mother bought bottled milk from the store for us.

I was prepared for the same thing to happen here, so I was pleasantly surprised to find that after the white liquid cooled in the refrigerator overnight, it tasted like "real" milk.

We enjoyed the milk the farmer brought. Paul and Nick drank it with meals and poured it over their cereal in the morning. We also made yogurt and yogurt cheese. We could have purchased canned milk from the store, but this was so much better. It tasted good, and we congratulated ourselves that we were giving our children good nutrition. We were also pleased to be able to help the farmer. He didn't talk much, but he had the appearance of a defeated man. Judging by his clothes and shoes, we assumed he was poor.

Little by little, Im Gaby gained the farmer's confidence. She chatted briefly with him each visit, each time just a little longer. I remember well the day that he finally confided in her. I was feeding Peter his bottle in the living room when the doorbell rang. Im Gaby came out of the kitchen, wiping her hands on her apron, and opened the door to the milkman. She greeted him, leading him down the now-familiar hallway and into the kitchen, where he placed his load onto the floor. He carefully emptied his buckets into the large pot Im Gaby had ready on the stove. He didn't spill a drop.

He turned to leave, but stopped when she offered him food. He declined, but accepted the pack of cigarettes she held out to him. She lit a cigarette for him and started speaking. He answered slowly at first, but with gradual confidence, coaxed on by her gentle words and generous manner. From where I sat with the baby, I could see his shoulders slump as he spoke. His eyes, always red rimmed, brimmed with tears as he told his tale to my mother-in-law in his raspy voice. He spoke as if he was choking on the words. Im Gaby put her hand to her mouth, and then both hands to the sides of her face.

The farmer spoke at length while his rapt listener encouraged him with petitions to the Virgin Mary and God. Tears ran down the milkman's creviced face, mirrored by those of my mother-in-law. I was silent. Even the baby seemed to sense the tension and was respectfully quiet. Nothing disturbed the drama as one poured out his heart, and the other tried to catch it.

Finally, he finished speaking. His listener ran to the back of the house while he waited, silently smoking another cigarette. Im Gaby reappeared, carrying a used pair of Nagib's shoes, an old sports jacket, and a carton of cigarettes. The solemnity of the moment made this seem appropriate, and I didn't even think to object. She pushed these on the farmer, and, turning to me, asked if I had any cash. I handed her what I had; she placed it, folded, in the pocket of the sports coat. He thanked her with dignity, bowing stiffly from the waist, and left.

Im Gaby sat down next to me, elbows on knees and legs apart. She leaned forward with both hands to her mouth, rocking back and forth, uttering entreaties to God and the Virgin. All the while, tears streamed down her face. She didn't try to make me understand, and I didn't ask. I knew that my limited command of the language was inadequate for this moment.

Later that evening, Nagib told me the story. The milkman had a few cows and some land on the hill in back of our building. He hadn't always been there. Not long ago he had enjoyed farming on a much larger tract of land in the Chouf Mountains. The land and the cows allowed him to support a large family: his wife, his sons, and their wives and children all worked together to make the farm a success.

For generations, the Greek Orthodox community lived side by side in the Chouf with the Druze, a sect of Islam. They had enjoyed a symbiotic relationship, respecting each other's values. But the relationship had become strained with the onset of the civil war, and when the Israeli army occupied the region, neighbors became enemies.

When the Israelis pulled out of Lebanon, they did so precipitously, giving no warning to the international community. The void they left was immediately filled with an eruption of hatred and unprecedented violence. The massacre of the Greek Orthodox, who had lived in the area for generations, was horrifying and complete.

The farmer had been too ill one day to get out of bed. His wife stayed home to take care of him and prepare lunch. His sons, their wives, and all the children went out to work the fields. When his wife rang the dinner bell at noon, no one responded. She rang it again. No response. The farmer finally went out to look for his family. He found them all in the fields, dead, their throats slit.

Horror seemed to permeate every walk of life. It seemed that everyone had a story or knew someone who did. I was told of a man in Saudi Arabia, known to Nagib, whose extended family lived in those mountains. He heard after the fact that his entire family—mother, father, brothers and sisters, grandparents, nieces and nephews, had been murdered as they tried to run away. It didn't matter if they were old and barely able to walk, or babes in arms. All were killed. It was too dangerous for this man to go back to the mountain to bury his family. He had paid a Syrian military officer to find and bury his loved ones.

War doesn't discriminate. I don't think there could have been a family in Lebanon left untouched by the violence and hate that had wracked the country for so long. Those who hadn't taken a personal loss might have been able to continue believing they had dodged the war for the time being. And yet, the psyche of the people had been subtly affected. It was evident in the edge in the women's voices, and the escalating heart attack rate in both men and women. It was evident in the children's unnatural knowledge of weapons and their uses.

Living in Beirut during the war, everyday irritations should have been irrelevant to me. There were so many tragedies, I felt I should have been above petty fears or trivial concerns. But I wasn't. We lived in the details, and it was more comfortable to focus on the little picture while tuning out the big one. Every time Nagib left the country, I was desperate. And so, planning our new house became too important. Even making lunch could take on an outsized importance.

This wasn't limited to me. The Lebanese women were unduly engrossed in the quality of the silk they wore, as well as the latest styles from Paris. Jewelry, hair, and nails kept their attention in a hysterical way that defied the death surrounding them. It was important, it seemed, to be superior to someone. Maybe it was just the need to feel in control of something; anything. All the while, a darkness loomed above and around us, like a thunderstorm waiting to break. Threatening.

My situation as a foreigner gave me plenty of time to observe. In some ways, I was psychologically removed from the reality of the people who had been born here. Even though we planned to make our lives in Lebanon, I knew we had a home and employment in Saudi Arabia. More importantly, we could always return to the States. We had options.

The Lebanese citizens did not. The inflation rate had caused the value of the Lebanese lira to plummet, and scores of people were out of work. One story we heard involved a man who could no longer support his ten children. He was a laborer who had managed a comfortable living for his family, even during the war. When he was no longer able to feed his children, he had no choice but to put them up for adoption.

My heart hurt when I read the story of this family's tragedy. I cried for the parents, and I grieved for the children.

One week after this story ran in the English-language Arab papers, a follow-up story announced that a Kuwaiti oil sheik had adopted all ten of the children and hired the parents to work in his house. There could be small mercies, even in war.

CHAPTER 19

The winter of 1983 was the coldest anyone could remember in a long time. I had only been there two months, so I had nothing to compare it to. But it did seem to me that a climate that could nurture date palms and banana trees should enjoy Florida-like weather as well.

Evidently the Beirutis never expected this kind of cold, either. None of the houses were equipped with heat. Suad had given me a heavy wool bathrobe for Christmas, and I wore it in the house over my clothes for warmth. Nagib bought a space heater, and Im Gaby and I would bring our coffee into the living room and huddle near it for warmth.

Zahle was now buried in snow, and the mountain was impassable. There was no way anyone could come down or go up. The blizzard had come up very suddenly, blocking the mountain pass at Dar el Baidar. Some two hundred people were trapped in their cars. Forty-two died before they could be rescued. For us, the winter days were excruciatingly long, and there was little we could do to alleviate the boredom or the cold.

One morning, looking forward to my hot bath, I turned on the tap. Nothing came out but air. The concierge of our building said there wasn't anything he could do about it. According to the radio, a water main had burst way up in the mountain, from cold and lack of routine maintenance. The infrastructure for utilities was antique. I wondered, how could anything be maintained with shifting government, assassinations, occupations, bombs...?

Still, we had plenty of bottled drinking water, so cooking and the all-important coffee brewing would carry on as usual. But we couldn't flush toilets, do dishes, wash clothes, or bathe. We already had clotheslines strung up across the bedrooms; it was too cold to hang the wet wash outside.

Not all towns were affected like we were. Sami al Soleh, where Nagib worked, had running water. It was only about twenty minutes west of us. Nagib bought some very large, hard plastic jugs; he'd fill them with water near his work and send them to us via Eli, the driver. Eli and Mahinda had to lug them up the stairs if the elevators weren't working. I hoped we wouldn't have to repeat this exercise too many times before the pipe was fixed. I was not particularly optimistic.

Still, we persevered. We were determined to be here for the long haul, and be part of the pioneer force needed to rebuild Beirut and Lebanon once the war was resolved. Arriving when we did, we had been fortunate to miss many of its horrors.

These things happened, for the most part, either before our arrival in the city, or after we had fled. Our residence was in a time of renewed hope, with a new government supported by the majority. The American women I had met told me it was better now. They showed me a bridge. During the worst of the fighting, "they" would come at night to dump the bodies of the dead young men, taken during the fighting, over the side of the bridge to the street below. In the morning the families would come searching for their lost loved ones, shrieking and keening in grief and disbelief.

Sometimes the stories came close to us. The war had been particularly hard on many neighborhoods in East Beirut. Teenagers that we knew had grown up with war as the norm.

They sometimes lived for days in their bomb shelters, huddling in fear and anxiety. One girl we knew thought she couldn't stand it anymore, and threw herself off the third story balcony of her family's apartment building. She was only thirteen. Her older brother, thinking her dead, went with a friend and put her on a door he found in a nearby construction site, bringing her body up to the house. Miraculously, she survived, but so many didn't. I heard stories like this over and over.

Finally, winter eased into spring, and I started to regain my bearings. Life in Beirut was different than in Zahle, and a world away from Saudi. This city was sophisticated and cultured. It reminded one of an aging socialite, once wealthy and sought after, but now down on her luck. She knew she would be back someday; she had seen hard times before. It was a big city with all of the accoutrements—an art museum, a casino, boutiques that sold designer clothes, as well as traffic problems and crazy drivers. I had my car and was not afraid to learn my way around. In the general mountain area surrounding us lived friends that I had made in Saudi, now back home in Lebanon. I made new friends as well, including Western women from Great Britain and the US. Some of them had been here for a number of years. They were tough and resourceful, and I looked forward to learning the ropes from them.

Shortly after Peter was born, I went driving in West Beirut with Colleen, an Irish-born friend married to a Lebanese dentist. Colleen had been there for more than ten years and offered to take me around, show me the sights and take me shopping.

After several years of occupation by the PLO, order was slowly being restored in this area of the city. The locals weren't yet used to obeying any traffic laws. Some of the youth may have never had to obey them.

We, however, were stopped at one of the few working traffic lights. Nothing unusual for me; they were a normal part of an ordered civil existence. We were probably five cars back from the light, next to the sidewalk on the left-hand side of a busy three lane one-way street. Colleen and I waited patiently for the light to turn green when a young man, impatient with the short wait, decided to pass us by driving on the sidewalk. In the process, he scraped

Colleen's new Mercedes. Colleen, Irish accent and all, was fluent in Arabic, and not shy.

As he stopped, she got out of the car and let him have it with both barrels. Hips and wagging finger keeping rhythm, she made her displeasure perfectly clear. I recognized, laughing, quite a few words she shouted at him. They were not complimentary. I decided she was going to be my model here in the Wild Wild East.

Another time when driving on the autostrada in heavy traffic. We were stopped by a policeman standing in the road, bravely directing drivers. As he began to wave on the cars coming from the other direction, a car behind us pulled around and started to pass, ignoring the policeman's up-turned palm telling him to stop. The officer whistled wildly and gestured frantically, but to no avail. The driver of the rogue car just went faster, apparently above the law. But his ride was short-lived. He came to a screeching halt when the policeman pulled out his gun and shot out the tires. This, I thought, must have been the same mentality that finally settled the old American West, shootouts and all.

I was adapting to the crazy drivers in Beirut, but the worst was still to come. Our property was in a suburb of Beirut called Suhaile. The terrain coming up from the Mediterranean Sea rises in tiers, making the city hilly. The neighborhoods stack one on top of the other at different levels. Suhaile was west and up from where we were living in Jounieh. The ride there was very picturesque, and we liked to sit under the trees on our property and picnic. The magnificent view of the Mediterranean was unobstructed. This was where we planned to build our house.

Nagib had been working in Saudi Arabia for two weeks. It was hard for me when he was gone, and the days often dragged on. But on this day, the weather had changed, bringing warm spring temperatures after the atypical winter. The sun shone brightly in a brilliant blue sky, and a light breeze was blowing. It was Sunday, and the boys wanted to "do something." So did I. Im Gaby and I packed a picnic lunch, bundled all three children into the car, and pointed its nose toward Suhaile. We were looking forward to our outing.

Im Gaby sat next to me and the three boys rode in back, Pete in his car seat. I felt proud that I had overcome my fears and could find my way around. Im Gaby would be no help in that department, as this area of Lebanon was foreign to both of us. The car found its way around the mountain without incident until the last few minutes of the drive. We had stopped to wait for a break in the south-bound traffic so we could make a 180-degree left turn to start the steep ascent up the mountain. The narrow road was one way in each direction, and I was not one to risk an accident by turning in front of the speeding oncoming cars.

There was a house and little store along the road where we meant to turn. Two boys played outside near the street against a stone retaining wall. At last, there was a break in the traffic, and I made my turn, just as the driver behind me ran out of patience. As I moved into the turn, he passed me on my left, hitting our car. Trying to avoid me, he drove right into the boys, pinning them against the wall.

As the two cars crunched, there was a squeal of brakes and the sound of glass shattering. I don't remember screaming, but I knew I couldn't watch as his big Mercedes plowed into those two children. I put my head down on the steering wheel and prayed.

I looked up only when Im Gaby started crying and shaking me. She had thought I was dead. All three of my boys were unscathed, as were Im Gaby and I. Peter was snug in his car seat and didn't even wake up. I pulled over to the side of the road to see to the young boys and wait for the police.

The scene was chaotic. The Mercedes, thank God, had been stopped by a curb right in front of the children. They had been pinned against the wall, but except for a few scrapes and bruises, weren't hurt. The driver of the Mercedes, on the other hand, was in imminent danger from the father of the boys. The father was a big man, a butcher by the look of his apron, and he came out of his shop shaking both fists and screaming. The crowd that had quickly gathered held him back.

237

The commotion, of course, was all in Arabic, but I could tell that no one was blaming me. In fact, everyone ignored me, except for the other driver. He kept coming over to me to say something I couldn't understand. Im Gaby sent him away every time and, finally, tapping my shoulder, gestured to me to write down his license plate number. A woman in the crowd gave us pencil and paper, and after we had written down the information and given someone our phone number, we left. The police, it seemed, would not be coming.

We arrived home greatly shaken. Im Gaby fixed herself a Scotch and poured a sherry for me. We called Nagib in Saudi Arabia. I spoke first, assuring him that everyone was okay. Even the car had almost no damage, only a broken taillight. He calmed me down and got the story in English, then I passed the phone to his mother. After talking to her, he spoke again with me and told me that the other driver had been trying to get me to say that the accident was my fault. We were insured and he was not.

We were shaken, but not harmed. I comforted myself with the knowledge that Nagib would be home in a couple of days, and wouldn't be traveling again for a while, I hoped. We all did our part to prepare for what felt like a long-awaited holiday. Mahinda cleaned, Im Gaby and I cooked, and all three children, affected by the exuberance of the adults, tried to help in their own ways: Paul did his schoolwork without a fight, Nick took a long nap, and

Peter was quiet and content. Eli picked me up early so we could have the car washed on the way. We chatted companionably on the ride to the airport, and Eli listened on and off to the radio. Halfway there, he started changing stations and became more tense, telling me that "something political" was going on, and he was trying to catch the news.

It was the Greek Orthodox Good Friday, a beautiful warm day in early May, with a blue sky and soft breeze. There was a crowd outside of the airport since, for security reasons, they didn't allow people inside to meet travelers.

Security had once again become vital. On April 18, I had gone to see an American friend in Ashrafia, a suburb of Beirut. During our visit, her fifth-floor apartment was suddenly rocked by a loud explosion; the American Embassy had been blown up. My friend's children were in the American school not far from there. We separated quickly; she moved frantically toward the explosion while I, with Peter and Nicky, swiftly headed in the other direction.

The picture of that day, screaming mothers running down the street pulling their hair as they ran is burned into my memory. Paul was in school further up the mountain. He was safe, and we were limp with relief when he arrived home an hour later, school having dismissed early.

On this day, however, things were calm. The plane came in without a hitch and the passengers hurried out to meet their rides. Eli quickly picked up on a murmur going through the crowd, told me to stay put, and went to see what was going on. I was just happy that Nagib was on his way home, and I thought nothing could spoil my good mood.

We didn't have to wait long for Nagib. After he hugged me, saying he had missed me, he had quick words with Eli, and we slung the bags into the car. Nagib made light of their hurry, saying they wanted to beat the traffic. I knew better, though, and began to feel uneasy. Eli said something to me about some shelling "not far from here." There had been some quiet consultations in Arabic between the two men, but nothing I could make sense of.

The road was flat and dusty, and every so often we heard an explosion. Craning our necks and looking back, we could see the mushroom cloud of dust and debris in the distance. It seemed to me that the "incidents" were following us, and that we were just managing to stay in front of them. This happened three times on the trip home, but I forgot about it when we walked into the house and the boys were turned loose on their father. We were happy.

Im Gaby had been cooking up a storm, preparing a fit repast for the returning traveler. The excitement bubbled over onto the two older boys who had run back and forth, watching out the window for the car to pull up. The table was set and everything ready to go when we walked in the door. Nagib greeted his mom and threw the two older boys up into the air, bringing their energy level to the max.

As we sat down to eat, a deafening explosion rocked our building. I ran to the balcony to see what had happened. This was a mistake, but I was new to war. I never did it again. I looked down the street to see the mushroom cloud of dust and smoke the missile had left in its wake. It still hadn't registered. I thought it must have been a car accident until my husband and mother-in-law dragged me back. The shell had landed about a mile from where we lived. Much too close for comfort.

We left our feast, taking the wine and Scotch with us, and moved into the hallway to be as far as possible from any projectile coming from the outside. *Right.* They never bombed Jounieh . . . until now.

We didn't dare venture outside, or even into the dining room, which was in the front of the house. We could make quick trips to the kitchen in the back, but for the most part preferred the safer option of the hallway; it had more walls. We sat and waited—cringing, listening, listening, holding our breath.

While we waited, I tried to capture what was happening, but I couldn't write. The bombs were coming every ten minutes or so, and we couldn't relax. After each explosion, we counted the minutes waiting, thinking, can this be the end? With each one, we tried to figure out where the bomb hit, then another would come. If there was a bright side, it was our knowledge that the Red Cross was out there helping the injured and rescuing trapped people from their buildings.

The night dragged on, totally surreal. My stomach hurt and I felt a wave of nauseous terror overtake me. I fought it back down every time. Hysterics weren't going to help anything. We never did get to eat any of that delicious dinner Im Gaby fixed. We left it on the table, afraid to go back into the front room. Once, during a lull, Im Gaby and I did run in quickly to grab the perishables off the table and put them in the refrigerator. When the kids woke up, we thought, we'd be able to feed them.

We had dragged the mattresses off the beds for Nick and Paul. As we huddled against the different walls in the hallway, the boys slept soundly. Not even the explosions right next to us could wake them. Im Gaby chose to sit on the toilet in the hall bathroom. Peter's bassinet went with her, putting an extra wall between him and any shell that might land on us. Mahinda had refused to join us, preferring to stay in his own room.

The power had gone out hours ago, and the house was dark. Our only light came from a little gas lamp, set on a small table we had brought in. We were sparing of the radio, since we weren't sure we had any more batteries. None of us really wanted to get up and look.

For the first couple of hours, I worked on my embroidery while Nagib played cards with his mother. They sipped on their Scotch, and I drank my Sherry. It soon became too dark to embroider, and I wished I could just go into a deep sleep like the boys; wake up and it would be all over.

The rest of the night and the next day the shelling was intermittent. The day of our celebration had become my night of initiation. Nagib and his mother listened to the *Voice of Lebanon*, a Phalangist-run radio show, that gave us the latest updates on the bombardment.

With the night, the shelling intensified. For what it was worth, we knew which neighborhoods had been hit and how many people had been killed or wounded. We knew who was sending the shells and what action was being taken to stop it. Somehow, just knowing something seemed awfully important.

Each night, the adults in our little group sat with our backs against the wall, waiting. The lamp's tiny glow gave our faces a surrealistic tinge of green, and I thought of Father Andre and his sermon to us about letting our light shine like a candle in the dark. We were grateful for that little light.

As the children slept in the hallway, Im Gaby and I took turns stretching out next to them. We dozed from time to time, each loud crash shaking us from our sleep.

The bombing lasted three nights and two days. Those hours were a frightening blur of exhausted dozing and terrified awakenings to the ear-shattering explosions. After each loud percussion, we analyzed its distance from us, as well as the length of time that had lapsed in between. It fooled us into thinking we could make some order out of this killing chaos.

The bombing finally halted when a valiant American Marine colonel took a helicopter up the mountain and shot out the nest from which the shelling originated. When it was over, Nagib went outside to view the damage. Our building, blessedly, was unscathed. There was an ominous circle of craters around it, a testimony to our many near misses. The rectory across the street, however, had taken a direct hit. A shell had gone right through the priest's window, exploding in his bedroom. Miraculously, he was not killed.

But our short-lived honeymoon in Lebanon was over. I couldn't trust the ensuing peace, knowing that the hostilities could be right around the corner. There was never a normal day after that.

Even after the war came to Jounieh, Nagib was still required to travel back and forth to Saudi Arabia. It was difficult for him, but he told me this was insurance for us. One could never know how long a political job would last, particularly in Lebanon. He was gone sometimes for as long as three weeks. I was nervous during these absences, particularly at night. No surprise at that—my confidence had been shattered. I couldn't trust the night anymore. Im Gaby could listen to the Voice of Lebanon if the shelling started again, but it would be difficult for her to make me understand the complex political situation.

I couldn't depend on the phones to call Nagib either, or even to call within the city. The phone system was literally propped up by two-by-fours, and chronically undependable. John, the nearest relative, lived at least ten miles south of us. If anything, the situation near John tended to be worse, and we couldn't depend on his help. I had always felt safe with my husband there, but like it or not, Nagib was gone, and I was in charge. I was the adult.

But I could deal with it. The weather was warming. I hadn't been in Saudi Arabia long enough to have forgotten spring! After the brutally cold winter, the children and I were happy to be without our layers of wool. Now, we enjoyed watching the dark clouds roll over the Mediterranean, churning up the waters and turning the waves a dark green that mimicked the ocean.

During those spring days, we opened the windows and let the sea breeze air out the house. I knew that in Saudi, Nagib was sweltering in 100-plus degree heat, with high humidity. Gradually, I let myself be lulled into letting down my defenses. Nothing had happened for a while. Maybe the war really *was* over.

One day, the wind blew harder as the evening became night. We closed the windows against the increasingly cooler air, and Im Gaby put on a sweater. The electricity went off at six, and I helped Paul do his homework by gas lamp light as best I could. I bathed Peter, then put Nick and Paul to bed at eight. Mahinda said goodnight then, and left. Im Gaby and I played cards for another hour and went to bed.

I felt uneasy, but couldn't put my finger on what was wrong. Nagib was coming home in a couple of days, and I should have been relaxed and excited. I had trouble falling asleep that night. When I finally did, it was a light sleep, with one ear open.

The first low rumbles broke the silence after midnight. It sounded far enough away that I just lay there and listened, my body tense, questioning what I had heard. It was quiet for a while, then another boom, this time louder and nearer. I lay in bed, willing the explosions to stop. But just then another, more violent cataclysm shook the house. This wasn't going away.

I got out of bed quickly, finding my robe and slippers in the dark. I tiptoed to Im Gaby's room to wake her; I would need her help to move the children's mattresses into the hallway. I was surprised that she had slept through this latest onslaught. I went into her room and gently shook her shoulder. Whispering her name, I entreated her to wake up.

"*Oumi, ya Tante!*" ("Get up, Aunt!")

"*Oumi, saadini*," I said. ("Get up! Help me!")

Im Gaby turned over sleepily and, opening one eye, told me "*Raad.*" As I became more insistent, she finally got out of bed. Taking me by the hand, she walked me to the front window, pointed toward the sea, and repeated

"*Raad.*" It took me a while, but when I saw the flash of lightning in the sky, I finally understood what she was telling me. It was a thunderstorm. Even so, I moved the children, and we slept in the hallway.

A few days later we weren't so lucky. The shelling started in the early evening. Predictably, the power went off and the phone went dead. Im Gaby and I took up residence in the hallway with the children yet again. This time the shelling seemed to be concentrated to the west of us, and we didn't feel quite as threatened. This was my first time facing the shelling without Nagib nearby. We were cut off from anyone who could have helped us by the lack of power and working technology. We didn't even know if our relatives in Beirut were aware that Nagib was gone. All we could do was play with the children and pray that this incident would be over quickly.

That night, we reconciled ourselves to the hallway again. We knew that sleeping might not be much of an option, but we would try. We settled in, reading stories to the children by candlelight, singing songs and trying to soothe them into sleep.

Paul and Nick were just rounding the corner to sleep when we were startled by a pounding on our door. I ran to answer it, shocked to see Nagib's cousin John in the doorway. John's section of East Beirut, I was sure, had been badly hit during the day.

His drive over had been dangerous and, to me, a spectacular feat of courage. He had made a promise to Nagib to keep an eye on his family while he was away. Always a handsome man, that night I saw an angel at the door. I continue to see that in him, even after many years.

Once he could see for himself that we were all okay, he gave us an update on the situation. It had taken him less than ten minutes to get to us. He was the only "crazy" person on the road, and had driven at breakneck speed. Despite our entreaties to stay, he left shortly after he arrived. We had no way of knowing that night if John made it back all right, and we worried until we heard from him the next day. I have never forgotten that night, nor the heroic risk John took for us.

When Nagib returned, he said it was time to go. We, unlike so many others, had choices. Nagib argued that we should just pack up and leave for Saudi Arabia. We had a home there. He had a job, and we all had friends waiting. We had a life there. The problem was, Peter didn't have a passport. As much as I wanted to leave, I couldn't risk taking the baby out of the country without a passport, even if the airlines would have let him aboard. The complications worried me. I wanted the American passport for him; I couldn't trust the Saudis to figure out any other scenario.

Weeks passed as we waited for the political situation to improve, and for the American government to open a temporary embassy. Eventually, after intense negotiations and a strong international presence, the hostilities settled into a tense truce. While we waited, life returned to a kind of normal, despite the military checkpoints and bombed out businesses.

When I took Im Gaby for her medical testing at the prestigious American University Hospital of Beirut, we endured a vigorous screening of our persons and belongings. When I wondered how they carried on with surgeries during heavy shelling, the doctor explained that anything delicate was carried on three floors below ground.

When the American government finally did open an interim facility, we waited a few more weeks to make sure the peace held. I was nervous about applying for Peter's American birth certificate and passport. On the day, I made sure I had all the necessary paperwork. I gathered my birth certificate and marriage certificate, two passport photos, and the baby's Lebanese birth certificate. I knew from experience that the embassy would require the baby to be with me.

Eli picked me up early that morning. I had the paperwork, plus a diaper bag full of Pampers, changes of clothes for Peter, and bottles. We had no idea how long we would have to wait, and I wanted to be prepared. The temporary embassy was in West Beirut, not far from the original bombed-out building.

As we approached, it was obvious that security had been increased. Barricades were set up, and tanks and sentries were in abundance. The area was closed off for a twenty-block circumference around the embassy. We left the car and walked—baby, carrier, diaper bag, and all. We picked our way through debris in the road and on the broken sidewalks, finding it necessary to climb over the larger pieces of stone and masonry. We moved carefully, stepping on rocks as we went and passing the baby from one to another, protecting him as much as possible.

The crowd around the entrance was daunting. I didn't think we'd be able to get in, there was such a long line. People had been camped out in front of the building. They were waiting for a chance to beg a visa to leave to the States, hopeful of winning the golden ticket out of hell. It hadn't occurred to my democratic mind that, by virtue of my American citizenship, I could go to the front of the line.

Eli shouldered a path for Peter and me, and we bulled our way to the front. There, a line of armed Marines kept back the crowd and let people enter in groups of five. As I looked at the raw pain, anguish, and desperation on the Lebanese faces surrounding me, I finally blinked. This wave of violence had left me numb for a bit, as if it were being experienced by someone else and I was gazing in from afar. As we approached the jammed entrance, Eli spoke to the corporal in charge. The Marine spoke softly, bending slightly at the waist while he asked if we were American. This brave young man had also seen too much. When I answered yes, Peter and I were admitted immediately.

The young Lebanese man who helped me looked worn and weary. He had deep circles under his eyes, and I wondered how many of his friends and coworkers he had lost in the recent explosion. Come back next week, he told me, and everything will be ready. It seemed that in my haste, I had forgotten an important paper, without which they couldn't proceed. But *don't,* he admonished, bring the baby. It's way too dangerous. Outside, I sheepishly confessed to Eli that it was my fault we had to come back. He was very kind, telling me chivalrously that he was at my service. What else could he say?

We picked our way back over blocks of rubble, while I carried my infant son, Eli carrying the useless stroller and diaper bag. In one fell swoop, my optimism melted away. It almost brought me to my knees, leaving me frightened and grief-stricken. I certainly couldn't analyze it then, but a patina, the same Mary had referenced so long ago, was being etched onto my soul. My spirits sagged.

Some months after we left the country, a truck loaded with explosives drove into the Marine barracks and blew up, killing 220 men. I sobbed when I read the news, thinking of those brave young men, wondering what happened to the ones who had helped me that day.

While we waited for our papers, the shelling began again. We were subjected to another round of assaults, one shell a day landing in different Christian neighborhoods. One late afternoon in June, I was sitting in the living room with Nick and Paul. Mahinda was on the back porch feeding Peter, and Im Gaby was in the kitchen. Nagib, of course, was still at work.

It was a Friday, and everyone looked forward to the weekend. The weather was good and our spirits high when the explosion rocked our house. There had been no warning or rumbles in the distance, no news from the radio. The rocket that day fell right in front of our house, landing on a car full of young teachers returning home from work.

The impact sent me catapulting me to the back of the house, grabbing the children as I went. The force of the blast caused Peter to projectile vomit the bottle of milk he had just drunk. The only rocket that day was also the last of our doomed sojourn in Beirut. It took more than a week before I could bring myself to go outside and walk past the wreckage.

By July, Peter had his American passport, and we left Beirut as soon as school let out. Our future was unsure, but we knew we had to leave. We decided on an extended beach vacation with my family in the States.

We left, barely clinging to our plans and our hopes. Peace was always just around the corner for the Lebanese, and I wanted to buy into that optimism, hard though it was. We still had the architectural blueprints to build a Tudor-style house on our land in Suhaile, but for now, battered, we put everything on hold.

We left Beirut changed. We didn't realize it then, but it manifested in the sharper way we began to deal with each other, in our trouble sleeping. We made light of our experiences; too many of our friends had seen much worse. Yet although we didn't name it, depression had set in. We left emotionally exhausted, psychologically assaulted, and spiritually bereft.

CHAPTER 20

SAUDI ARABIA

FUDGE: (*verb*)

2. An instance of faking or ambiguity. Present or deal with something in a vague, non-committal or inadequate way, especially so as to conceal the truth or mislead.

"I'm not really making it; I'm only just faking it. I'M FUDGING IT!"

We landed at Dharan Airport in Saudi Arabia without event. The heat and humidity enveloped me as we stepped off the plane. But this time, instead of a slap in the face, it was like a hug. It felt familiar and safe. And dare I say, like home? Maybe Beirut would retreat into the recesses of my mind like a bad dream.

A storm was brewing inside of me. I was anxious and depressed, but I pushed it aside, preferring to believe that fleeing the war toward peace in the emotional distance of Saudi Arabia would make everything okay. I subconsciously erased the horrors of the past year, and it was surprisingly easy for me to pretend that the friction between Nagib and me would stay behind. I knew he was deeply disappointed by the turn of the political situation in Lebanon. And me? I was confused and frightened by what I had experienced. It would take some time to process everything; the shock and chaos that we were trying to flee traveled with us. My thoughts increasingly wandered toward home. But home was in the States, not the Middle East.

And yet, our return to Saudi was like a homecoming. Word spread quickly, and soon our days were filled with visitors and well-wishers coming to get the news, welcome the new baby, and pick up where we had left off. I was happy to be back in my old surroundings with my old furniture, seeing my old friends and even viewing the same, tedious vistas.

Nothing had been said about our plans to settle in Lebanon. We wouldn't, couldn't admit we were no longer on the same page. We were developing different agendas. We had been here before, but this time it was more serious. We needed to catch our breath, and I didn't want to rock the boat after the past year. Ostrich-like, I could just stick my head in the sand and pray that events would solve the problem for me.

I wasn't the only one suffering from fears for the future and nightmares from the recent past. Being absent for a year made me sensitive to the nuances of mood that cloaked my friends. The Lebanese in our community were collectively depressed and reevaluating their post-Saudi plans. Many had lost family members or friends in this most recent round of hostilities, and they were reluctant to commit to a return to Lebanon. The elusive peace continued to elude.

Despite the sagging spirits of its guests, Saudi remained, frustratingly and amusingly, the same. Same sleepy humdrum existence, same everyday routine, same brown and gray landscape. Unfortunately, also the same frustrating molasses bureaucracy. One speed for everything: slow.

Saudi was a stopover for us on our way to the Maryland beaches. We had rented an oceanfront condo. We were expected there within another week, excited at the prospect of seeing family and friends. These plans had been made while we were still in Beirut. But we were in Saudi now, with Saudi rules and Saudi time. An exit visa was required in order to leave the country. Not a problem, Nagib told me. Just give it a day or two. Day after day, Nagib heard tomorrow, God willing. But he kept not being willing... and so we waited, with the rental date looming near.

Once our predicament was known, people came out of the woodwork to tell us their peculiar stories. Over dinner one night, the husband of an American psychologist regaled us with his bizarre story. He had worked as a civil engineer in the Kingdom in the early years of its boom. He was a bachelor for many years and lived the loneliness of single life in Saudi. The Christmas holiday was particularly hard for him. To cheer him up, his family in England conspired to surprise him and sent him a Christmas tree. Not the aluminum or plastic type, but a real one. Of course, it couldn't be a surprise, since he needed to claim it at the airport. And indeed, it came in due time. However, in true Saudi bureaucratic style, they wouldn't release it to him. It didn't have a death certificate.

Another woman told us about bringing her pet cat into the Kingdom. She had expected it to be quarantined and submitted to tests, and be obliged to fill out reams of paperwork. She was unprepared though, to submit the requested birth certificate.

The most preposterous of all the stories came from my friend Tahseen. Just a couple months earlier, a middle-aged man who worked in her husband's company died suddenly of a heart attack. Tahseen's husband Wasi was the manager, responsible for reporting the death and making arrangements to send the body back to the man's family in Pakistan. Incredibly, the shipment of the body and subsequently the funeral, were held up for weeks while Wasi endeavored to obtain the dead man's exit visa.

As I heard these stories, I started to despair about leaving in time to make our beach reservation. The reservation couldn't be postponed, though, so we told my mom and siblings to go ahead. We would, *bukra in'shaAllah*, meet them there.

In undue time, we were released by the Saudi bureaucracy, only a day late. Complicating the delays, we were to transport Nagib's teenage cousin Rita from Beirut to the Dammam Airport to meet us. She was accompanying us to the States as a mother's helper. It was an amazing opportunity for her, but a puzzle for us. She couldn't possibly get a Saudi visa and could only transfer planes within the airport. What a complete mess!

We solved that puzzle by coordinating her layover in Saudi with our departure to the U.S., and at long last arrived at the beach. We were finally able to relax. At least I was. Nagib descended to the street every other day armed with quarters to use the payphone and call his work. Even on vacation, he had a business to run. We saw everyone: aunts, uncles, brothers, sisters, and cousins. It was wonderful. I was sad when we had to leave, but these days Paul's school dictated our schedule. Nick, too, would be starting school this year.

The morning of our scheduled departure, we woke early. We had stayed in a hotel in Washington, D.C., after leaving the beach. There were too many to be comfortably housed with relatives, and we preferred the downtime before traveling. Rita had enjoyed the trip of her life. She was also a great help with the children. We had three adults, three children, and many bags of luggage to get ready. Rita was a lifesaver.

We had tickets to fly out of Dulles Airport to Beirut. Our plan was to return to Beirut to pack our belongings and for Nagib to tie up loose ends, since our departure had been rather precipitous. With the myriad political failures, Nagib's job in Beirut was at an end. He had been wise to keep one foot in Saudi.

I was surprised when the phone rang in our hotel room, even more so to hear the voice of a friend from Beirut on the other end. She was an American married to a Lebanese like I was. And like me, she was from Maryland, home visiting family.

"Where are you?" she asked.

"We're in D.C., but we're getting ready to go to the airport in another hour or so. We're leaving for Beirut," I answered.

"Haven't you heard?" she shouted with a hysterical note in her voice. "Turn on the news. Beirut is under siege and the airport is closed. I don't know what we'll do."

I turned on the news. Hostilities in the region had escalated. Four days of bombardment in Beirut would be followed by the withdrawal of the Israeli army and massacres of Christians and Druze in the Chouf mountains. The images in the papers made knots in my stomach. I was conflicted—so glad we weren't there for this round of war, yet revolted. I feared for friends and family, grateful I had somewhere else to go. At the same time, practical considerations had to be addressed: what about Rita? She couldn't come back to Saudi, and Lebanon was closed for the time being. And what about our tickets? We scrambled to make arrangements.

We returned to Saudi the next day, leaving Rita behind with my sister, Betsy, since she had no visa to go with us. She stayed in Washington for two weeks, frantic about her family, staying with strangers, albeit kind ones, before the airport in Beirut reopened. We were lucky to have Saudi as an option, since we didn't know how long the airport would be closed. All our belongings, including most of our clothes, were still in Beirut.

It felt strangely good to wake up in my old bedroom in Dammam. I was happy to see familiar faces everywhere I went, and to be back in the lazy routine. I still found myself jumping three feet and hiding behind the couch every time I heard an empty dump truck go over a speed bump. I thought of Anna now, understanding her in a way I never could have before. I wondered if I'd ever get over thinking I was hearing bombs.

The boys were happy too—back with their friends, swimming in the pool, getting manushi, an herb-coated pita that the Europeans here called "dirty bread." It was delivered on Friday mornings, still warm from the bakery oven. Their favorite, though, were the Thursday evening buffets at the Carlton. The year in Beirut seemed like a dream. I made the rounds of visits to friends I hadn't seen for a while, in between receiving the Carlton wives for coffee as they came to welcome me back.

Despite all the changes we'd been through, life must go on. It was late September and school was back in session, lending a rhythm of normalcy to our lives. Nick was lucky to have Madame Ava as his teacher; the same teacher Paul had had when he started at the French School. This time she was the head teacher, not the aide. A call from the teacher in the evening is mostly a concerning thing, so when I realized who Nagib was speaking with in Arabic, my antennae went up.

But when he hung up the receiver, he was smiling. Ava, he said, had called to tell us something nice. She told him that when the boys arrived on their bus to school in the morning, Paul would help his little brother off the bus, taking his hand, making sure he didn't fall. Paul would then take Nick's lunchbox from him, carrying it for him while holding his hand, and take him to his classroom door. There he would place Nick's lunch box in his hands, kiss him goodbye, turn him by his shoulders, and stand there until he saw him safely into the room. Only then would he turn around and head for his classroom.

Nagib beamed; I cried.

Regardless of circumstances, seasons still change, years turn around, and life goes on. After what we had experienced in Beirut, I was determined to make the approaching holidays special. Nick's birthday and Halloween coincided, putting a charge of excitement into our community as costumes were planned and made.

As in the past, Thanksgiving was the kick-off to the Christmas season. I looked forward to hosting, but so many people had left. However, my brother would join us this time, bridging the gap between my homes.

What a bonus! Chris had just graduated college with a degree in graphic arts. Nagib had gotten him the job with one of the sister companies. It was wonderful to sit in the evening with him and talk about home. He had never been away from home for any length of time, and adjustment to this life was hard for him. Conversations with Chris showed me that life in Saudi for bachelors working here bore no resemblance to what I was experiencing.

"Cath," he told me after a family dinner, "I'm exotic to the people I'm working with!"

I laughed, remembering my first visit to Lebanon several years ago. I could relate. But Chris wasn't married to a Lebanese; he wasn't in this for the long haul. I could see by his serious expression that there was more to come. "It's mentally exhausting," he continued. "I'm having a hard time understanding what people are saying in English! Even the native speakers from Scotland and Australia!"

Again I could relate, but I held my peace and let him talk. He was lonely, he said, and homesick. The men he worked with were kind and friendly but couldn't fill the void. After venting, he shook himself, laughed, and let his natural good humor take over.

"Thanks for listening," he said. "I needed that. Please don't tell Nagib. I know he's pulled strings to give me this chance. You know, it's not all bad. I'm saving a lot of money and seeing things that most people could never experience! Like the drive through the Rub'al Khali."

The Empty Quarter, Rub'al Khali, is all desert and takes up most of the southern third of Saudi Arabia, extending into the United Arab Emirates and Yemen.

"Who gets to see that?" he exclaimed. "It was awesome! But don't worry about me. I'm just blowing off steam. It's great that I have you and the kids here, and I'm really looking forward to Thanksgiving dinner!" Yes, he was definitely a bonus.

Thanksgiving arrived with enough of a warm breeze to keep the ladies sweatered and shawled, but not enough to blow out the candle flames on the candelabras, set at both ends of the table. After dinner we all sat sipping drinks, enjoying each other's company, and looking up at the star-studded night sky. At times like this, it was easy to forget the ugly views revealed in the daylight. Looking up just in time, I saw a shooting star. I had never seen one before and gasped loudly. Tahseen looked up and saw what I saw. Turning to me, she beamed and announced that this was, indeed, a very good omen. *Wow!* I thought. *What a night!*

My shipment of personal belongings had finally come back from Lebanon, minus any Christmas decorations. The Saudis had confiscated them. In the absence of purchasable ornaments and decorations, I decided to make my own. I didn't even try to shop for them, although I had found some lovely things in the past. I heard that the Mutawa, the religious police, had raided several stores in Al Khobar. They burned any Christmas items right on the street, and the shop owners had been punished.

Instead, I went to Al Zamil's, the craft and fabric store. There I was able to find magazines and craft books from all over the world, including many with Christmas ideas. I immersed myself in patterns and fabrics. I began to sew red gingham ornaments for the tree and a stuffed Santa Claus, as well as a stuffed quilted fabric Christmas tree.

I was busy most mornings with this colorful task, and so it was a natural evolution that, as the women came to pay a visit, they would find me hard at work. One by one, they came and stayed, shyly asking if I minded teaching them how to make the ornaments I was working on. Eventually it looked more like Santa's workshop than anything else. It segued easily into weekly sewing meetings.

The hotel ladies met at my house to work on their projects. Some of the women, like me, were making ornaments and decorations—embroidered table runners and winter-themed hand towels. I had collected a pile of books and magazines to choose projects from, and we would sit companionably after the children went to school. As Christmas music played, the sewing machine whirred while we laughed and talked.

I had told some of them about the traditions we had at home for Christmas Eve, including the pageant we put on, reenacting the Christmas story. Somehow, in the telling of the story, we all became excited to do that here. There was no religious celebration, and we thought that it would be a wonderful thing if we could have the children put on a pageant at our big hotel Christmas party.

As everything else in Saudi, the Christmas pageant took on a life of its own. The tailor at the hotel offered to make costumes, parts were invented to accommodate the number of children, and of course Santa Claus would need to make an appearance.

The little boys, Nick included, were to be the sheep, and some of the older children would be the shepherds. Nick, even at age three a force to be reckoned with, had to throw a wrench into the works. He insisted that he was *not* a sheep. He would be a cow.

I had already purchased the fabric for the sheep costumes and argued with the little boy, telling him we couldn't do anything about it. But the tailor, on hearing the story, laughed and proclaimed that Nicholas, indeed, was not a sheep. Nor has he ever been since. He would be a cow. He went out that day and bought some dark fabric, and a very happy Nick was the only cow at the Christmas pageant. Pete, of course, was too little to participate. Paul, as befitted his age and status as the boss's son, as well as his personality and status in our family, was a king.

Christmas came and went, bringing the end to our excitement-packed year. In my heart, I prayed that this new year would see us leave the Middle East and go back to the

United States. I didn't voice this, coward that I felt I was, but I thought that Nagib had to know.

New Year's came, and our party that year was exhilarating! It felt good to carry on our New Year's Eve tradition of hosting the party at our place, and to be celebrating with our friends. The year in Beirut, we didn't celebrate at all. It had been two weeks before Peter's birth, and we had gone to bed at nine. It's amazing, I thought, how the total direction of your life can change in a heartbeat.

The ladies dressed for the party in their silk creations and jewels and gold. The waiters moved the family room furniture onto the balcony and set up buffet tables in that room. The chef prepared lobster Thermidor and petit filet mignons for our main course and had a gorgeously arranged salad and fruit table. The appetizers included the Lebanese staples like tabouli, hummus, Baba ghanoush, and kibbeh balls, but there was also an elaborate platter of smoked salmon. I noticed the absence of caviar. When I asked Nagib why we didn't order it for the parties anymore, he explained that it was the best caviar, from Iran, that we used to have. Since the war with Iraq, the Iranians had stopped trade with Saudi Arabia.

We had moved the furniture in the living area around and made a large dance floor, cranked up the music rather louder than was comfortable for me, and, needless to say, a good time was had by all. Nick and Pete slept through it, but Paul came to join the festivities for a bit. I teared up when we sang "Auld Lang Syne." I was happy to be with these friends again, but emotional over the family and friends that I missed. I wasn't the only one. There was a different tone this year, and many eyes were damp as we sang the familiar song. All of us sensed that this would be our last New Year's celebration together.

CHAPTER 21

ZAHLE, LEBANON, SPRING 1984

In the spring of 1984, we returned to Zahle for a visit. Nagib had had an offer in the States, and he wanted to pursue it. I didn't say much, but he knew I was hoping and praying that a move would be in our near future. After our experiences of the past year, we were ready for a change.

The boys and I stayed with Im Gaby, Maroun, and Suad in their little house. I waited eagerly for his phone calls, expecting good news any day. But the phone system was even worse internationally than it was internally. I had to be patient.

The electricity went off regularly now. You could set your watch by it. Every evening at six, we would gather for the nightly ritual of waiting for the dark.

It was warm that spring, even in the mountains. We would sit in Im Gaby's marble tunnel-like hallway in the evenings, watching the light slowly fade into darkness. This area separated Im Gaby's apartment from Gaby's. A stairway led up to the roof, where the laundry was hung on lines, and the hallway ended at the street. The ceilings were high, and we were able to catch a breeze from the street without too much dust.

We would sit by the light of a camp gas lamp in the twilight. All the work of the day was done, and it was time to relax. Im Gaby would prepare the argileh, the Turkish water pipe she liked to smoke in the evenings. She would heat small coals on a metal tray in the kitchen, then place them carefully on top of the already-packed tobacco. The tobacco had been pre-soaked in water and wrung out.

This was a household ritual. Im Gaby was very fond of the hubbly-bubbly, and was the undisputed expert on the best way to prepare the water pipe for smoking. The preparation of the pipe was always accompanied by a lot of joking and laughter.

While Hanani, Im Gaby's niece, or Maroun, sucked on the hose coming out from above the glass body of the pipe, she would fan the coals until the tobacco caught. The smokers would take turns drawing on the hubbly-bubbly, alternately sucking in the smoke and then exhaling. The coals glowed orange in the shadowy dusk of the evenings, and the water in the pipe bubbled, giving a rhythmic gurgle to the slow evenings.

A round tray holding a pot of Turkish coffee and empty demitasse cups were placed on the floor beside Im Gaby's chair. She would place a small saucer on top of the coffee pot to keep it hot, ready to serve to anyone who dropped by. Often, I would have prepared a cup of freeze-dried

American coffee for myself. The bitter coffee's pungent aroma mingled in the dry, dusty night air with the smoky fragrance of the burning tobacco, an odiferous beacon of invitation to those wandering by. The children drank juice and ate cookies as they waited for the adults to dictate the evening's entertainment.

This summer night, we took turns telling stories in the semi-darkness. Suad and I sat, each with a baby enthroned sleepily on our respective laps, keeping an eye on the older children as they played with toy trucks or jacks on the cool marble floor. An adult foot was always at the ready to block any balls or trucks headed for the water pipe or the gas lamp.

Maroun and Suad told their stories in English alternating with Arabic so everyone would understand. When it was my turn, I told the story of the Trojan horse. Maroun translated for Im Gaby, and it was well received by the children and the adults. Storytelling had been included in my job description as a children's librarian back in Baltimore. Back in another life. But that night, Im Gaby enthralled us all with the story of her brother, Hanna.

"My father, Ibrahim El Fahel," she began, "was a merchant and a sheep farmer in the early 1900s. He dealt on a large scale with the government of the Ottoman Empire, and specifically, with the wali (governor) of Lebanon and Syria. The wali was the highest authority representing the empire. Ibrahim used to supply sheep for meat and dairy products to the Turks for use by the military and officials. His reputation as a man of integrity preceded him wherever he went. He was known for his generosity and honesty. Eventually his name reached the High Chair in Istana, the headquarters, and he was rewarded with a rare and incredible gift."

Here Im Gaby paused for effect, making sure that the grandchildren were caught up in this dramatic telling of family history.

"The gift," she continued, "was a coal-black Arabian stallion. Ibrahim, pleased, accepted the horse for the honor it was. When he took it home, you can imagine the reaction from his sons and daughters. But it was Hanna who he asked to take care of the horse.

"Hanna was a young, strong, and ardent young man in his early twenties. He immediately fell in love with the magnificent beast, devoting every possible minute to its care and training, wanting nothing more than to be with the horse.

"He started slowly, not pushing hard lest he scare the animal, and little by little, gained its trust. He took gifts of carrots, apples, and sugar to the stallion, speaking softly to him as he ate. Gradually, the wild horse began looking for his visits and started to respond to the sound of his voice.

"At this point, Hanna knew they were ready to start training. Slowly, he taught the young stallion to accept his weight on his back. He started riding him, training and testing the beast's capabilities on many levels. Everyone could see that Hanna loved the horse, and it appeared that the horse loved him back.

"The horse and Hanna had become a customary sight in the village, and people would stop by to watch Hanna put him through his paces.

"'What are you doing with this horse, Hanna?' they would say. 'Why are you teaching it tricks?'

"It seemed to everyone that Hanna had something in mind, but he never said a word about his plans, even to his family.

"Now Zahle, where we lived, was the capital of the Bekaa area. Back then, as now, it was a Christian city. Each year since 1890, the Zahlewese were known to celebrate the Feast of Corpus Christi. Every year on the first Thursday of June, a festival was held. This was to celebrate the deliverance of the town and the surrounding villages, by Christ, from the plague. In thanksgiving, the people commemorated being spared by reverently carrying the body of Christ, in the form of the host, in a solemn procession through the streets.

"The priest would walk at the head of the procession, formally robed and holding the monstrance high. He would be preceded by a deacon or altar boy waving incense. The faithful followed behind, chanting and praying. The bishops and clergy would gather in the early morning for the long march.

"Zahle is divided into sixteen neighborhoods, each of which would create a holy stand. The people would stand and wait, holding pictures of the Virgin Mary and other saints. They would decorate the streets with ribbons and wait for the arrival of the Holy Eucharist to bless the people and the neighborhood, all the while chanting holy songs and prayers.

"After the blessing took place, the people would join the procession, swelling the ranks of the faithful as they passed each stand. They would process from one stand to another until the entire city had been covered. Some eight hours after it began, the ceremony would end with an outdoor Mass, attended by all the people of the town.

"The fun would begin in the early evening, after the Mass. The crowd would surge to another part of the town to spend the rest of the day watching games and competitions performed by the talented and strong men of Zahle.

"As the story goes," she went on, "the rumor was spreading around the town that Hanna El Fahel was going to do something that had never been done before in those games." She paused again for effect.

"Unfortunately," she continued, "this turned out to be true."

The children now were leaning forward, anticipating the climax.

Im Gaby took a deep breath and a sip from her coffee before she continued the story of the brother she had had for such a short time.

"Hanna had been training his horse to perform a dangerous stunt. Hanna would lie down on the ground, and at Hanna's signal, the horse would come running at his master at full speed. He had trained the horse to step on his chest without putting any weight on him.

"The rumors had done their job. People gathered from all over in eager anticipation of whatever exhibition Hanna and the horse would offer.

"Now, Hanna had a sweetheart. Her name was Nasiha, meaning pure. Her hair was long and black, and her eyes a deep brown. Hanna loved her very much, and she him.

"As Hanna prepared for his stunt, Nasiha held her breath, her clenched fists pressed tight against her mouth. But as the powerful horse came thundering closer and closer to her beloved, she couldn't help herself. Just as the horse came up on his master, she cried out Hanna's name. Hanna, startled, jerked his head around suddenly to look at her, causing the horse to lose his rhythm."

Here Im Gaby started to cry. She had only been a little girl, but that day was burned in her memory.

"The crowd gasped, and Nasiha screamed as the stallion's hoof slipped and came down on Hanna's head.

"Hanna was rushed immediately to the hospital, where his distraught father was told there was no hope. Hearing

274

this from the doctors, Ibrahim cursed them and ordered his son moved to his house. 'God will heal him,' he shouted. 'You will see!' After all, weren't they celebrating the divine intervention of Christ, saving his people from the plague? Today was a holy day, and Ibrahim had always had a close relationship with God. He was sure that God wouldn't fail him now.

"After seeing his son comfortably moved to his home, Ibrahim went in search of the horse. He found him, as usual, in his stall. As he untied the horse and led him out of the barn, Ibrahim cursed himself for the misfortune brought on his son and his whole family.

"Resolutely, he led the horse down the street. The crowds, recognizing him, parted silently to let him pass. Many crossed themselves as they prayed silently for the young man, so recently vital. But Ibrahim saw none of this. He looked neither to the right nor to the left, but straight ahead, making people wonder what he had in mind to do with the horse.

"Straight to the church Ibrahim marched, leading the horse behind him. He neither hesitated nor stopped when he approached the front of the church, but strode straight up the marble stairs, the horse's hoofs making a loud clopping noise as it followed. In the front door and past the priest, down the aisle and right up to the altar rail he went. Only then did he stop. After tying the horse to the altar rail, Ibrahim stepped back respectfully. He spread his arms wide and with head thrown back, loudly implored his God to accept the horse in exchange for the life of his son. His plea was passionate and eloquent. There was nothing more to do. After bowing to the icon of Christ, he turned slowly and left the church, alone.

"Ibrahim returned home to wait and to pray. When he saw the horse walk down the street toward the house, he knew that this offering had been rejected. He ran into his son's room to find the women weeping and keening. Hanna had just died."

This story of faith resonated deeply with me. I had a deep faith, but I didn't know if my relationship with God would have taken me to the church to implore in such a way. I was awed by this man, my children's great-grandfather, who could talk to God as the patriarchs of the Bible did. One on one. I wanted to know more about him. What happened after? How did anyone go on when God's answer was no?

We had only been there a week when all three boys got very sick. They developed high fevers and vomiting. First Nick, then Pete and finally Paul. Maroun took me and the children to see a doctor, who prescribed antibiotics for them. Night after night I walked the halls with Peter in the dark, after the electricity went off. In between, I would comfort Paul and Nick, trying to bring down their fever. Im Gaby was there to help me, but the children only wanted their mother.

The situation took on a nightmarish quality when after three days of antibiotics, the boys were no better. I didn't trust the doctor; I wanted a pediatrician. The only one I trusted to know what to do was Nagib, and he was conducting important business in the States. I didn't want to call him if I didn't have to. What could he do, so far away?

But, at my wits end, I begged Maroun to take me to the phone company to call Nagib at my sister Betsy's house. We couldn't get an international line from the house.

When Betsy answered the phone, I told her the situation. She quickly got Nagib, who was staying with her, on the phone. We talked at cross purposes. I was annoyed and upset when he told me he'd be gone another week, but I didn't tell him the children were sick. He, in turn, was annoyed at the pressure I was putting on him and didn't want to tell me his bad news; he had turned down the job offer.

My sister, thank God, didn't think this was the time to keep a confidence. When she saw his confused anger, she quickly told him what was going on. By the time I got back to his mother's house, the phone was ringing. It was Nagib, saying he had booked a flight and would be back the next day.

He was true to his word and quickly took the children to another doctor, who diagnosed them correctly. They were all well enough to travel within ten days. Exactly fifteen days later, all three boys came down with chickenpox, compliments of their Rouhana cousins.

CHAPTER 22

It wasn't until we returned to Saudi Arabia that Nagib wearily sat down and explained his bad news. He had been in contact with top officials in the American government since his days in Beirut, working for the ministry.

The children were asleep, and we were in the living room holding our coffee mugs protectively. He looked tired and gray, and my stomach was doing flip-flops in anticipation of the news he was preparing to give me. I already knew by his demeanor and unhappy look that this wasn't going to have the outcome we had hoped for.

"You know," he began, "why I went to the States. First, someone else has been asked to be the ambassador to Washington, D.C." He raised his hand to stop any comments from me. "You know, Cath, that nothing went as we planned. There's nothing they can do. They offered me the second position in the embassy, but I turned it down."

I knew that when the triumvirate from the World Bank had taken on their political positions in the Lebanese government of Amin Gemayel, the three had been promised plum political positions. Amin Gemayel had been elected after the brutal assassination of his very popular brother, Bashir. One was to be the governor of the Central Bank,

278

the second, the National Security Advisor, and Nagib had been promised the ambassadorship to D.C. But all of this had been planned with a different president in mind, Bashir Gemayel, and not his brother. Sadly, nothing had happened as planned.

"That's first. Next, my meeting in the States. They would not give me my job with the World Bank back. They said their hands are tied."

Nagib had been in contact with the top officials in the American government since we came to Saudi, and soon after, working in the ministry in Beirut. He, along with his friends from Washington, had been instrumental in opening doors for an American presence in Lebanon. We had felt confident that should all else fail, the American government would find a way to restore Nagib and the others to their previous positions in the World Bank. But the World Bank had a policy that if an employee left to pursue any kind of political position, they could not be re-employed.

"Second," he continued, "you know that the Americans were grateful for our help and had said they would help us to re-establish ourselves in the States. Well, they had a job offer for us. But before you get excited, I have to tell you I turned it down."

My heart sank as he prepared me for this disappointment. I hadn't realized until I heard his words how desperately I had wanted a different outcome.

Nagib had told me before he left that he was expecting a job offer. We thought that we would have two offers to choose from. Now it seemed we had none. I had known by his demeanor when he returned that there was no pot of gold at the end of this rainbow. I was reluctant to bring up the subject while we were still in Lebanon, but now there was no avoiding the bad news.

"We met with Philip Casey," he continued. "You know who he is, don't you? He is the nephew of the director of the CIA. They use him as a secret liaison. He's not official, but he carries a lot of weight."

I didn't like where this was going; I had goosebumps. I leaned forward on the couch and gripped my coffee cup tighter. I had noticed that my hand was shaking, and the hot liquid had started to splash over the sides.

"I don't know any easy way to tell you this, Cath. They want us to become arms dealers for them. They want us to be the middlemen between them and third world militias and armies. They would have control of everything going out, and would be able to keep tabs on these arms, through us. Of course, we would be instant millionaires."

"Sure," I answered bitterly. "Sitting duck millionaires."

He held up his hand, palm out, stopping me from interjecting. His face was dark, and the vein in his temple that was always a barometer to his anger was bulging.

"Let me finish. I can't say this twice."

I sat back, took a breath, and let him continue.

"Yes," he repeated. "We would be instant millionaires. I would have to go through extensive CIA training.

"But Cath," he continued darkly, "as you guessed, no one survives this job for more than five years, to say nothing of the threats to the family. Anyway," he continued, "I haven't spent the last few years trying to make things better just to put guns in the hands of terrorists, murderers, and children. It's just a game to them," he continued angrily. "I won't be a part of it." He sighed and sat back, seeming to relax for the first time since he had come back from the States.

"I support your decision one hundred percent," I told him quietly. "No money is worth that job. I won't lie to you—you know I'm disappointed. But we won't leave here on that ride."

"Huh," he snorted. "Maybe we'll get a flying carpet and a djinni all in one. We're in the right part of the world for that. Don't worry, habibti. We'll work something out. Let's get some sleep."

As crushed as I was over the outcome of his trip, Nagib had had so much more at stake, more than I knew at the time. Now, he told me what he had not been able to share before. He had been deeply involved in secret negotiations between Lebanon and Israel to broker a peace settlement that would have put Lebanon on par with Egypt.

In 1982, Israel invaded Lebanon, resulting in Israel gaining military outposts from Lebanon's southern border to Beirut. The invasion served a dual purpose. Their first goal was to remove the threat to their borders by neutralizing and then removing the PLO from Lebanon. Their second goal was to begin negotiations with Lebanon to lay the foundations for a relationship that would result in a lasting peace between Israel and Lebanon.

Nagib's principal mission during our residency in Beirut was clandestine. Publicly, he was an advisor to the minister of telecommunication, industry, and petroleum, George Frem. George's appointment was one of the many favors cashed in for past monetary donations. But privately, Nagib was there to facilitate the plans that had been formed in Washington, D.C., before we ever left the States. These plans were made with Bashir's vision for a greater Lebanon in mind, still alive under his brother's administration.

The "godfather" of the negotiations was Philip Habib, a man of Lebanese descent, named special envoy from the United States to Lebanon for these purposes. His mission was to facilitate the exit of both Israel and Syria from Lebanese territory, using peaceful tactics.

We had arrived in Lebanon in November, shortly before Thanksgiving of 1982. The first meeting took place on December 28, 1982. At the outset, three committees were formed; a Lebanese contingency, an Israeli group and, of course, the American contingency,

Their stated goals from the beginning were to cancel the state of war between Israel and Lebanon. This achieved, they looked for the entire withdrawal of Israeli troops within a period of eight to twelve weeks. A no-man's land was to be created at the southern border with Israel, making it a military area to prevent infiltration into Israel by neighboring combatants. Furthermore, a fourth technical subcommittee was arranged, establishing neutral relationships between the two countries. These would deal with commerce, telecommunication, transportation, and other areas, helping to ensure normal relations between Israel and Lebanon.

Nagib was the lead on this fourth committee.

The negotiations continued until May 17, 1983, when it was signed by the three committee chairs. This was known as the May 17 Agreement. The Lebanese Cabinet, headed by Prime Minister Chefik El-Wazzan, approved the accord. From there, it went to the Lebanese parliament and then the Arab League, who, with the sole exception of Syria, approved the plan.

There were thirty-five meetings in all, held alternately in Lebanon and Israel. The Lebanon meetings were held in the town of Kaldhe, in a hotel called Lebanon Beach. The location was chosen to be near the American installation. There, the Americans had a diplomatic and military presence, complete with office and full staff. The Israelis held their meetings in a settlement called Keryad Chomona, near the border with Lebanon. The meetings in Israel were held on a military base in a hangar-like, prefab facility, stark and equipped with the necessities. This location was near a place called the Northern Hotel, where the delegation would go for lunch. The delegates were ferried back and forth by military helicopter, and they almost went down in bad weather on one trip. Each helicopter could carry up to twelve men at a time, and three or four helicopters were needed per trip. Nagib always traveled with the nine men who reported directly to him. Years later, he recounted to me that the Israelis brought in a belly dancer as entertainment at the last meeting.

The feeling at the meetings was amiable, particularly with the technical committee. They were highly motivated to set up a mutually acceptable plan and needed to support the military and political side of the proposal.

The U.S. was the middleman for this treaty. George Shultz, the sitting Secretary of State in Ronald Reagan's government, lent both his presence and the power of his office to the proceedings.

The May 17 Agreement would end the state of war between Israel and Lebanon, a state that had endured since the 1948 Arab-Israeli War. It provided for a planned withdrawal of Israeli troops on the condition of an established Lebanese "security zone" in South Lebanon.

In February 1984, the Lebanese government collapsed. The army had been slotted to take over Israeli positions, but this made it impossible for Lebanon to keep their side of the bargain, and the agreement was doomed.

Syria was particularly vocal, refusing to move its troops from Lebanese soil. To make matters more complicated, Israel increased their demands. This effectively stopped the treaty from going through, since Israel's withdrawal was contingent on Syria doing the same. But Israel insisted on the implementation of the treaty and threatened to go ahead with or without Lebanese cooperation. So, despite public protest and the start of the end of a fragile and elusive civil peace, the parliament ratified the agreement. But it was the Lebanese government, reacting to the withdrawal of the American presence in Lebanon and under pressure from Syria, who abrogated their agreement on March 5, closing the Israeli mission that had been opened to administer the treaty.

Chills went up my spine when he told me this story. I imagined all the things that could have gone wrong, all the factions that wouldn't have wanted this treaty to come to fruition.

Had it gone through, the treaty would have changed the course of Lebanese politics, tilting the Arab world a good deal toward the West.

At the end, each of the three friends met separately with George Shultz. Promises had been made many years before when Bashir was alive. The three had risked and sacrificed much, despite seemingly insurmountable odds, to push forward for their country's sake. For them there was no shame in this failure; rather, the shame would have been in the failure to try.

But now, with the collapse of the agreement, the American Secretary of State didn't have much to offer the trio.

He met with the men individually, offering alternatives to his original promise. The ambassadorship to Washington for one, and a green card for another were offered and accepted. But Nagib had lost the ambassadorship he had expected, and reinstatement at the World Bank was not possible. He certainly didn't need a green card. Mr. Shultz then offered the position of deputy to the ambassador in D.C., but Nagib bitterly declined. He had been led to expect the top position. In the end, Nagib walked away with nothing.

CHAPTER 23

Shortly after that trip, my mom was diagnosed with liver disease. Now there would be no "going home" for my brother Chris or me. Nothing would ever be the same.

The news of my mother's illness continued the downward spiral in my Arabian adventure that had begun in Beirut. Among the many casualties of those events was the unraveling of our peaceful family life. After our departure from Lebanon, the fabric of our plans began to come apart—just a loose thread at first, but we began to unconsciously worry at it. As one disappointment piled on top of another, it was as if an unseen hand were slowly pulling the thread and damaging the cloth. You could put a halt to the damage, but the cloth would be permanently scarred.

I had always figured that these adventurous years were parenthetical to my real life. In the back of my mind, I pictured myself coming home to take up where I had left off. But the seeds had been sown by the events in Beirut that past year. Although I still had a chin-up mentality, I was learning about the real markers of adulthood—babies, a job, and independence were all well and good, but now I was facing the looming loss of a parent. My life would never be the same.

In my absence, other things had changed as well. My cousins Mary Beth and Jack had both died of leukemia, my sister Franny moved far away to Oregon, and my sister Anne and brother Tom had each gotten married. I was starting to understand the adage, "You can't go home again."

I was lonely in Saudi Arabia, despite the attention and status that, through Nagib, had always been mine. This wasn't my world. It wasn't even Nagib's world. I would fantasize from time to time about sitting around my mother's kitchen table with my sisters, drinking tea, and wowing them with my stories. In these daydreams, Mom was always there. It became increasingly urgent to wrap up this chapter in our lives and head for home.

I wasn't the only one in this state. Anxiety and grief went through our little group like a virus. Tahseen's mother was very sick as well. The doctor in Pakistan had done extensive blood work, but it had to be sent out to the lab in London to be analyzed. Her family was told that the tubes of blood had been broken in shipping, and they were back to square one. They didn't have the diagnosis of leukemia for six weeks.

One friend had been excited about taking her children to visit her mother in Haiti. She hadn't seen her for a couple of years and was glowing with happy anticipation. She got a phone call giving her the news of her mother's death just days before her scheduled trip.

My mom had her results back within four days, diagnosing cirrhosis, and was set up with one of the best liver doctors in Baltimore, a prestigious medical town. I was blessed to be born an American.

It was hard to be so far from home and the people we loved during these times of personal crises. What was so different this second time in Saudi? Our first round had been filled with hope, goals, and excited anticipation of the future we would build. It was our big adventure, the financial springboard to create a different way of life. For Nagib, the challenge of catapulting up the ladder as an executive in the business world was coupled with being front and center on the stage of a political arena he had helped initiate.

We wanted to see our children grow up multilingual in a multicultural environment. Nagib and I had hoped to be free of the financial burdens that our parents had shouldered. Our first trip had achieved much of this.

But this time nothing was the same, including our relationship. We had arrived as equal partners, and now, at least in my mind, I was subordinate. Was I any more than a bystander watching his parade? Nagib had his work, his politics; he had control. I had given up my work, my language, culture, and all that was familiar and loved. I was not, I feared, a good modern-day Ruth. My mouth had once upon a time said, "Whither thou goest, I will go." Now, my heart said no.

What had changed? We had left the protective bubble of the illusion that was Saudi life. Outside, we had been assaulted with the harshness of world reality.

I never actually said this to Nagib. I was afraid of confrontation and thought he should have known how I felt. The fact of the matter was that going home to him was no longer in the same direction as going home for me.

To make things worse, the Lebanese situation was precarious. The expatriates in Saudi would still gather around the radio in the evenings to listen intently to the "Voice of Lebanon." They never gave up hope that peace and prosperity were just around the corner.

But we were human, and life had to go on. Our little group of ladies had decided to use our collective sewing skills to help the orphans in Lebanon. So, led by Marita, the women of the hotel and associated companies gathered their forces and talented acquaintances to start work on a huge charitable undertaking: a bazaar.

Marita used her contacts within the Lebanese community to augment the contributions. We initially met at her house to map out the scope of the bazaar, and each group committed to certain crafts. We gave ourselves three months to get it all together, including the creation of the goods we would be selling.

I purchased patterns to make baby quilts and pillows. I had never made anything like that, but I was sure I could figure it out. I made two baby quilts for the sale. One was white with a red and yellow rocking horse; the other was a light background with an appliquéd sleeping teddy bear.

I made a tooth fairy pillow with an embroidered poem and a pocket, next to an elf, to put the tooth in. I sewed a stuffed hen pillow with baby chicks to tuck under her wing, as well as a stuffed hippo, which was spoken for by a Canadian friend who had just found out she was pregnant. I hadn't even finished it. My final contribution was a beautiful Jacobean-design crewel embroidered cushion. I did the embroidery, and Tahseen did the zipper and the sewing.

Some of the women knitted intricate lace tablecloths and doilies and made fancy stuffed hangers and soap holders. With the goodwill and energy that poured into this project, we knew it was bound to succeed. Nagib was a big hit with the women when he announced that the hotel would donate the use of an empty apartment in our building in which to hold the sale.

I was pregnant again. We had been surprised this time and hoped that we could have the girl we both wanted. It didn't slow me down though. I never felt better than when I was pregnant. Progress on the plans for the bazaar was better than expected. We had had more donations of handmade goods than we anticipated and had set the date for the sale. Boxes of donations were piling up in Marita's house, and pre-event sales didn't make a dent in our inventory. The female half of the multinational expatriate community was abuzz with excitement.

I, too, was feeling better. I was making some headway getting out of the funk I had descended into after our year in Lebanon. Also, Nagib, always planning, had made a proposal to me over the weekend.

"What would you say," he began, "to starting our own business?"

"Okay," I answered tentatively, giving him the chance to collect his thoughts. "Where, when, how?" I shrugged and put my hands out, palms up.

"In Zahle, by next summer, using our savings and my share of Mom's land in the *croom*." (orchard)

I drew a breath to speak, but he stopped me, saying, "Wait. Before you say anything."

Classic. But I played along and shut my open mouth. I shrugged. "Okay. Speak. I'm all ears."

"You know where the *croom* is, above Zahle, up that steep hill? We went there for a picnic."

"Do you mean where all the fig trees and grapes are?" I asked.

"Yes. That hill is known as Fahel Mountain. Fahel for my mother's family. You know she is a Fahel."

"I know. Ibrahim's family," I said.

"Good girl," he smiled. "You have been listening. Anyway, when Ibrahim died, his huge land holdings were split up among his children. The land in the croom belongs to

Mom and Tante Nabiha. So, when they die, it would go to my cousin George, Gaby, Maroun, and me.

"I have proposed, and Mom and my aunt have agreed, that they deed the land to us now, and you and I will build a business on that land that overlooks Zahle. It will be a resort-type place, initially with only a large swimming pool and snack bar, but as we progress, we will add cabanas and condos, something like we have around the pool here. We don't have anything like it in the area."

I was intrigued. I knew my husband had a gift for business.

"What about George and your brothers?" I asked.

"Gaby already has his own business, so we would buy him out of his share of the land. Maroun and George would be partners with me, and Maroun would manage the project. Of course, we would be the majority owner, since we are funding the venture. So, what do you think?"

I was slow answer. He read me immediately and reassured me that his brother would manage the project, and he was still looking for an opportunity in the States. He had been telling me for a while that he just didn't want to be employed by anyone again. He wanted to be his own boss.

I had a lot to think about, but in the meantime, we had a bazaar to put on. The eventful day finally dawned, bright and sunny as usual in the Kingdom at this time of year. The collective of ladies, of multiple nationalities, representing various industries and companies within this part of the Eastern Province, had done themselves proud. Led by Marita and the women of the hotel and its sister companies, we had set up the borrowed apartment for the sale. We were hopeful that it would be wildly successful, and, if rumor bore out, it would be.

But halfway through a crowded, promising day, with presenters and buyers alike bubbling over with enthusiasm, we got word that the Mutawa were coming to shut us down. Nagib had received a call from his friend in the police department and came to give us the bad news.

The Saudis put an end to the bazaar, but they couldn't put an end to the sale. Marita had everything moved to her home, where she continued to receive visitors intent on making a purchase. They came from near and far—European, American, Lebanese, and Saudi women alike. When the last item was sold, Marita counted over thirty thousand dollars. It was a terrific boon for the orphanage in Lebanon.

But the action of the Saudis still took its toll. We had our sale, and the orphanage got its money, but they were successful in quashing the momentary, fleeting lifting of our women's spirit. That spirit had been derived from a renewed sense of purpose and achievement, and from that, a sense of empowerment long dormant.

We were deflated. But I was given no time to dwell on this indignity, or to participate in the outcome. I had received a call from the States telling me to come *now*. Mom was in the hospital, and it was touch and go. With my brother Chris, I traveled the next day.

Mom survived that hospitalization, but I came back to Saudi knowing that her disease was terminal. We didn't know how long she would be with us, but we kept our hope. I felt like I was on an emotional rollercoaster. Our spirits had been high when we went to Beirut, thinking of new beginnings. These were dashed by the political upheaval. Once again in Saudi, I found joy working with friends to raise money for a worthy cause and plunged again with the news of my mother's illness. This ride was making me dizzy.

CHAPTER 24

SUNNYLAND, 1985

In the spring of 1985, we went to Zahle for the opening of the project that would become our new business, Sunnyland. We would be staying for three months while Nagib traveled back and forth between his work in Saudi and the new project. There was still work to be done before the grand opening. Finding water was a major concern, and we held our breath until the find was made. I went with Maroun one day to view the progress.

It was a huge venture, necessitating digging, earth moving, and cement pouring. That day, Maroun showed me how they had finally found water on the land by using the old-fashioned method of divining. He had taken a fallen tree branch and shown me how to hold it. I was dumbfounded when the forked branch pulled downward without any help from me. Maroun laughed at my amazement, telling me that that was where they would be digging.

Sunnyland opened on June 25, 1985, to much fanfare and a large crowd. We were graced with blue skies and prayers from the church higher-ups as well as the general community. I was there with a couple friends from Saudi, who had come help us celebrate. It was a good day.

At the time, we were living in a rented house in the heart of Zahle. It was wonderful to have a space of our own, instead of at my mother-in-law's house. I'm sure they were grateful too. Our family had grown, and so had Maroun's, who lived with Im Gaby. The new place wasn't far from hers, but far enough to need a car.

We had decorated our house with new furniture that was custom-made by our landlord, a cabinetmaker. Just inside the front doorway was a spacious living-dining room. The dining room was just behind the living room, at the opposite end of the house from the front entrance. A beautiful handmade banquet table, Louis XIV style, stood grandly in front of the large double windows, light flooding over it during the day.

At the end of the hallway was a roomy kitchen, unique in that it was underground. It would make a natural bunker in case of trouble. The kitchen cabinets against the right wall were so high that I had to stand on an ever-ready ladder to bring down any dishes from even the lowest shelf.

We were here for the summer, but we expected to come back and live in this house. We sent Peter to a nursery school run by nuns. He was picked up every morning by the school van at eight a.m. He was happy to go and would board the bus with his breakfast *aroose* in his hand. An *aroose* is a sandwich made by filling half of a pita with whatever filling you chose, then rolling it tight so the bread would contain the filling. Peter liked his *aroose* filled with labneh for breakfast, or sometimes he would take one filled with scrambled eggs.

Pete would arrive home around 12:30, and Nagib would come in at one, and we would have the big meal of the day. Peter was a pleasant, happy little guy, popular with everyone, and he enjoyed his daily outing. Paul and Nick fought hard against going to school. They didn't know the children and preferred the company of their cousins, or, in Nick's case, the neighborhood urchins.

Having a place of our own in Zahle was a mixed blessing in many ways, but for the older boys, it was decidedly a bonus. The little street we were on was closed to traffic and filled with children. It never ceased to amaze me that my children could adapt to new situations so quickly.

Coming to spend the summer in Zahle was, in many ways, a challenge. I felt clumsy and inadequate. I was still an outsider, even though speaking some Arabic made me feel somewhat better. Not so my boys. Nicky, for instance, was in his element wandering the neighborhood with the other children. He seemed to revel in a freedom not allowed in Saudi. His command of the Arabic language surprised me; he hadn't had any reason to use it before, since his friends in the Kingdom all spoke English. Everything was new and exciting for him, and he was only too happy to be part of the gang.

Our landlord's mother lived across the narrow alley from us. Her name was Aunt Marie, and she was in her mid-sixties when we were there. She worked hard around her house, and I could hear the rhythmic thud of the large wood pestle she used to make kibbeh the old-fashioned way, as it came down with force onto the meat in the mortar. Kibbeh, the cornerstone of Lebanese cuisine, is made by grinding lamb or beef very fine and mixing it with ground onions, spices, and burgle. In the days before the food processor, this was done by hand, such as Aunt Marie did. Aunt Marie had taken a liking to me and had taken it upon herself, like a good neighbor, to watch out for me and the children. This was a somewhat funny situation since Im Gaby considered this her sole territory. Aunt Marie would run over often to warn me of pending danger to me or the children. ("Don't buy from him, he's a cheat!" or "Don't let the children eat ice cream. It will give them a sore throat.")

On this day, she ran over very excited. She wore a dark bandanna tied around her steel-gray hair. She had her apron on over her house dress since it was near noon and she was cooking lunch for her son. She was excited and agitated, with beads of sweat forming on her forehead. It was obvious that she was anxious to talk to me, but this was no easy task. My Arabic was much improved, but she was speaking very quickly, and it was hard to understand. When I did understand, I had a hard time not laughing. I didn't want to be disrespectful since she was so worked up.

Three dirty-faced little boys had come to my door earlier in the day asking for Nicky. I guessed their ages to range from six to nine. They lived in the neighborhood, and he had been playing with them the day before. Nicky went happily with them, and I didn't see him come back in to collect all the eggs we had in the refrigerator. Nicky didn't speak much Arabic, but he was basking in his new-found celebrity. Then, as now, he could always be counted on for a little mischief.

The boys had cooked up a money-making scheme and figured that if they let the blond American be their front man, they might have better success. After Nick had brought out the store-bought eggs from our kitchen, they put them in a basket and went door to door selling them as fresh eggs. Even now, I can't help laughing when I think of Nicky pushed forward, not understanding a word of what was being said, standing before door after door with his basket of stolen eggs. This worked well until Aunt Marie got wind of it, and that ended Nick's first entrepreneurial endeavor. And I had to buy more eggs.

The boys waited about a week before they launched their next money-making scheme. This time they went door to door begging. They didn't get as far with this plan as they had with the last. Nick was quickly recognized by a friend of Nagib's. One phone call to Nick's dad broke it up. We were getting ready to leave in another week to return to Saudi Arabia and I figured that it was for the best. If we stayed much longer, Nick would be well on his way to a life of crime.

With Nick's adventures, I continued to delve into Lebanese culture. Folk medicine was important to the people living in the mountains. When Nick was born in Saudi Arabia, he was colicky. Im Gaby had word sent to us on just what to do. She instructed us to rub warm olive oil on his stomach and then wrap his torso in a scarf. When Paul was in middle school in the States, he liked to have his stomach aches treated this way. It seemed to help and comfort him. We used strained carrots and water from boiled rice to treat babies' diarrhea, and tea made from anise seed to settle an infant's upset stomach.

When one of the children on the compound in Saudi Arabia fell and cut his head, it bled profusely. The Lebanese ladies brought ground Turkish coffee and poured it into the wound. The pulverized powder stopped the bleeding, as intended, and they took the child to the emergency room to be stitched. The doctor there told them that the coffee did indeed stop the bleeding, but it was a lot of work to clean out the wound. He said that this was a suitable method in a place where they might be far from a hospital or medical care, but since they were five minutes from the hospital, next time use a compress.

We used homemade mustard plasters and poultices for coughs, we boiled eucalyptus leaves and inhaled the steam for congestion and drank mint tea to soothe our stomachs. The people there had learned to depend on themselves.

Nagib told me the story of his paternal grandfather who, while chopping wood in a secluded, unpopulated area of the mountain, was bitten on the thumb by a snake. He recognized the snake as extremely poisonous and knew he had little time to decide. Putting his hand up against a tree, he quickly chopped off his own thumb, saving his life. He bound his hand in a tourniquet, which kept the bleeding under control while he boiled some oil. He plunged the wounded hand into the hot oil, cauterizing the wound. He became renowned in his area and lived to an old age.

Many of the women were respected herbalists. Not surprisingly, Im Gaby was one of them. I was grateful for this when we stayed in Lebanon that summer. Peter was a very physical child. He walked at nine months and never walked if he could get there running. He could ride a two-wheel bike without training wheels when he was three. He was the youngest of three boys and six years younger than his oldest brother, but when they were older, in the States, Nick and Paul were trying to get a ballgame together, they were known to offer Pete a bribe if he would play with them.

While we were in Zahle, Pete came home from nursery school with a badly scraped palm. The teacher said he had fallen while running and had caught himself with his hand. We cleaned it up and treated it with antiseptics, but he fell on the gravel outside the next day and hurt his hand in the same place. Small pebbles and dirt had been ground into the wound, and by evening, despite our best efforts to clean and disinfect, it was red and infected. I wanted to call the doctor but was told he was out of town for the weekend. What to do? We called my mother-in-law instead.

His grandmother answered our call at a run. She cleaned his hand well, but was unable to remove all the particles of dirt and stones. Of course, the three-year-old wasn't cooperating. Never mind, she told me. Not to worry. We'll take care of it after he falls asleep. In the meantime, she mixed up some flour with a little bit of yogurt and water to make a sticky dough.

After Peter fell into the deep sleep of babyhood that night, she put antibiotic cream and a black salve made of spider webs on his hand. On top, she placed the dough and bound his hand with strips of cotton cloth to keep it all on while he slept. The next morning when we removed the bandages, the dough came off with it. Pete's hand was healed with no evidence of the red puffiness of infection that had been there the night before. I had many occasions over the years to use this remedy while raising three active boys.

My Arabic had improved immensely by now, so I could take part in the mundane banter and chatter that make up ninety percent of everyday conversation. I couldn't talk rocket science, but then, I couldn't do that in English either. I did very well with my "kitchen Arabic." I was fairly fluent in anything to do with cooking, babies, and weather. I could tell time and give simple directions, and I wasn't shy to go shopping by myself.

We had come for several weeks while the construction on Sunnyland was being completed. Nagib was back and forth between Zahle and Dhahran. I knew that he would be late one night from the project, but as the evening wore on, I started to hear thunder in the distance. I didn't think anything of it at first. The boys were asleep, and I was content to read my book until Nagib arrived. I hadn't been aware of anything out of the ordinary until Nagib called to see if everything was all right. The thunder I had been hearing in the distance was from shelling on the opposite side of the town. He told me he couldn't come back yet because of the danger and told me to listen, and if the shelling sounded any closer, to move the children into the kitchen.

The house was built into a hill and the kitchen was bunker-like with no windows. I had been warned that if a situation became dangerous, several of the neighbors would congregate with us for safety. I knew the drill.

This episode didn't last long; it had been unexpected and blessedly brief. When Nagib made it home, he told me that the view from Sunnyland, way up on the mountain and unobstructed, was like watching fireworks on the Fourth of July, but without the *oohs* and *aahs*. He also told me that one shell landed dangerously close to Gaby's house, and the percussion of the explosion had thrown baby Grace right out of her crib and onto the floor. She was unhurt but scared, as were her brother and sister who were babysitting while their parents were drinking coffee in an outdoor café. Of course, Gaby and Salwa had started to make a frantic return home at the sound of the first explosion. About a week later, while Nagib was in Saudi, I was awakened from a deep sleep by a commotion outside. Our bedroom window looked out over the street, and having been awakened by the loud noise, I sat up and turned on a small light.

From my bed, I saw a young man running by at breakneck speed. He was carrying a bazooka on his shoulder. Shortly after that, a pounding on my front door roused me out of bed to find Nagib's cousin, Hany. He had promised to look after us while Nagib was gone. Luckily, no one was hurt. We were all lucky that night.

But luck didn't last. The stresses and disappointments that accumulated after Beirut began to wear us down. I had lost the baby I was carrying when I came back from the States. Mom's condition had deteriorated again, and I knew time was short. The boys had been having problems in school, and Chris broke it to us that he had had enough of Saudi and was going home.

For us, the writing was on the wall. We decided that I would return to the States with the children. My mother's illness combined with the deteriorating social situation in Saudi Arabia helped us decide. I would find a house in the States and move my mom in with me, and Nagib would follow after he finalized his business in Saudi and got his project off to a good start. He had pursued the prospect of developing land in Montgomery County and a group of associates was ready to invest in it as well.

But once again, nothing went as planned. The land investment went sour, costing us thousands of dollars. The project in Zahle had problems, and Mom died before I could move back to take care of her.

After Mom died, I could hardly stand the grief. My natural optimism went out the window. Nagib and I were fighting constantly. The more I cried and tried to talk it out, the worse it got. I had trouble sleeping, and when I did sleep, I dreamed of being buried alive. I was depressed, lonely, and having panic attacks. Nagib made himself busy with his work, as his blood pressure began to skyrocket. I craved emotional intimacy that my husband wasn't able to give.

The days were excruciatingly slow, like running through waist-high water. Our move was planned for June to coincide with the end of the school year. In the meantime, I needed something to hold onto. To get myself started again, I searched for and found piano lessons. A wonderful American woman, Ladine, living in the Aramco compound was a talented musician and gave lessons in her home.

Ladine convinced me to take her seminar for beginning teachers. She said there was a greater demand for beginner teachers than there were teachers of more advanced students. I soon had six students, both adult and children. Ladine saw how unhappy I was and asked me one day as we worked on a Chopin étude if I had tried praying. Defensive, I immediately answered yes, of course I had prayed.

But I lied. I didn't know how anymore. I felt dead inside. Anyway, God didn't live here. He didn't even visit. Trying to cheer me up, Ladine asked what I was good at. I was dismayed that the only answer I had was at playing bridge.

My sense of self was gone. Who was I? I was a mom, wife, sister . . . madame. I was defined only by the roles I played. But could I be me if there was no one who knew me? No friend who understood my thoughts, my pain? My brother Chris had found it very lonely here as a single man. I missed him. He spoke of home to me, and now he had gone just like so many others. Could there be a me out of context? The call to prayers was a daily reminder of my mental imprisonment. Slowly, I felt myself fading, knowing that parts of me were scattered all over the world, and wondering if a whole was ever to be had again.

I felt like a failure as a mother; my children had to be tutored because I didn't speak the language they were studying. Someone cleaned my house, and if I didn't cook, the chef would send something far superior to anything I could concoct. I was superfluous, purposeless. I tried to be a good wife, whatever that was—that mythical creature that men, for centuries, have dreamed of. A chameleon, a chimera, sometimes even a phoenix.

Nagib saw my distress, but he was at a loss. He was dealing with his own problems. It was obvious that we were at the end of our great adventure. We agreed that I would go to the States and rent a house. The schooling for the boys was deteriorating, work was disintegrating, and I was grieving and desperately unhappy. Nagib suggested that I go to Lebanon since it would be closer for him to come and go, but I needed the safety of home. Right now, that was the States.

I found a house to rent close to family and friends. It was an old, three-bedroom house with a huge family room, fireplace, and large backyard. Nagib was scheduled to follow in two years.

It was midnight when I left the Kingdom. This time, I was alone. From my seat on the airplane, the runway lights sparkled on an otherwise very dark, moonless, night. It was midnight and the rest of the Kingdom slept as I sneaked away, without fanfare, feeling like a criminal. I didn't know what would come next as I left this life to fly into another.

My eyes were red and my soul sore. I had watched, helpless as our papier mâché life crumbled around us. We were undone, at last, by wealth, war, indolence, and monotony. Divorce was never a consideration. He had told me when we met that Rouhana, in Arabic, meant our two souls. I had liked it then and embraced it now.

A gentle breeze had blown off the water relieving the heat as we made our way into the airport. It had blown the ends of my blue abaya as if I had a Superman cape, forcing me to gather it tightly around me, lest I be immodest. I wouldn't need the abaya anymore, I thought as we made our way silently through the necessary lines. At the boarding gate, Nagib hugged me tightly and kissed me goodbye. He had turned quickly away, but not before I saw the tears in his eyes telling me he cared.

Somehow, that look gave me hope. I knew we weren't finished yet, only this chapter. We were scarred, but intact. I hugged that image to me that night as I flew west into a less glamorous life.

CHAPTER 25

Decisions! My boys, now young men, scream gleefully at the opposing team's quarterback whenever they throw an interception.

Decisions. The building blocks of life. Things we make on a minute-by-minute basis. Some are small and inconsequential; others are life changing. Sometimes for the better, sometimes not. Sometimes you can battle back from a bad throw, but other times the outcome of a single decision can change your whole game plan. In the end, sometimes you just have to punt.

And punt we did. Back and forth Nagib went. I explained his absence by saying that he commuted between Lebanon and Baltimore. It was a struggle, but he and I had made the decisions that brought about our circumstances, and we were determined to keep our family together even while we were apart.

It was a bittersweet homecoming for me. My friends and family rallied round, understanding without speaking. First things first. A dwelling must be found and established quickly as a home. Mary took that in hand. She pointed out the best schools for the boys, and we went looking within those districts.

I found a house to rent, not far from Mary's. The boys were registered for school, and I threw myself into the fray by volunteering as a den mother for the local Cub Scout pack. The Scouts were delighted that I volunteered and astonished when I told them I already had the den formed. Maybe if I ran fast enough, I thought, I wouldn't have to feel.

But it didn't work.

Dread, loss, anxiety, and worry were my daily visitors. I was unemployed and dependent on a very slow money transfer system. I felt paralyzed; I not only lost a way of life I had become accustomed to, but my dreams and plans for the future. *Our* dreams and plans. I had three little boys who were dealing with similar issues, and I tried to hide my ever-present anxiety. But at night, when the old, rented house moaned and groaned, I pulled the covers over my head. I wouldn't go downstairs.

I was home. But what was home without Nagib? Watch what you ask for, you might get it. I missed him dreadfully.

Time leaked away. Nagib was owed a substantial sum by the Frems and the Saudi companies. It was his ticket home. That money would tide us over while he looked for employment in the States and until Sunnyland would be able to sustain us. But for now, the Frems didn't want to part with the money. They put him off, calling meeting after meeting, each one the last, until Nagib lost his temper.

He tore out his Saudi visa from his passport and quit. He would never get that money.

Two years came and went. But he did not return to live in the US. There were problems at his new project, and he was required to stay and manage it. He worked hard, establishing the new business he'd built in Zahle as a viable enterprise, making him able to support his family. It wasn't easy for either of us. Him, separated from his family, and me, missing him and carrying the sole responsibility of childcare. To complicate things further, the hostilities flared and waned, then flared again, making instability the norm. Nagib came as often as he could and sent money regularly.

Communication was difficult. Every week I held my breath, hoping he'd be able to call. But Lebanon's damaged phone system meant that the country relied on undersea cables. They weren't yet connected to the world by satellite, and I took what I could get.

What could I do? What I had always done. I put one foot in front of the other and trudged on. By nature, I am a glass-half-full type, romantic and sentimental, but practical. The eternal optimist. I believed in us, and I believed in family. When he finally called that spring of 1988, he said that he was coming for Easter and would arrive the following week. The boys and I were thrilled. They excitedly discussed what gifts Dad would bring for them, and I set about shopping and preparing food for the event.

But our happiness was short-lived. I liked to get up early in the morning and wake up gradually, helped by my morning caffeine, while I watched the news. That morning, I nearly choked on my coffee. Just days before he was to arrive, fiery images of buildings and burning cars came on the screen. I read the caption: *Beirut under siege.*

I was glued to the TV, searching news programs for updates. I couldn't get through to Lebanon and made myself crazy waiting for word . . . any word. I hoped against hope that he hadn't been caught in the conflagration on his way to the airport and was safe in Zahle. But I knew that if he was in Zahle, he would have found a way to call.

When Nagib finally called, he confirmed my fears. Caught between the airport and home, he had sheltered where he could. For the next ten days, he stayed in an underground garage, surfacing during the lulls to call and let me know he was alive.

Those were very difficult days, and I found myself on the verge of hysterics too often. My father was a great help to me. He, a recovering alcoholic, gave me a book of spiritual essays and sayings to help me cope. When I opened the book, my eye fell to the words, "With the help of my Lord, I will leap over this wall." It became my mantra, calmed me down, and helped me get through each day until I finally heard that he was back home in Zahle, safe. God was whispering to me. Maybe I would reconnect.

Nagib's own troubles were piling up. Problems with Sunnyland and his work in Saudi put tremendous pressure on him. It seemed like nothing went right, no matter what he tried. As time passed, he became increasingly irritable, then ill. His blood pressure skyrocketed, and he had nerve damage. We didn't have a name for the emotional upheavals we were both experiencing. Was it PTSD?

Years passed. We muscled through the hard times, and I limped through boy world, learning on the job. I became a baseball fan, cheering on little league games and serving as the designated scorekeeper. Later, when my boys entered high school, they taught me football. They managed to accomplish what my husband never could. I became a sports fan. After all, if you can't beat them, join them!

And so flowed the seasons of little boys waiting for Santa, the seasons of knobby-kneed adolescents waiting for their driver's license, from license to cars, to graduation to college to girlfriends to fiancées. Now here I was with my boys and Corinne, Pete's fiancée, heading east to Lebanon for Paul's wedding. I felt like I had come full circle.

CHAPTER 26

ZAHLE, LEBANON, 2007

It was a long trip with a six-hour layover in Heathrow Airport. Television screens throughout the concourse announced that a bomb had exploded on a plane in nearby Scotland. We knew that tensions were high around the world. Those same tensions had precipitated trouble in Lebanon. My aunt told me that she had wanted to see Lebanon ever since she met Nagib so many years ago. But he was forced to cancel my family and friends' plans to travel for the wedding. It was too dangerous. Adrenaline and the God-given gift of sleeping soundly on airplanes brought me through my flight. Again, after all these years, I landed at Beirut International Airport. It had only taken twenty-four hours of uneventful travel to sail me back into my past.

One foot in front of the other, my old habit, had finally brought us to this life-changing occasion. It would be the first in a cavalcade. Paul's marriage first, then Pete's in six weeks. Nick, the first to be engaged, would be the last married the following June. I looked out the window of the airplane. The butterflies in my stomach were making their presence known. Outside was bright sunshine, warmth, and humidity. In Zahle, away from the Mediterranean, it would be cool and dry.

This airport didn't look anything like it had looked years before. I had left a Beirut recently under siege with an airport struggling to maintain its function under the direst circumstances. Now, deplaned and inside, I gawked in admiration at the ultra-modern facility that could rival any in Europe or the U.S. The customs process was professional and thorough, but efficient. All of the personnel we encountered spoke English. This was lucky, since none of our bags arrived with our plane. After much discussion, we were told they'd been left in Europe, and we should call about them tomorrow.

"Where is everyone?" I asked as we pushed our almost empty luggage cart through almost empty corridors.

"Outside," Paul answered me. "For security reasons, anyone picking up passengers has to wait outside." It made sense. This was still an unstable region. "Poor Dad," I said. "He's got to be worried that we're not out yet."

Paul didn't answer. He knew I was right and just picked up the pace. Searching for our lost bags had eaten up a lot of time, and we were, indeed, the last ones out.

Nagib was waiting anxiously. When he saw us, his face split in a grin of instant relief as he waved excitedly. He was standing next to a statuesque young woman holding a bouquet of roses. The roses were for me, the girl was for Paul. Rosie welcomed me with a kiss on each cheek as she presented me with the flowers.

"*Hum d'Allah salami*," she said in the traditional greeting. Thank God for your safe arrival. "Welcome," she continued in heavily accented English. "I am so happy to meet you." She was well rehearsed. Her coach and father-in-law-to-be nodded.

Nagib guided us into two cars: his and a taxi. I rode next to Nagib, with Paul and Rosie in the back seat. I snuck a look from time to time at the two behind me. They were holding hands and seemed totally absorbed in each other as they chatted in Arabic and French. It was dusk now; the bright sunny skies of late afternoon had receded.

This was the more dangerous leg of the trip. As we passed through Shiite slums, I noticed a revolver sitting on the console next to Nagib. I didn't comment; none was necessary.

As the car wound around the hills and out of the city, always upward, I remembered the first time I had made this trip. Now I took in the sights, welcoming old friends. No longer intimidated, I smiled to myself, thinking I had won the battle. Yes, I had run away, but I was back now.

"*Ahla, ahla,*" (welcome, welcome), Nagib said as we arrived at his condo. Throwing open the ten-foot double doors, he ushered us in, giving instructions in Arabic to his housekeeper. He led us to the banquet she was spreading on the dining table for us. Happy and excited, Nagib started pointing out all the boys' favorites. They had placed their orders weeks in advance, as had I. Our mouths were already watering.

Night had set in, but our internal clocks said it was midday, and we had no problem digging into the bounty. Kibbeh, baba ghanoush, hummus, tabouli, and kabobs ensured the happiness of the hungry and travel-weary young men.

Once sated, I allowed myself to relax and look around at my home-away-from-home. It had been so long since I had been here that this part of Sunnyland hadn't yet been built.

Persian carpets covered the marble floors and gave warmth and color to the family room to our left. A large-screen TV took up most of one wall, while oil paintings of horses, by famous Lebanese artist Haidar Hamawie, decorated others. A sliding glass door led out to a balcony. Next to the dining area, a small kitchen was hidden from view by screens. A more formal living area just beyond the family room boasted Moroccan couches, teakwood carved end tables and a lovely carved ivory coffee table. I recognized the lacquered card table that Emil, the carpenter, had made for us as a gift. On top of it sat a handmade backgammon set, inlaid with mosaic work. This was the formal living room for receiving guests. The argileh sat in the corner, ready for use.

I sighed in contentment and joined the young people on the balcony. Sunnyland was on top of the mountain, and Nagib's third-floor condo brought us up even higher. The cool, dry summer air of the mountains brushed like a whisper as I gazed in awe at the lights beneath us. Somewhere in the distance an event, possibly a wedding, was being celebrated with fireworks. The lights from thousands of homes and businesses twinkled at me, and I remembered another time without electricity. But the *coup de grace* was the moon, its golden brilliance spilling a sparkling welcome all over Zahle.

I am finally here again, I thought. I found it hard to process all the emotions running through me. I was in a new space, but it felt as if time had stood still. Nagib was giddy. This was the first time in years that we were all together here in Lebanon. Everything that I loved about this country and town came flooding back to me. The smells, the sights, so many memories came crashing in all at once; bad and good combined. It was no use trying to separate them, they were two parts of a whole. But this trip was about the good—a gift.

Nagib came outside and quietly put his arm around my shoulders, understanding the emotion of the moment.

"Gaby and Salwa send their love," he told me. "I told them not to come over tonight, that everyone's tired. They'll be over to say hello tomorrow. It's too late to do anything about your lost luggage tonight. I'll make phone calls in the morning." All our wedding finery was in our lost bags. For all we knew, they were in Europe somewhere. But he was right. There was nothing that could be done tonight.

"That's fine," I replied. I wasn't tired, but Nagib looked beat. Tomorrow was a workday for him. "Don't stay up for us," I told him. "It's still early by our clocks."

"Good idea," he said. He kissed me, hugged the boys and Corinne, and left for the bedroom, leaving us to our devices.

After an hour I began to yawn, admitted defeat, and joined Nagib. But the boys and Corinne were too excited. They stayed up late, playing cards on the balcony overlooking the sleeping city, relishing the moment and raiding the wine cabinet.

I awoke the next day in Nagib's king-sized bed, refreshed. Nagib had been up for several hours helping his boys, as he called his employees, to clear up around the pool and make some repairs. He made a cup of American coffee for me and brought it out to the balcony, with a plate of *kak halib*, the not-so-sweet pastries I had enjoyed so long ago. He remembered.

Paul had already gone to Beirut with a driver to retrieve our luggage. It had finally arrived from London, and only he could pick it up since he was the one who had checked them all in. These were days of high security—even in Beirut, where you used to be able to buy anything.

I was relieved to hear that our bags were now confirmed to be in the same country. It would feel good to shower and put on clean clothes. I had started to dress as soon as I got out of bed, but Nagib stopped me, saying, "Why? This is your house." He knew I never dressed until I'd had my coffee. And this was vacation. Nothing better than sitting around in jammies. Be comfortable, he told me. Stay in your pajamas all day if you want. That wasn't likely to happen. I was sure people would be dropping by to greet us, including Rosie's family.

One by one, the boys and then Corinne joined us as we drank coffee on the balcony, relishing the freedom of not having to be anywhere but here. I was still wearing Nagib's t-shirt that I had slept in the night before, and had pulled on the sweatpants I had traveled in and had been living in since Saturday. It was now Monday. We had lost Sunday somewhere along the way.

The balcony was up high, overlooking the pool and the St. Joseph Monastery just down the hill from Sunnyland. The view by day wasn't as magical as under the stars, but breathtaking nevertheless. If you looked straight ahead, Nagib told me, you were looking down the valley all the way into Israel. To one side was Syria and to the other, Baalbek.

"You see that mountain right there," he told me, pointing. "That's where the Syrians set up to bombard Zahle in the eighties." How could I forget? I shivered in the warm breeze as we leaned against the balcony railing looking down on the landscape of the breadbasket of the Middle East.

"This, where we are, where Sunnyland is built, is called Fahel's Mountain in the land registry in the courts. It all belonged to my grandfather, Ibrahim. Of course, as you know, he had twelve children. Only eleven inherited, because Hanna died, but the land was split up among the surviving siblings, according to custom. Sunnyland was built on my mom and Tante Nabiha's land."

"Where are the others?" I asked.

"I'll take you around after the wedding," he answered. "But my cousin Louis and his brother Maroun are just down the road and around a bend. You know how the mountain roads twist and turn, and how the Lebanese build their houses on top of hills."

I did know. The Lebanese made the most of their inherited property by brothers building their condo/apartments one on top of the other. Generally, they would build in phases as they had money for the construction. When the money ran out, the construction would stop until the next infusion of capital.

Nagib went back to work after that short coffee break. He had much to do to prepare the property for the wedding reception. I went back inside and looked around the well laid out apartment. Nagib had enlarged it in anticipation of our arrival. A hallway leading from the front door passed two bedrooms; Nagib's overlooking the pool area, and Paul's on the other side, looking down the mountain going away from the project. Paul's room was new, built in anticipation of the marriage. He would be bringing his wife back with him. Both bedrooms were large and had their own bathroom and balcony.

We travelers started the second day like the first—lazy, relaxed, and happy. Nagib was relaxed as well, despite his work and the details of putting on a wedding in just a few days. As in Saudi, his office was just downstairs on the first floor so he could come and go quickly.

Paul was too busy being the groom-to-be, but Nick, Pete, and Corinne couldn't be pried from poolside. Our luggage had come back from Beirut and the important pieces had been retrieved. Bathing suits in hand, vacation could now start in earnest. The tuxedos had been unpacked, along with my dress—all sent to the cleaners to be steamed and pressed.

I had forgotten how civilized the Lebanese protocol of visits is. Rosie's mom came around noon to say welcome. Nadia, a thin, tiny woman, was very friendly, but she couldn't hide a deep sadness. Sending her oldest daughter so far away was breaking her heart, and it showed in her eyes. My own heart went out to her. Even if I hadn't been inclined to friendship for any other reason, this would have sealed the deal. I hugged her hard, not just the kiss-kiss of first-time meeting, squeezed her hands, and trotted out my kitchen Arabic. I wanted her to feel more at ease with the woman to whom she was entrusting her beloved daughter.

Two of Rosie's sisters came with their mother. They were darling girls in their early twenties, very cute and vivacious. We served them Turkish coffee, my first since I left the Middle East twenty-two years ago.

I napped after they left, jet lag having taken its toll. I felt as if I should have so much to do. Our oldest son was getting married in a few days, and we were throwing the party. But I really couldn't do anything other than receive people as they came. Nagib was completely in control. It was his show.

The custom in Lebanon is for the groom's parents to host the wedding and reception. This made it our responsibility. Aside from the normal wedding chores, there were additional complications. The groom would need to produce church documents verifying he had never been married before. More importantly, the bride would need a visa, *and* she would need to learn English, pronto.

The preparation/scramble had started six months prior. Nagib took care of affairs in Lebanon, dealing with the bride-to-be and her family as well as wedding preparations. I took care of the States. I had quite a list as well.

The custom in Lebanon is for the groom-to-be to give his fiancée her engagement ring in the church in front of the priest. An old-fashioned betrothal. The bride-to-be also presents her fiancé with an engagement ring—the wedding band—and after the priest blesses them, they wear the rings on their right hands until they transfer them to the left at their wedding ceremony. This ritual is serious and considered by the church to be almost as binding as the marriage ceremony.

Jen, Nick's fiancée, liked this custom, and was careful to make sure that her Nicky wore that engagement ring on his right hand before he left. She wanted to make sure that any young beauties who cast their eye on him would immediately see he was taken. No fear there. Nick only had eyes for Jen. As events unfolded in Lebanon, he saw things through her eyes, saying over and over, Jen would love this!

But once, Paul broke custom. In the spring, he went to Lebanon for the express purpose of proposing. After excusing himself in the name of his American tradition, he took Rosie out to dinner the night before the scheduled ceremony and, going down on one knee, asked her to marry him. She said yes.

They had set the date for July 7, a mystical number—7/7/07 at seven p.m. The date was much sought after by engaged couples around the world. After some negotiating, Nagib secured the church. St. Anthony's was where Nick and Pete had been baptized, the same church that was across the street from my mother-in-law's former house. She had died just a few years before, but I felt her presence throughout my visit.

The next day, we went to the Croom to have dinner with Salwa and Gaby. Salwa had told me previously about their new summer house and showed me pictures. The view was amazing and the property very pretty. A lawn off the back of the house was accented with rose bushes, fig trees, and grapes planted along the edge. Gaby picked some ripe figs for me and put them on the table. It was the honey from the land of milk and honey.

The lower garden boasted a variety of vegetables and more grapes, and in the back, Gaby showed me a spring. The elevation, on par with Sunnyland, gave an unobstructed view of the Bekaa Valley. Gaby promised that he'd show me a moon as soon as the sun went down. We have come a long way, he and I. I guessed age had mellowed us both. I enjoyed the attention he gave me. We hadn't always been friends.

Salwa set the tables outside on the patio, overlooking the garden on one side and Zahle from the other. I sat on the side looking down the steep slope of the mountain at Zahle. I kept telling the boys and Corinne how privileged they were. The boys had enjoyed this for a number of years, but now they were of an age to appreciate the uniqueness of the situation. It was a gift from their father.

Gaby and Salwa's youngest daughter, Grace, was there. I hadn't seen her since we opened Sunnyland when she was a baby. Salwa told me that Christine, Grace's sister, was on a business trip to Dubai and couldn't be here tonight but would be back for the wedding. Khalil, their oldest, and his wife Cynthia would be here for the wedding too. I saw them from time to time since they lived near D.C. Karmen was living in Texas and was very disappointed that she couldn't travel this year because of her work. Magily, Khalil's oldest daughter, was to be the flower girl in the wedding.

The weather was always perfect in Zahle this time of year, and this night was no different. A soft breeze blew, but even so, it was comfortable to sit outside without a sweater. There was no humidity to make us gasp as in Baltimore in July. We walked around chatting companionably while we waited for the dinner to be served.

When the sun went down, I went to stand next to Gaby at the railing to look down over a sparkling Zahle. Another breathtaking view! Salwa had put music on the stereo, and it drifted out to us as we gazed below. Gaby nudged me and pointed up to the sky.

"Look," he said.

The moon had emerged, full and brilliant.

"Look," he said again. "Didn't I promise you the moon?" He grabbed me and spontaneously started waltzing me around the patio. Détente!

As surprised as I was, I found out once we were home that the children on both sides were even more astounded. Paul told Nick, "Look! It's Reagan and Gorbachev." Grace

ran to find her uncle Nagib, laughing, "Look at Tom dancing with Jerry!" It really was a magical night.

Salwa served the traditional foods, and we drank arak,
toasting the bride and groom, and remembered old times.
When it was time to go, I was surprised that we'd been
there so long.

I woke up that morning and wished the boys a happy
Fourth of July. I asked Nagib if there would be any fireworks around Zahle for our wedding or some feast day.
He told me no, there'd been too much death in Lebanon,
and the country had been thrown into a general mourning.
Out of respect for the families of the soldiers from all areas
that were grieving, they had stopped selling fireworks in
the town.

We went to Rosie's parents' house for dinner the next
evening. The ride was typical of any drive in Zahle: down a
steep hill, round a sharp curve, up a steep hill. At the sound
of our car crunching the gravel, she and her family came
out to the front porch to greet us and offer us drinks. There
was a lot of kiss, kiss, hug, hug, and introductions made
in Arabic. There were around twenty people altogether, I
estimated. I smiled and struggled through with my now-
rusty Arabic. I had met Rosie's mother and sisters, so after
the initial greetings, I followed them into the kitchen to
offer help. Nadia emphatically declined my offer, and I was
shooed outside.

Chairs had been set up outside and we were made welcome. Rosie's grandmother, aunts, uncles, sisters, and brothers fussed around us, making us feel like visiting royalty.

It was gratifying to realize how comfortable I had become with this situation now, after all these years. I could understand the gist of every conversation, and even to participate a bit if I wanted to. And God bless Corinne. She wasn't shy at all and plunged into conversation with anyone. She just looked them in the eye and talked away. She might not have had the language, but she communicated nonetheless. It was a gift.

Nagib, on his part, took the opportunity to make amends for leaving me in the dark all those years ago. He readily left any conversation to translate when asked, and sometimes even when not asked! Times had really changed. I was touched by his attention and grateful for the chance to repair history.

Peter started feeling sick before we left the dinner. We had told the boys to take it easy on their favorite foods, but the raw kibbeh was too hard to pass up. Pete had a bad night and in the morning, Nagib called the doctor for antibiotics. He stayed either in bed or on the couch in the house with us for the next two days. He had to be well for the wedding.

The wedding day dawned as every other summer day in Zahle: beautiful bright blue sky, a cool breeze in the morning, and no humidity. It was a bit windy, proving Nagib right yet again in advising against a convertible for the bride's ceremonial ride to the church.

The boys and Corinne slept in, but Nagib and I were up early. He had a lot of details to see to, and I got up to drink coffee with him. It was a luxury to come out onto the balcony every morning in my pajamas and linger over my coffee, enjoying conversation with Nagib. We were at such a high elevation that it lent itself to finger pointing in multiple directions, asking, "What's that?" Nagib enjoyed answering and painted a colorful picture of the area, its history and geography, and his family's role in it.

But this morning was particularly poignant. Our beloved oldest son was getting married to a girl who promised to be a good companion on the rest of his road. She shared his interests, was educated and beautiful, and I thought, would support him where he most needed it. I hoped that these qualities would be mirrored in him for her. Isn't that what marriage is supposed to be? That is, other than the roller coaster of ups, downs, joys, and shared sorrows that anyone who has survived this gauntlet can testify to.

So far, we had been unable to pin Nagib down as to what to expect. He had promised a wondrous surprise and refused to even give a hint. This made Paul rather nervous, and he told his father in no uncertain terms that he did not want birds of any kind involved. Nagib just laughed and promised no birds.

What we did know was that by Lebanese tradition, the groom's family and friends would gather at our place over a period of two to three hours to congratulate the groom, give their best wishes for a happy married life, and have formal wedding pictures taken with him.

When the boys woke up, they went immediately out to the balcony to see the happenings around the pool below us where the reception would take place. Nick began to laugh, calling me out to see. His father was below us, dressed in sweatpants and no shirt, directing his workers with an abundance of energy. They had set up a stage the night before, and now were setting up the tables and testing the sound system. It nearly blasted us out of our seats when he turned it on. It worked!

But Nick was laughing because his father, in his typical exuberant way, was wildly gesticulating with the saber that was to be used to cut the cake at the end of the evening. Hair, what was left of it, stood straight up off his head. He looked like some crazed facsimile of Zorba the Greek. We all ran out to see the sight from our bird's-eye vantage point, and with delighted peals of laughter, the day was off to a good start.

I had been to weddings in Zahle before, but nothing had prepared my boys for the coming day. Even though the wedding ceremony wasn't until seven p.m., we were dressed and ready to receive company by two. Nagib had warned us that the photographers would come early to set up, and the family that had come up from Beirut would most likely come early as well.

Huge bouquets of flowers had been arriving all day, and the small condo soon was quite festive. The photographers set up lights in the Moroccan room, Nagib's formal living room, and were taking practice shots of Paul, Corinne, and Paul's brothers. By three, trays of fancy candies had been delivered, and yet more trays were being arranged with champagne and fruit juice glasses, ready for the pouring.

Groups of family, hitherto unknown to me and the boys, arrived and were introduced. They stood, stiff and formal, to be photographed with the groom. It was hot in the room with the photographer's lights and a steadily increasing crowd, especially dressed in a black tuxedo. Paul had stated early on that if he had to be photographed, so did his brothers. After all, misery does love company, and Pete and Nick, unable to deny their brother on his day, joined Paul under the lights. They livened the proceedings up, clowning with each other and their dad, and generally keeping themselves, the photographers and everyone else amused.

Nagib's apartment was filling fast, as each group finished the photography session, and joined the growing crowd in the living room. Groups spilled out onto the balcony, and guests watched from that height as the final touches were made around the pool. The mood was festive and jocular, and family members from both the Fahel side, and the Rouhanas greeted each other. Family jokes and rivalries were revisited, and the mood in the apartment was joyful, as befitted the occasion.

For me, it was a homecoming. I was full of emotion. My first child was about to be married, and I had returned to Lebanon, reuniting with the friends of my youth. So many here today were dear to my heart and I had missed them.

I hadn't been sure how I would be received after all the time I'd been away, but that fear was quickly addressed. I was embraced with love and affection from everyone who had known me. It was as if time hadn't even passed.

Behind all the joyous bedlam, the bells rang out over Zahle, announcing other weddings taking place this day. Bells have always moved me, and in Zahle they brought up nostalgic memories. Coupled with the emotions of the day, this was too much for me to keep to myself, and I found myself wiping the happy tears that kept overflowing.

By five the house was full, and the hilarity ratcheted up a notch when different ladies in the family began to chant for Paul. This was an old tradition whereby the women would take turns reciting rhymes extolling the virtues of their kinsman. It was a dying art, and many of the guests told me that Im Gaby had been the best of all, even standing up and chanting at Khalil's wedding shortly before she died.

So many old friends. My heart was full. Nagib's cousins John, Louis, Maroun, Badr, and Leila. Tante Marie, Louis's mother, Hanani and Elias, and many more. I felt like Dorothy returning from Oz to Kansas. They all hugged me warmly and said they'd missed me.

Shortly before six, Nagib announced it was time to go. Cars began lining up outside as guests prepared to descend on the bride and her family. The young men stayed behind with Paul and his brothers. It was their job to make sure he got to the church safe and on time.

With horns blaring, the rest of our entourage wound our way noisily down the mountain and then up again to the bride's house. It was our responsibility to swarm the bride's parents' house and take her away "by force." But they were waiting for us, and as Nagib and I led the procession, Rosie's parents came out to greet us, walking between the double rows of relatives lining the patio.

Nadia carried a tray of sweets. Her dress was a soft gold color, three-quarter length that she had bought with Rosie. Her hair had been coiffed to perfection, but her eyes were red rimmed from hours of crying. She broke my heart.

Rosie's father, a tall handsome man, carried on the ceremony for both of them. He welcomed us into the house where Rosie and her bridesmaids waited to take formal pictures with us. It was obvious that all the girls had been crying as well. But our soon-to-be daughter-in-law was not red-eyed. She looked tense but happy. The sadness of the women she loved was difficult, making her wedding day bittersweet.

Rosie looked radiantly beautiful, as a bride should. She carried herself like a stately Lebanese princess, receiving her admirers as her due. She had painstakingly picked out every part of her bridal finery, conscious of cost, but stylish.

We presented her with our gift: a necklace and earrings of diamond and moonstone. She thanked us and put them on, posed for pictures, and then put them away.

Now the real battle of the two families began, as the poetry-chant began again. This time, I realized that the recitations at our house had been a warmup. The two sides now took turns, extolling their relative in glowing terms rhyme and rhythm. The groom's side praised his strength, intelligence, and ancestry, while the bride's family, accepting the wonderful qualities of the groom, made sure that the groom's family knew what a treasure they were getting as they celebrated her beauty and kindness.

It was a sight to see and hear. A competition of words, mostly made up on the fly. As each recitation ended, the women on the appropriate side threw back their heads and ululated loudly, their cries punctuated by the bass tone of the men's exclamations. I wished that I had been better able to understand the nuances of the chants.

Much laughter, back-slapping, and jokes later, Rosie walked the relative-gauntlet. Her parents were behind her, but right on cue, Paul's substantial family fell in behind the bride, effectively blocking off her parents and attendants. Laughing, I grabbed Corinne's elbow and followed the crowd to our car, where the bride was already ensconced.

We left her parents' house with the bride and her sisters, Lore and Rita. Our entourage had captured the bride, driving away with her in our car, with Paul's family and friends loudly following. The rest of the wedding guests joined in procession as we slowly made our way down the mountain toward the church.

As we encountered drivers coming the other way on the narrow roads, they accommodated the wedding party by politely pulling onto the sidewalk. There was barely enough room for the oncoming cars. From my perch in the front seat between Nagib and the driver, I had a wonderful view of the road. Neighbors heard the universal signal heralding the coming of a bride and hung out their windows and lined the streets, throwing rose petals and flowers, chanting prayers and blessings. Many of them nearer to Rosie's house were crying. Our kind-hearted bride was a favorite.

Many blocks from the church, I could hear the pealing of the bells. Rosie, Nick, and Pete had been baptized there. I sat, overwhelmed and humbled, savoring these moments of joy. I made a conscious decision then and there to keep this memory in a safe place, close enough that I could bring it out, over and over again, to refresh and replenish me in times of drought.

Given the din along the streets, it was obvious that we had been expected. The noise from many, many cars blasted the quiet evening, announcing our coming from blocks away. There had been more than the usual number of weddings for this seventh day in July, and the air was festive.

We arrived at the church, horns still blaring. Guests laughed and hugged each other while Nagib, not so discreetly, tried to herd people toward the door and inside the church. Such a difference from the day of Maroun's wedding twenty-some years before. That had been a much smaller affair, and all the bride and groom had had to do was walk a short block to the end of the street.

But there had been no military presence at Maroun's wedding. On this day in 2007, there were soldiers in front of the church now and across the street, almost blocking the entrance. I didn't immediately register their presence as a threat. I was used to seeing soldiers stationed everywhere I went in Lebanon.

As Nagib got out of the car and strode over to the captain, I whispered, "What's going on?"

"It's okay," he replied. "There have been some problems at other weddings in Beirut. He wanted to know if I wanted everyone checked at the door. I told him no, just keep a close eye on the street."

I sighed. "Even at our son's wedding we can't have a reprieve?" It was a rhetorical question. Later that night, when all the events were over and everyone had gone home, he told me that the army had been posted outside all weddings that day. Threats had been made prior to this mystical date.

Rosie had decorated the church herself, with ribboned archways along the aisle, flowers, crystals, and candles. Now she walked proudly down the aisle on the arm of her father to her smiling groom. Fearlessly vowing, as so many women had done before her, before God and everyone she knew, to follow this man to the ends of the earth, for better or worse.

It was dusk when we emerged from the church. The vows had been exchanged and pictures taken. I was surprised that the day had turned so gray in its final light, a sharp contrast to the vivid warmth we had left inside. It was as if the colorful pageantry had sucked every hue from the outside, leaving it dull and lifeless by contrast.

But it didn't last. Nature was only taking a time out, and by the time we reached Sunnyland, it had its second wind. I watched, awed, as stars, one after the other, popped out of the velvet black sky to shimmer overhead, as if loathe to miss anything.

Nagib had been teasing us for months, promising a surprise. It was now or never, and the air tingled with excitement as we stood receiving our guests at the pool entrance. Nagib had had the tables set up around the pool, reminiscent of the barbeques in the early days in Saudi. The tables on the far side had a spectacular view of the light-bejeweled city below and the valley beyond. From our elevated setting, we were caressed by a light breeze. The tables were covered with white linen tablecloths, a flower centerpiece in the middle. Each table held a bottle of scotch and several bottles of water. A separate area, to the right of our head table, had been sectioned off as a stage. It was surrounded by spotlights near the ground and huge speakers toward the back. This was to be the dance floor.

The evening air was dry and cool now that the sun had gone down, and the breeze that wafted over us seemed to bring with it an air of expectant anticipation.

At exactly nine, with the guests seated, spotlights came on, illuminating the stage area. It was showtime. Music started, and an announcement welcomed the guests to the reception, and congratulated the bride and groom. Spotlights focused on the second- and third-story balconies where flags were flying. I gasped and clapped as bugles sounded the charge. A turbaned man, garbed in black, rode out on a white horse waving a flag with writing in Arabic script. He put the horse through his paces as bagpipes replaced the bugles. This was the surprise, no doubt about it. Nagib was so excited he could hardly sit in his seat.

I barely had time to wonder where Paul was when dancers appeared, briefly joining the horse and horseman before he rode off into the shadows at the far end of the pool. The performers, male and female, did a lively dance to traditional Arab music, punctuated by the steady beat of a drum. The girls, dressed Scheherazade-like, and the men dressed like Aladdin, wove in and out under the lights. I felt my skin tingle as a thrill went through me. The guests clapped and cheered as they watched this talented group of men and women.

As the dancers left the stage, one stayed behind. This was the narrator. He had complete command of the audience as he began his singsong narrative. It was done in Arabic, but even though I couldn't understand the words, I felt the gist of the story he was weaving.

This was the *zaffe*, the traditional escorting of the bride to her husband. In years gone by, the whole village would participate as the groom's family "kidnapped" the bride, carrying her through the flower-strewn streets, safely to her groom.

Traditionally, the wedding celebration also involved the whole village and would take three days. On the third day, the groom would be escorted to the bride's house by dancers and musicians as he and his family claimed the bride and took her to church.

Now the narrator told the story of two lovers, brought together at last after a long wait and longer journey. His singsong style had the audience mesmerized, making Paul's entrance even more dramatic.

The spotlight directed our attention, and I watched in delighted, gape-mouthed amazement as my son made his entrance riding the white horse, escorted by the tambourine-banging, drum-thumping, cavorting male half of the entourage. It was not a small thing for this rather large group to pick their way along the narrow path between the pool and the seated guests. Nick and Pete worried that either the horse and rider would fall into the pool, or the horse would get skittish and knock into the tables on that side.

But arrive safely to the stage Paul did, and, dismounting, received his bride as she floated down the stairs, escorted by the females of the dance troupe. Paul and Rosie danced for what seemed an eternity with each other and with the performers, Arabic style. When Paul finally took his seat next to me, I congratulated him on his endurance and his dancing skills. But when I asked when he had known about his entrance, he shook his head. It was only when he saw the horse that he knew.

On the other side, the excitement was high as well. Pete's uncle John was putting heavy pressure on him and Corinne, insisting that Pete have his wedding in Lebanon as well. Pete laughed and told his uncle that he would only do that if he could make an entrance on an elephant instead of a horse. His brothers, on hearing the story later, did their best to procure an elephant. Thankfully, they were not successful.

In a moment of quiet, I reflected on how many people had walked in and out of my life. So many here tonight I had thought I'd never see again, yet here they were and here I was, saying hello again. For many, it would be the last time I would see them.

I was left that magical night with snapshot images to pocket in my memory, available to look at on a later day. Corinne, dancing with abandon, hair flying, feet bare, arms raised overhead as she wove in and out Arabic style; Paul's famous entrance on the white horse; Nick and Pete's toast to their brother, delivered in English and translated by their cousin, Khalil, into Arabic, the reunion with old friends and old self, and finally the image of Paul dancing slowly with his bride to "Come Away With Me" by Nora Jones as flares went off around them. What a night!

A young mother will dream of this day for her son or daughter, thinking that at this point she will have brought the ship to dock in a safe harbor. I felt content and hopeful for the two just starting out on their journey together, and I prayed their road would be smooth.

I left Lebanon with the bride and groom and with a full heart. Nagib would follow in a few weeks. So much had happened over so many years, joys as well as sorrows. We were coming from a wedding and going to a wedding. In the darkness of the plane, I hugged the memories close to me.

It was dark when we finally arrived back in the States. Time to shift gears. We had been traveling for twenty-four hours and were exhausted. I had been busy and excited while in Lebanon, but now I had a quiet chance to let it all sink in. I allowed my mind to walk through the past. I was rich in memories and experience. I still grieve for the girl I was, but the woman she became rejoices. I can now accept, with bowed head, that "without the hurt the heart is hollow." Ah, our patina is burnished now, our metal having been shown to be sterling.

I looked at the young woman, sleeping now in the front seat next to her new husband. She was brave to leave everything familiar and loved to join us on the other side of the world, to come blind and trusting into a new life. She would have tools available to her that I hadn't; Skype, a cell phone, email, and internet. Even so, in time she would find, like I had, that she would have to redefine herself.

We had come full circle now, and the story had reversed itself. I closed my eyes and thanked God for the richness of this life and the blessings that had been heaped upon me.

Like the cocoa bean, life could be bitter. But once that cocoa was mixed with butter and sugar, the sweet confection was worth the labor. And so with life. The bitter disappointments and sorrows mixed with the rich experiences and joys had brought us to this happy point. We would be going forward now to two more weddings, Pete and Corinne in four weeks, and Nick and Jen in eleven months. The fudge trees had now bloomed, and Nagib and I would be reaping the sweet harvest into our old age.

The treasure we had naively sought in Saudi Arabia was not monetary after all. It was in the sacrifice made for family . . . for our children.

I looked at Rosie again, and tears came into my eyes with the knowledge of what her road would be like.

I would take good care of her.

We had endured and we had persevered, and life renewed itself when I held my first grandchild, Paulie, in my arms. . . followed by Alex, Ruthie, Petra, Michael, Evan, and Jesse. The fudge was far sweeter than anything I could have imagined.

ACKNOWLEDGEMENTS

My literary journey began in the late eighties when I returned to the U.S. with my boys. I wrote the first ten pages that fall. I didn't hide those pages under my bed, but I did put them away in a box. There they stayed until I found them and showed them to my sister Betsy (Elizabeth Cohn). Her enthusiasm and encouragement gave me the motivation to continue this project. So, thank you, Betsy, and thanks for your continued encouragement.

Many thanks also to my Aunt Dorothy Pula Strohecker, PhD, for her advice and lessons on writing. She was a reader early on and offered invaluable help. Thanks to my Uncle George Strohecker for his enthusiasm for this book as well as Mayo Lucas, a published author, and friend, who generously and enthusiastically read the draft and shared her advice.

Many thanks to my sister, Terry Heller, who was one of my valued readers and critics, as well as my brother, Edwin Watson, and sister Mary O'Banner. My cousin, Judi Zamzow, was an early and enthusiastic reader. Without her push to complete, *Fudge Trees* would still be sitting in purgatory.

345

My sons, Paul, Nick, and Pete, and their wives, Rosine, Corinne, and Jen, have been there for me all along. Thanks to my family here and in Lebanon and my friends on both sides of the ocean for believing in me.

I am eternally grateful to Barbara Regan for her tireless puzzle-solving help in rewrites. She took a chaotic draft and made sense of it.

Finally, many thanks to Nagib for his staunch support and for his substantial contributions to this book.

About the Author

Catherine Rouhana is an American author, adventurer, and entrepreneur. She is also a wife, mother, and grandmother of seven. She has lived in Baltimore, Zahle, and Beirut, as well as Dammam, Saudi Arabia. *When the Fudge Trees Bloom* is her first book.